Secondary Headship:
The First Years

Secondary Headship: The First Years

Dick Weindling
and
Peter Earley

NFER-NELSON

Published by The NFER-NELSON Publishing Company Ltd.,
Darville House, 2 Oxford Road East,
Windsor, Berkshire SL4 1DF, England

and in the United States of America by

NFER-NELSON, 242 Cherry Street, Philadelphia, PA 19106 – 1906.
Tel: (215) 238 0939. Telex: 244489.

First Published 1987
© 1987 D. Weindling and P. Earley

Library of Congress Cataloging in Publication data

Photoset in Times by David John Services Ltd., Maidenhead, Berks.

Printed in Great Britain by A. Wheaton & Co. Ltd, Exeter

ISBN 0-7005-1071-0
Code 8249 02 1

Contents

List of Tables

Acknowledgements

The success of a project involving a national study of secondary heads obviously relies on the cooperation of a large number of people. We would like to thank all the heads and local education authority officers who completed questionnaires or participated in the interview programme. In particular, we wish to record our debt to the 16 newly appointed heads of the case study schools, who not only welcomed us into the schools, but also gave up a considerable amount of their time for the research. We should also like to express our gratitude to the case study school teachers and chairpersons of governors who agreed to be interviewed and provided valuable information. Similarly, we would like to thank the more experienced heads and staff involved in the four case studies of innovation.

Considerable help was given by Margaret Reid, the project director, who provided constant support and guidance throughout the various stages of the research. Other colleagues at the National Foundation for Educational Research contributed their time and expertise; we should especially mention Lesley Kendall for her assistance with the statistical analyses; Graham Ruddock and Penelope Weston for reading the manuscript and making extremely helpful suggestions; and Janet May-Bowles and her colleagues for providing excellent library support. Finally, our special thanks go to Stephanie Box for her superb secretarial support and administration of the project, and Ann Symmonds who helped produce the final draft of the report.

CHAPTER 1
Headship in the 1980s

The headteacher has always been seen as a key figure in the school and the importance of leadership has been stressed by numerous writers and in almost every government publication on education. Thus, the Department of Education and Science (DES) in the Green Paper, 'Education in Schools' (1977) pointed out that, 'The character and quality of the headteacher are by far the main influence in determining what a school sets out to do and the extent to which it achieves those aims'. Her Majesty's Inspectorate, reporting on 'Ten Good Schools' (HMI, 1977), felt that, 'without exception, the most important single factor in the success of these schools is the quality of leadership'. It is generally recognized that heads – together with the senior management team – play an extremely important role in today's secondary schools.

It is equally clear that the role of the head has changed. For Hughes (1973) the position has moved from the autocratic 'headmaster tradition' described by Baron (1956) to one where the secondary head is both a 'leading professional' and a 'chief executive'. More recently, a study by Taylor (1983) showed that 'the diminishing freedom to manage' was the greatest concern of the heads he interviewed.

A variety of factors has been suggested to explain the change in role. It has been attributed, for example, to the change in school size and composition associated with the establishment of comprehensive schools and also the demand for greater accountability. More recently, falling rolls, legislation such as the Health and Safety Act, greater parental choice of school and the increased use of industrial action by the teacher unions have all affected the work of the head (e.g. Lambert, 1984). Useful summaries by Morgan, Hall and Mackay (1983) and Buckley (1985) show that the role has increased in complexity and scope and that heads are facing increased pressure both from within and outside the school.

In the last few years increased attention has been focused on headteachers and school management, partly as the result of the government's initiative on funding for senior management training, and a number of books have recently been published focusing on management issues and the selection and training of heads (e.g. Hegarty, 1983; Morgan, Hall and Mackay, 1983; Dean, 1984;

Paisey, 1984; Blatchford, 1985; Buckley, 1985; Frith, 1985; Everard and Morris, 1985; Hoyle and McMahon, 1986).

Despite the current interest and recognition of the key role played by heads, surprisingly few major research studies have been carried out in this country. While this chapter provides a brief overview of recent work on headship, it is not intended to give a detailed review of the literature. (References are quoted for the reader who may wish to pursue these further.)

Baron (1979) and Hughes (1983) provide good summaries of existing work, most of which has been undertaken for higher degrees and noticeably has concentrated on secondary rather than primary heads. The DES commissioned Lyons (1976) to examine the administrative tasks of heads in large secondary schools and Morgan *et al.* (1983) to look at the selection of secondary heads. Ethnographic studies, involving 'shadowing' or following heads for prolonged periods of time are rare. In this country, Burgess (1983) as part of his research, observed the head of a Roman Catholic secondary school and a very detailed observational study of four secondary heads has been conducted by Hall, Mackay and Morgan (1986).

In the US a great deal of research has been undertaken and, in contrast to the UK, this has mainly focused on elementary heads or principals. Greenfield (1982) provides a good review of the literature but points out that one of its shortcomings is the prevalence of survey methods; 'case studies and longitudinal investigations are practically non-existent in research on the school principal'. Exceptions are the ethnographic studies by Wolcott (1973) and Morris *et al.* (1981) and the case study approaches of Blumberg and Greenfield (1980) and Hall *et al.* (1984). Other researchers have used techniques of structured observation and analysis developed by Mintzberg (1973) in his studies of managers, and applied these to school principals (e.g. Willis, 1980; Martin and Willower, 1981; Kmetz and Willower, 1982). The different observational approaches have generated very similar findings and have shown that most of a principal's time is taken up with short, unplanned, face-to-face verbal contacts – the head's life is hectic and unpredictable.

Effective schools and effective heads

Although the NFER project was not designed to study effective schools or effective heads directly, it was thought that a review of the literature would provide useful information for heads and others. The following section therefore discusses attempts to locate the role of the head in relation to school effectiveness and shows that many of the significant factors can be influenced by heads.

Research in the 1960s on student achievement found that the main explanatory factors were ability measures such as IQ, and home background variables such as social class. The message which resulted from these studies was that 'schools make little difference' to educational attainment. The main US research was carried out by Coleman *et al.* (1966) and Jencks *et al.* (1972).

In this country the Plowden Report (1967) and a re-analysis of the data by Acland (1973) found similar results, with family background factors accounting for most of the variance in test scores. Glasman and Biniaminov (1981) reviewed 33 US studies conducted between 1959 and 1977, all of which used an input–output model, and confirmed the main effects of family background on students' attainment.

Studies in England (Brimer *et al.*, 1978) and Ireland (Madaus *et al.*, 1979) found greater between-school or between-class differences than those obtained by Coleman. These researchers argued that the standardized achievement tests used by Coleman and most other US workers were not good measures of the content and skills which schools attempted to teach and that public exam results were a better measure of student outcomes.

More recent work (e.g. McPherson, Gray and Raffe, (1983; Reynolds, 1985), while confirming that variables outside the school were a major influence, also showed that 'schools do make a difference' and has stimulated a search for factors within the school to explain the differences. This line of research suggests that students' academic performance is affected by the school culture and that successful schools have a climate or ethos conducive to teaching and learning. The studies in the US have mostly been carried out in elementary schools (e.g. Austin, 1978, Edmonds, 1979 and Brookover *et al.*, 1979). In this country, research of this type has been conducted in secondary schools by Reynolds *et al.* (1976), Galloway (1976) and Rutter *et al.* (1979). Schools in which students achieve good academic results after controlling for home background factors and ability measures are termed 'effective'. While a number of methodological problems exist, including the narrow definition of outcome measures largely in terms of academic achievement, the different studies have produced fairly consistent findings and have identified a set of factors which seem to be related to pupil performance. (Excellent reviews of the research are provided by Purkey and Smith (1983) and Rutter (1983).)

'Effective' or high attaining schools tend to be characterized by some or all of the following:

Academic emphasis
- High academic expectations by teachers, a belief that all students can learn and a belief that teachers can teach. In the US literature this is often termed 'efficacy'.
- Regular setting and marking of homework.
- Visible rewards for academic excellence and growth.

Classroom management
- High proportion of lesson time spent on the subject matter of the lesson (as distinct from setting up equipment, dealing with disciplinary matters, etc.).
- High proportion of teacher time spent interacting with the class as a whole as opposed to individuals.
- Lessons beginning and ending on time.

- Clear and unambiguous feedback to students on their performance and what is expected of them.
- Ample praise for good performance.
- Minimum disciplinary interventions.

Discipline and pupil conditions
- Keeping good order and maintaining appropriate rule enforcement in the school, i.e. promoting an orderly and safe climate.
- Building kept in good order, repair and decoration.

School management
- Positive leadership by the head is necessary to initiate and maintain the improvement process. US studies use the term 'instructional leadership', which is the attention the head pays to classroom instruction and the amount of classroom observation by the head. In secondary schools, a number of other staff in addition to the head, take on leadership roles.

Clear goals and monitoring
- It is important that all staff know what the goals are and that they focus on the tasks they deem most important.
- Continual monitoring of students' progress is necessary to determine whether goals are being realized.

Staff development
- To influence the whole school, staff development has to be school wide, rather than specific to individual teachers, and closely related to the curriculum.

LEA/district support
- Fundamental changes require support from the LEA/district office. Few of the variables listed are likely to be realized without this support.

Parental involvement and support
- Evidence is mixed here – Purkey and Smith suggest that parental involvement is likely to influence student achievement positively, but is not in itself sufficient to produce a major influence on performance.

While all the above appear to be related to school effectiveness, the following factors have been found *not* to be associated with pupils' academic performance:

Resources
- Fairly consistent findings that factors such as the pupil–teacher ratio and expenditure on resources and salaries have little effect on school effectiveness.

School size
- The evidence is not clear, e.g. British studies have generally found no size effect, but US studies have shown some effect with smaller schools being more effective.

Class size
- Some studies suggest children in large classes make better than average progress, others that very small classes are better. It seems probable that there is little difference within the range 20 to 40 pupils.

Organzational structure
- Factors such as mixed-ability teaching, house/year systems and single sex versus mixed schools do not seem to be related to school effectiveness.

Rutter (1983) argues strongly that school effects are not simply the sum of separate teacher or classroom effects. He believes that there are school-wide influences which extend beyond the classroom and beyond direct teacher–pupil interactions and thus it is meaningful to speak of the ethos of the school as a whole (while still recognizing marked variation among teachers and classrooms within any single school).

While one of the factors found in almost all the work on effective schools was positive leadership by the principal, most of the others can also be influenced by the head and related research has tried to identify factors associated with effective principals (e.g. Blumberg and Greenfield, 1980 and Dwyer *et al.*, 1983). Useful reviews of the literature have been produced by Persell (1982), Rosenholtz (1985) and Manasse (1985). The various studies show that effective principals have high expectations for all the children and hold a clear conception of the achievement levels they want to attain in the school, and are able to share this goal with their staff. They concentrate on the curriculum and classroom instruction rather than on administration. Research on the personalities of effective principals reveals that they seem to have strong, dynamic personalities. They do not sit back and wait for things to happen. Instead, they take the initiative and take charge of their schools. They need to achieve a balance between authoritativeness and listening to what the staff have to say on a given issue. Effective principals are able to facilitate the actions of the teachers and encourage them to feel they have a significant part to play in achieving various agreed objectives. If disorder is hindering learning, principals work to establish discipline and order and strive to reduce interruptions to the classroom. Effective principals continue their own growth and development and encourage staff development and INSET. Rosenholtz (1985) sums up her review by saying,

Principals of effective schools have a unitary mission of improved student learning, and their actions convey that these goals can be attained. Such actions include recruiting outstanding teachers who have goals similar to their own and to those of other staff, organizationally buffering teachers to ensure that their efforts are directed towards raising student achievement, maintaining the academic progress teachers make, supplying additional technical assistance to needy teachers and providing – mostly in concert with teaching colleagues – the opportunities to establish strategies to achieve instructional goals.

Leithwood and Montgomery (1985) have reviewed previous work and carried out their own research in Canada to produce a 'profile of growth in principal effectiveness'. The study attempts to identify which principal behaviour is linked to school effectiveness. The profile involves four levels which, moving from less effective to more effective, are called the Administrator, Humanitarian, Program manager, and Problem solver. The higher levels represent an accumulation of skills, knowledge and attitudes from the lower levels as well as some significant changes in the principals' beliefs.

Level 1, the Administrator – these principals believe it is the teacher's job to teach and the principal's job to run the school. Their main goal was to maintain running a smooth ship. Change was a source of annoyance.
Level 2, the Humanitarian – they believe strongly in the importance of interpersonal relations and that the effective school is a happy school.
Level 3, the Program manager – they are particularly concerned about implementing the program requirements as outlined by the central office administrators.
Level 4, the Systematic problem solver – a small group of principals who had a philosophy of education which involved high expectations for *all* pupils. This was used as a frame of reference to provide the best educational experience for students and they were receptive to changes which might achieve these goals. They used a wide range of strategies and were aware of the variety of factors which could be used to improve classroom teaching.

Leithwood and Montgomery point out that only 10 per cent of the 200 principals on whom they have data worked predominantly at the highest level. Most of the school systems involved in the study considered the lowest level in the profile to describe minimally acceptable, rather than unacceptable principal behaviour. In their more recent work principals were interviewed to ascertain their current position on the profile and then a training programme was devised in an attempt to move them up to a higher level. While some doubts exist about the theoretical model, it will be interesting to see how useful the current training scheme proves in practice.

In the US a new field of research on 'leadership succession' has developed to examine the effects on an organization of a change in leader. Gordon and Rosen (1981) provide a review of the literature from a variety of different fields, while Miskel and Cosgrove (1985) summarize the research from school settings. One of the major debates concerns whether a change in leader causes positive, negative or no effect on the organization's effectiveness. At present, however, the data do not provide a clear answer to this complex problem. The reviews are useful in constructing a conceptual model which divides the process into two phases; the set of events which occur before the arrival of the new leader and those which occur once they have taken up post. The pre-arrival factors include the reasons for succession, the selection process and the reputation and orientation of the leaders. The arrival factors include the organizational structure, school culture and the actions of the new leader. Both reviews indicate some of the methodological problems and end with a list of useful hypotheses and a call for further research to build on the relatively small number of previous studies.

The NFER study

The project was concerned to document the demands made on heads in their first years of headship; to describe the range of strategies employed to cope with them; to identify the requisite skills and knowledge needed to carry out their new role and to provide guidelines for in-service agencies concerned with senior management training in secondary schools. As stated earlier, the research was not planned as a direct contribution to the effective schools or leader succession debate and, given the time-span of the project, it is difficult to see how it could have made such a contribution. Although some information was collected on pre-arrival factors and post-succession effects, it is necessary to go beyond the first two years of headship to gauge the effects of a change in leader on that which takes place within the classroom. As later chapters demonstrate, a change in leader is invariably accompanied by much activity, but the extent to which such activity led to more effective schools was not part of the present project.

The NFER study concentrated on newly appointed secondary heads as very little research had been conducted in this area and it was felt that the transition to headship would highlight a range of training needs. The only previous work identified was that of Nockels (1981) and Turner (1981) who interviewed and surveyed heads during their first year. Although small scale, both pieces of work identified many of the themes that were found in the NFER study. In the US, Duke *et al.* (1984) have begun a study called 'Transition to Leadership' which in its initial phase obtained the views of a small number of recently appointed principals and compared these to a group of 'veterans'.

The NFER research involved three groups – newly appointed secondary heads, secondary heads with three to eight years' experience and local education authorities (LEAs). The project was designed to include survey and case study methods in order to obtain the benefits of both a cross-sectional and a longitudinal study. The questionnaire surveys of all three groups involved in the research were used to provide basic information and obtain comments on specific areas, while the case studies attempted to elicit fine detail at the school level over a two year period. Further details about the research methods used

Table 1.1   Research methods – an overview

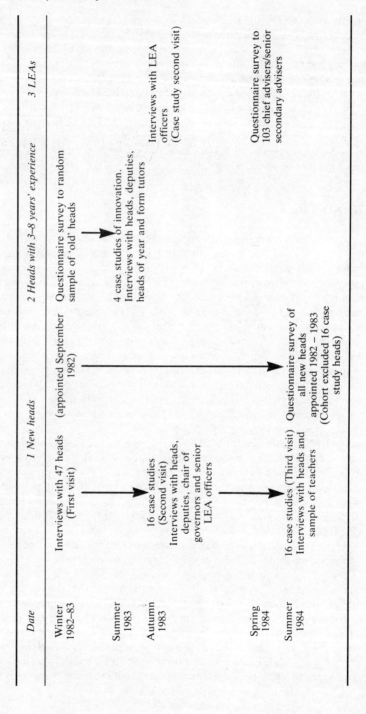

Date	1 New heads	2 Heads with 3–8 years' experience	3 LEAs
Winter 1982–83	Interviews with 47 heads (First visit)	Questionnaire survey to random sample of 'old' heads (appointed September 1982)	
Summer 1983		4 case studies of innovation. Interviews with heads, deputies, heads of year and form tutors	
Autumn 1983	16 case studies (Second visit) Interviews with heads, deputies, chair of governors and senior LEA officers		Interviews with LEA officers (Case study second visit)
Spring 1984	Questionnaire survey of all new heads appointed 1982 – 1983 (Cohort excluded 16 case study heads)		Questionnaire survey to 103 chief advisers/senior secondary advisers
Summer 1984	16 case studies (Third visit) Interviews with heads and sample of teachers		

with each group are given in the following sections, while an overview is presented in Table 1.1.

Newly appointed heads

The project intended to study the 1982–83 cohort of secondary heads: i e. *all* secondary heads who took up their first appointment in England and Wales during the school year 1982–83. The research began in July 1982 by asking LEAs to provide details of those heads taking up their first appointment in secondary schools in September 1982. Education authorities were also asked whether the heads had been previously employed within the LEA and if they had been promoted from within their present school. An analysis of the returns showed that approximately 100 new secondary heads were in post by September 1982.

In the initial phase of the project, the team visited a number of experienced heads to discuss a variety of issues associated with headship and each spent a day 'shadowing' a secondary head. An interview schedule was then constructed and pilot interviews undertaken with seven randomly chosen newly appointed heads. On the basis of the responses, the schedule was refined and a further 40 new heads visited to obtain their initial views of headship. A stratified sample of heads was produced to correspond to DES national data in terms of school size and age range of pupils (e.g. 11–16, 11–18). Visits were made to 47 schools in 32 LEAs thoughout England and Wales and the sample consisted of heads appointed from outside and within LEAs or schools and included all newly appointed female heads. Other selection criteria included catchment area and geographical location. In all cases except two, the schools were co-educational and the 47 interviewed were comprehensive school heads. Heads of selective schools were deliberately excluded at this stage, although *all* newly appointed secondary heads were involved in the questionnaire survey administered at a later date.

The interviews, which lasted from one-and-a-half to over four hours, took place towards the end of the head's first school term or, more commonly, during their second term in office. The interviews were semi-structured and consisted of a series of quesions covering the following areas: previous experience, preparation for headship; information on the present school and problems on arrival; style of headship, communication and delegation; relations with outside agencies; planned changes; possible future career plans and advice to a new head. After being asked if there were any particular aspects of headship the project team should investigate, the heads were informed that the design of the research was to follow a small number of heads over their first two years of headship. When given further details and asked if they would be interested in continuing to participate in the research, almost all the heads said they would and many thought such participation would be valuable both for themselves and for the schools.

From the 47 initial interviews with comprehensive school heads, approximately one-third were selected to be visited by the researchers on two further occasions. The 16 case study schools were chosen using a variety of criteria and located in 16 different LEAs (shire counties, metropolitan district councils and London authorities). The schools covered the range of factors mentioned earlier (e.g. sex of head, school size, age range of pupils, catchment

Table 1.2 The case study schools

	NEW HEAD			LEA		SCHOOL
	Age (approx.) Sex	*Within LEA appointment?*	*Within school appointment?*	*Size**	*Area/District structure*	*Age range*
1	35 Male	No	No	3	Yes	11–18
2	45 Male	Yes	No	1	No	12–18
3	38 Male	No	No	2	Yes	11–16
4	39 Male	Yes	Yes	4	Yes	11–18
5	43 Female	No	No	1	No	12–16
6	38 Male	No	No	2	No	13–18
7	34 Male	No	No	2	Yes	11–16
8	42 Male	No	No	2	Yes	11–16
9	40 Male	No	No	3	Yes	11–18
10	43 Male	Yes	No	3	Yes	12–16
11	45 Male	No	No	3	Yes	11–18
12	44 Male	No	No	3	No	11–18
13	36 Male	No	No	1	No	11–18
14	40 Female	No	No	1	No	11–18
15	41 Male	No	No	2	Yes	11–18
16	40 Male	No	No	2	No	11–18

*LEA size: band 1 = up to 30,000 secondary pupils + 16- to 18-year-olds in non-advanced further education:
        band 2 = 30–66,000
        band 3 = 67–100,000
        band 4 = 100,000+

Table 1.2 (contd)

	SCHOOL					PREVIOUS HEAD	
Size (approx)	*Previous status*	*Falling roll?*	*Split site?*	*Location*	*No. of teachers*	*Years In post*	*Destination*
950	Secondary modern	Yes	No	Medium size town	60	22	Retirement
1080	Secondary modern	No	No	Suburban	65	5	Another headship
530	Secondary modern	No	No	Rural	31	18	Retirement
1700	Amalgamation	Yes	No	Medium size town	93	8	Retirement
800	Grammar	Yes	No	Suburban	53	11	Retirement
1400	Grammar	No	No	Inner city	80	20+	Retirement
520	Secondary modern	Yes	No	Rural	28	17	Retirement
710	Secondary modern	No	No	Rural	43	21	Retirement
860	Grammar	Yes	No	Small town	52	22	Retirement
810	Secondary modern	Yes	No	Suburban	44	7	Another headship
1380	Amalg. of grammar + 2 sec. mods.	Yes	Yes	Small town	82	8	Retirement
1060	Secondary modern	No	No	Rural	60	10	Retirement
490	Secondary modern	Yes	Yes	Inner city	55	3	Another headship
1170	Grammar	No	Yes	Inner city	72	20+	Retirement
920	Grammar	Yes	Yes	Rural	56	28	Retirement
1350	Grammar	Yes	Yes	Small	81	20+	Retirement

area, outside LEA appointments, internal promotions, etc.) and, as the project team now possessed additional information, it was possible for other criteria to be taken into account. The initial interviews had obtained data on, for example, the previous head at the school, problems faced by the new head and changes to be introduced as well as more basic information on such matters as falling rolls, the school's previous status and whether or not it was on a split site. This information, together with the criteria mentioned earlier, was used to select the 16 case study schools and background details of the new head, LEA, school and previous head are shown in Table 1.2.

After selecting the schools, the heads were contacted and all 16 agreed to participate in the case study phase. The researcher's second visit took place in the new heads' fourth term in office (autumn 1983) and involved staying at the school for four days. During that time, interviews were conducted with the head, members of the senior management team (deputy heads, senior masters and mistresses, and occasionally senior teachers), the chairperson of governors and a senior LEA officer (usually the head's first line of responsibility, e.g. an area education officer or a senior secondary adviser). All interviews were voluntary and the usual canons of anonymity and confidentiality guaranteed. The central theme of all the second visit interviews was the school and the new head, with particular emphasis given to a comparison of style between the new head and their predecessor, problems facing the school, changes planned and general staff reactions. In addition, chairpersons of governors were asked to comment on governors' meetings, the support heads received from governors and the relationships between the new headteacher and themselves. The LEA officers' interview focused on questions relating firstly to LEA provision and support for heads and secondly to the school and its heads, both past and present. The interviews with the senior management team and chairpersons of governors lasted approximately one hour, while those with the LEA officer were lengthier. The second interview with the headteachers, which took place at the beginning of the visit and lasted up to four hours, raised some new issues, but pursued many of the themes discussed at the first interview. With the head's permission, opportunities were also taken during the course of the second visit to talk informally to other staff and where possible observe meetings. School brochures, working party papers and other relevant documents were also collected.

The researcher's third visit to the school took place towards the end of the head's second year in post (summer 1984). Again, the researcher spent four days at the school, during which time interviews were held with the head, usually at the beginning and the end of the visit, and with a cross-section of the teaching staff. To ensure consistency between one school and another, it was decided to interview in each case study school at least four heads of department (mathematics, science, English and humanities), four heads of year (1st, 3rd, 4th and 6th year) and eight scale 1 or scale 2 teachers. The heads and staff were all extremely cooperative and arranged a timetable for the researcher's third visit so that during the course of the week it was possible to see 16 or so staff during their free periods. No teachers refused to see the researchers and the individual interviews lasted between 35 and 60 minutes.

The heads were able to choose which junior teachers the researcher would see, but were asked to exclude probationers and recent arrivals and to include teachers of both sexes and of various ages and subject background. The heads were also asked if they would object to the researcher approaching 'known opponents' or critics of the heads and in all cases the team were given the opportunity to see any member of staff they wished. In most cases, the heads remarked that they had included 'opponents' in the schedule for the week. The interviews with teachers focused on the types of changes introduced and the change process; compared the styles of the new head and the old; sought information on levels of consultation and involvement in decision-making; and collected general staff reactions to the new head.

The third and final interview with the heads continued themes raised during the previous sessions, but also asked questions that attempted to gauge the extent to which matters had changed over time, e.g. perceptions of professional isolation, relations with other heads, positive aspects of headship and whether or not the job was getting easier. During the course of the week there were opportunities for further contacts with the head and the staff and therefore by the end of the third visit, the researchers had obtained an overall picture of the school. By interviewing a variety of people, it was possible to obtain their perceptions of the situation and gain an understanding of the events that had occurred during the new head's first two years.

Finally, with the exception of the 16 case study heads, *all* new secondary heads appointed in the academic year 1982–83 were sent a questionnaire. LEAs had previously been asked to provide details of all secondary heads in the authority who had taken up their first appointment between September 1982 and July 1983. The questionnaire was of a similar design and content to that despatched to the sample of more experienced heads and therefore enabled comparisons to be made between the two groups. The intention was to compare the kinds of issues and problems faced by the new heads with their more experienced colleagues, as well as seeing the extent to which the main themes identified in the 16 case studies were applicable to the cohort as a whole. The questionnaire was piloted on two groups of new heads; all those who had earlier been interviewed (excluding the case study heads) and a randomly selected 'uncontaminated' sample. Only minor amendments were

Table 1.3 The questionnaire surveys

	1 New heads	*2 Heads with 3–8 years' experience*	*3 LEAs*
Date of survey	Summer 1984	Winter 1983	Spring 1984
Numbers sent	233	304	103
Numbers returned	188	228	80
Response rate	81%	75%	78%

required and the questionnaire was sent to the remainder of the cohort in the summer of 1984. A total of 188 replies (including the pilots) was received giving a response rate for the national cohort of 81 per cent (see Table 1.3).

Heads with three to eight years' experience

A group of more experienced heads was chosen to provide a comparison with the newly appointed heads. It was thought that heads with between three to eight years' experience would have moved through the initial phase, but still be able to remember their early years. The initial task was to identify the heads who could be included in the survey but there was no simple way of finding this information, as the DES do not collect data on years in post. The sample of more experienced heads was therefore identified from the following sources. Two recent NFER projects on school reports and provision for slow learners had each drawn one-fifth random samples of all secondary schools in England and Wales and these surveys had obtained information on how long the heads had been in post. These data were supplemented by randomly sampling heads who had become members of the headteacher associations during the relevant period.

A questionnaire was constructed and after piloting with a random sample of 20 experienced heads, the revised version was sent to the selected group of 'old' heads. The questionnaire dealt with the following areas: previous experience and biographical details; preparation for headship, delegation, management skills and training; support for heads and relations with various groups; changes introduced and basic school details. Other sections focused on the difficulties experienced during the first two years of headship as well as seeking comments on contemporary concerns (e.g. staff morale). The heads were also asked what advice they would give to new heads and other general comments and opinions were welcomed. The questionnaires were despatched in January 1983, and after removing the small number of responses that did not fall into the three to eight years' experience category, 228 were returned, giving a response rate of 75 per cent (see Table 1.3).

In addition to the questionnaire survey, a small number of case studies were carried out in the summer of 1983 to study issues associated with innovation. It was the team's intention to investigate in depth the process by which experienced heads introduced change. For this purpose, the section on change in the questionnaires was analysed and using a variety of criteria, four schools were chosen that had recently changed their pastoral system. The schools were visited towards the end of the first year of the innovation and a total of 60 interviews conducted with heads, deputies, heads of year or house and a cross-section of form tutors.

Local education authorities
As previously mentioned, interviews with senior officers were conducted in 16 LEAs as part of the new heads' case studies. However, in order to build up a national picture of the support and training opportunities offered to heads and senior staff in secondary schools, a questionnaire was sent to education authorities in spring 1984. The questionnaire survey formed a very important third strand of the research project.

Three authorities declined to participate in the questionnaire survey and completed returns were obtained from 80 LEAs, giving a response rate of 78 per cent (see Table 1.3). As with the other two surveys, the questionnaire was designed to include a combination of precoded and open-ended questions and information was obtained on LEA background, support for both new and established heads and courses on school organization and management offered for senior secondary staff.

Outline of the book

The research project generated a large body of data derived from education authorities and new and more experienced secondary heads. The combination of quantitative and qualitative research methods enabled a broad national picture to be documented as well as providing detailed information on the heads' early years. The results of the research are presented in the following sequence. Chapter 2 focuses on the period prior to headship and examines this chronologically under three headings: career paths and background factors, the appointment process and the head designate period. Preparation and training for headship are explored in Chapter 3, which examines the tasks and skills of headship and how these are acquired through a combination of prior experience and off-the-job training.

The next three chapters all centre on staff-related issues. Chapter 4 considers the crucial area of relations with senior management teams and shows, amongst other things, how important these are in determining how quickly new heads are able to settle in and implement future plans. Teachers' perceptions concerning the arrival of a new head, the criteria employed in judging them and the difficulties they see resulting from heads' actions are all explored in Chapter 5. Chapter 6 focuses more on the heads' perceptions and examines staff-related difficulties as well as considering staff morale and the strategies used to improve it.

Chapter 7, after reviewing the literature on educational change and innovation, looks at the changes introduced in the head's schools and gives particular attention to the management of the change process. Detailed references are made to the new head case studies and these are compared with the case studies in innovation carried out with the more experienced heads.

The following chapter looks at the professional isolation of heads and considers the forms of support currently available as well as discussing how that support could become more effective. Chapter 9 continues the general theme of support and considers the role played by education authorities. In particular, it examines means by which LEAs introduce new heads to the workings of the authority. Relations with external agencies, particularly governors and the community are examined in Chapter 10 and attention is given to what was seen by the heads as an important area – namely public relations and the improvement of the school's image. Chapter 11 considers some of the vexed issues associated with headship style and examines, amongst other things, levels of consultation and communication.

Each chapter ends with a summary and discussion of the main points, while the last chapter illustrates some of the more positive aspects of headship and lists a series of recommendations for heads, prospective heads, LEAs and course providers.

CHAPTER 2
The Path to Headship

It is the intention of this chapter to focus on the period *before* a new secondary head takes up post. For analytical purposes, the research data have been divided into three chronological phases: 1) career paths to headship; 2) application for headship and the appointment process; and 3) the head designate period.

The first section of the chapter looks at the routes to headship and provides background data on, for example, posts previously held, subject backgrounds and the educational qualifications of heads. Although educational researchers have collected data on teacher careers in this country (e.g. Hilsum and Start, 1974; Lyons, 1981; Sikes *et al.*, 1985), there is little information available specifically on heads and their career paths. The main purpose of this section is to provide empirical data to assist in filling this obvious gap in our knowledge. The second and third sections of the chapter deal with headship applications, interview experiences and the period before the successful candidate took up post. The head designate period has been further divided into school visits and introductions to local education authorities (LEAs) prior to taking up post.

Career paths to headship

Each year approximately 300 secondary headships are advertized (Morgan *et al.*, 1983; Lodge, 1986), which suggests about 7 per cent of *all* secondary schools experience a change in leader (DES, 1983). The NFER data show that 249 heads entered their *first* headship in 1982–83, which means that of those taking up headship, approximately eight out of ten were new to the job. What is known about such individuals, how do they compare with other teachers and which career paths have they typically followed in order to achieve headship?

During the interviews with the 47 new heads they were asked at what point in their career they decided to become a head. Their replies fell into two main categories: the majority said they had *not* deliberately planned to become heads; while others saw the achievement of headship as an ambition they had held from an early stage in their career. Of the first group, many heads made reference to their period as deputies when they first became aware, or convinced themselves, they had headship potential. For one respondent this became apparent when a new head arrived at the school and he was certain he could perform better or at least no worse! For many it was only when a position had been successfully filled or a task competently completed was it felt appropriate to apply for more senior posts. Others pointed out they had never 'gone out of their way for promotion' or they 'just happened to be around at the right time', while for some it was encouragement from their heads or the need for a fresh challenge that caused them to contemplate a career move.

A case study head decided to become a head only when he became a deputy, but once the decision had been made he set himself a target time of five years and was prepared to move anywhere in the country to fulfil his ambition. Others were less mobile or unprepared to achieve headship regardless of cost, seeing the quality of life and family considerations as more important.

The other main response from heads was to suggest that once they had decided on a teaching career, the next obvious step was to aim for the top. Some had always wanted to be in charge or hold responsibility and enjoyed seeing tasks through or persuading others to accept ideas. The decision to become a head was made in one instance during the second year of teaching, and it was thought once headship had been achieved it would prove possible to facilitate certain desirable changes. The new head added that now headship had been achieved he was much more aware of constraints and how difficult it was to effect change. Others had ambitions not only to achieve headship, but achieve it by a certain age – usually 35 or 40. The few heads who thought this way had made deliberate attempts to acquire the necessary curricular and pastoral experiences to enable them to realize their ambitions and prepare them for headship.

Table 2.1 shows the path to headship for the cohort of new heads who took up their first appointment in 1982–83 and responded to the questionnaire survey. The table also provides a comparison with information for the other group of heads involved in the research – namely, the 228 heads with three to eight years' experience who were appointed between 1975 and 1980. The first line shows a small, but statistically significant difference in the age on appointment. The average for the 'old' heads with three to eight years' experience was 40.9 years of age, while that of the 1982–83 heads was 42.1 years. Further examination showed this was largely accounted for by the fact that on average the 'old' heads had spent five years as deputies, whereas the average for the new heads was 6.5 years. On average the new heads had spent nearly two years longer in teaching than had their more experienced colleagues. The 'old' heads therefore, had not only been appointed at a slightly younger age than the new heads, but also had taught for less time.

Table 2.1 also shows that 25 per cent of the cohort compared with only 15 per cent of the sample had been acting heads – of these 11 per cent of the new heads and 6 per cent of the 'old' moved straight to their first headship (Table 2.2). The remainder after a period as acting head usually returned to deputy level and then later became heads. The statistically significant differences between the percentages who had been acting heads might possibly be explained by the

Table 2.1 The path to headship

% of Cohort	Average[1] (Yrs)		Average[1] (Yrs)	% of Sample
	New Heads		'Old' Heads	
100	42.1#	Age on appointment	40.9#	100
100	19.1#	Years in teaching	17.2#	100
25*	0.8	Years as acting head	1.0	15*
97*	6.5#	Years as deputy head/senior master/mistress	5.0#	88*
26	3.2	Years as senior teacher	3.1	18
44	4.4	Years as head of house and/or head of year	4.0	47
86	6.4	Years as head of department	6.0	86
	(N = 188)		(N = 228)	

[1] *NB* Average refers only to those with relevant attribute.
* Chi-square significant at 5 per cent level between the two groups.
# t-test significant at 5 per cent level between the two groups.

Table 2.2 Post held immediately before becoming a head

	Percentages	
	New Heads	'Old' Heads
Acting head	11	6
Deputy head/senior master/mistress	86	81
Senior teacher*	1	7
Other (e.g. education officer, adviser, head of department)*	2	6
	100%	100%
N =	188	227

*Chi-square significant at 5 per cent level between the two groups.

larger number of schools more recently involved in amalgamations and mergers resulting from falling rolls, and therefore the greater likelihood of becoming a temporary or acting head until this process had been fully completed.

Table 2.2 also demonstrates that the entry point to headship from a senior teacher post or 'other' (e.g. head of department, education officer) appeared to have declined over the time period between the appointment of the two groups of heads. A further interesting statistically significant difference was that 97 per cent of the cohort compared to only 88 per cent of the 'old' heads had been deputy heads (see Table 2.1). For both groups the most common route to headship was from head of department rather than from head of house/year, i.e. 'academic' or curricular, as opposed to 'pastoral'. Almost all of those who had been head of house/year had also been head of department. The normal progression to headship was via a head of department and deputy headship and it appears increasingly unlikely headship will be achieved unless a period has been served as a deputy. The move directly from departmental head to head, possible in the 1950s and 1960s prior to the comprehensive reorganization of schools, is now virtually impossible. (Data from a survey by Hilsum and Start (1974) carried out in 1971 showed that only 52 per cent of heads had been appointed from deputy headships and as many as 21 per cent directly from head of department level.)

For the heads in the NFER study, only 26 per cent of new and 18 per cent of 'old' heads had been senior teachers and the data therefore gave some support to Straker's (1984) thesis that this position is rarely seen as a stepping stone to deputy headship; rather, it is suggested such posts are used by heads to reward heads of large departments and/or senior staff members. Straker's small-scale research found many senior teachers perceived this appointment to be their final one and further career moves were seen as most unlikely.

Educational qualifications and subject background

The educational qualifications of the two headteacher groups are shown in Tables 2.3, 2.4 and 2.5. Statistically significant differences were found between the groups with a greater proportion of new heads holding certificates of education, advanced diplomas and higher degrees (Table 2.3). Significant differences were also found when the data were further analysed in terms of the highest level of qualification gained by the heads. Table 2.4 shows that very few heads possessed only a certificate of education, but whereas a half of the more experienced heads had a degree or PGCE, only 39 per cent of the new heads were similarly qualified. Conversely, only 21 per cent of 'old' heads possessed a higher degree whereas this was the case for as many as one-third of the new heads. The data on educational qualifications, therefore, suggest that a greater proportion of new heads than 'old' have upgraded their certificates to degrees or taken higher degrees after first acquiring an advanced diploma.

The vast majority of both groups surveyed had first degrees and the percentage figures were higher than the national picture which showed 80 per cent of all secondary school heads (excluding middle-deemed secondary) were graduates (DES, 1983). The differences between the national and NFER statistics may be attributed to the fact that it is now more difficult to obtain a headship without a degree and that teaching is generally becoming an all-graduate profession.

Table 2.3 Educational qualifications

	Percentages	
	New Heads	*'Old' Heads*
Certificate of education*	27	18
First degree	90	93
Postgraduate certificate in education	62	65
Advanced diploma*	25	10
Masters degree*	33	21
Doctorate	3	2
N =	187	227

*Chi-square significant at 5 per cent level between the two groups.
NB Percentages do not total 100 per cent as more than one qualification can be held.

Table 2.4 Highest qualification held

	Percentages	
	New Heads	*'Old' Heads*
Higher degree (masters/doctorate)	33	21
Advanced diploma	13	7
Postgraduate certificate in education	39	50
First degree	13	17
Certificate of education	2	5
	100%	100%
N =	187	227

Chi-square significant at 5 per cent level between the two groups.

Not only were the heads in the NFER study virtually all graduates, but over a third could be classified as having 'good' degrees (i.e. a first or upper second class degree). There are no directly comparable national statistics on headteachers' class of degree. However, if DES figures for all teachers in England and Wales are compared, they show that the heads in the NFER study generally had better qualifications than the profession's average (see Table 2.5). Of the heads in the NFER study with degrees, 15 per cent of the new and 17 per cent of the 'old' had been educated at Oxford or Cambridge. (Oxbridge MAs were categorized as first degrees.)

Table 2.5   Educational qualification – class of degree held by graduates

| | Percentages | | |
	New Heads	'Old' Heads	All Teachers*
1st class	6	4	3
Upper second (2:1)	31	32 ⎫	56
Lower second (2:2)	46	34 ⎬	
Pass/ordinary	15	24 ⎫	41
Other (e.g. general, aegrotat)	2	6 ⎬	
	100%	100%	100%
N =	170	211	136,621

*Extract from Table B148, 'Full-time graduate teachers in maintained secondary schools' (DES, 1983).
(Headteachers are included in these figures.)

Both NFER groups of heads were asked to indicate the departmental area in which their secondary teaching had been mostly concerned. The results are shown in Table 2.6 which indicates a reasonably close correspondence between the two groups. The table shows that three subject areas – humanities, English and science – accounted for the majority of the heads in the surveys. Once again, there are no directly comparable national data, but DES statistics can be adapted to permit a crude comparison of the subject backgrounds of the heads involved in the NFER research, with those of teachers in England and Wales (DES, 1982). (The DES data from 505 secondary schools refer to 'main subject of highest qualification', whereas the NFER's refer to 'main teaching areas'.) Table 2.6 shows the four major subject areas of English, humanities, sciences and mathematics to be, on average, over-represented amongst heads, while aesthetics and craft and, to a lesser extent, physical education are grossly under-represented. The over-representation is particularly noticeable in the humanities. Hilsum and Start's (1974) survey in the early 1970s also looked at subject background of teachers and found headships were concentrated disproportionately in a few subjects and in particular history.

Explanations to account for the differences in the subject background of heads have been couched in terms of personal characteristics possessed by such individuals and the different tasks which they carry out within the school (Bernbaum, 1973). It is interesting to note, that while the percentage of heads in the NFER study with a humanities background has remained unchanged, there has been a slight increase in those with a mathematics, science or English background.

Table 2.6 Subject backgrounds

	Percentages*		
	New Heads	*'Old' Heads*	*Teachers***
Aesthetics and craft	3	3	21
Classics	3	5	–
Commerce and business studies	4	2	–
English	24	21	11
Humanities (other than English)	38	38	18
Mathematics	15	11	9
Modern languages	10	11	9
Physical education	6	5	8
Remedial education	3	2	–
Sciences	25	23	15
Other	2	8	9
N =	188	228	**

* Percentages for the heads' surveys do not add up to 100, as more than one area could be listed.
** Adapted from DES Statistical Bulletin, 'The Secondary Staffing Survey', 5/82 Table 4 (1982), based on a survey of 505 secondary schools in England and Wales.
Chi-square not significant between the two groups of heads.

The majority of the new heads' cohort took up a headship in a different local education authority from that in which they were previously employed. Of those remaining in the same LEA in which they held their last post (41 per cent), approximately a quarter were promoted from within the same school. For the cohort as a whole, just under one in ten heads were internally promoted.

A significant relationship was found between internal promotions and the position heads had previously held, with a much larger proportion having been acting heads immediately prior to their appointment as head. There was also a significant relationship between internal promotion and gender. Only 10 per cent of the men within the new head's cohort were internal promotions, compared to 25 per cent of female heads. A further difference was that just under a quarter of males compared with 40 per cent of females had been acting heads at some stage prior to taking up their first headship. The importance of gender is further discussed in the next section, while a discussion of the differences between internally promoted heads and others, in relation to the change process and headship styles, is found in Chapters 7 and 11 respectively.

Gender differences

Relatively few women are found in the upper echelons of the professions or management and administration. The teaching profession, although different from most in having a high female membership, is not exceptional in that few women achieve headships, especially at secondary level. Social scientists have made use of a variety of explanations to account for the low representation of women in positions of seniority. (Useful summaries of the literature relating to educational management can be found in Adkinson, 1981; Fauth, 1984 and Haven *et al.*, 1980. For a brief British overview, see Sayer, 1980.) However, it is not our intention to discuss critically such explanations, but rather to describe the main gender differences between the groups surveyed in relation to career paths to secondary headship.

Only 25 of the 188 new heads were women (13 per cent), whereas a higher proportion was found amongst the sample of 'old' heads (18 per cent). Education statistics for England and Wales showed that nearly 16 per cent of heads of maintained secondary schools (excluding middle-deemed secondary) were female, whereas for comprehensive schools the figure fell to 13 per cent (DES, 1983). The main differences between the career paths of male and female heads are shown in Table 2.7. The table shows significant differences in career paths, notably in relation to age on appointment to headship, years in teaching and years as deputy head.

Table 2.7   Path to headship – gender differences

New Heads				'Old' Heads		
Male (87%)		*Female (13%)*			*Male (82%)*	*Female (18%)*
Average[1]					Average[1]	
41.8	#	44.6	Age on appointment		40.2 #	43.9
18.6	#	21.9	Years in teaching		16.7 #	19.6
0.8		0.8	Years as acting head		1.0	1.1
6.3	#	7.8	Years as deputy head/senior master/mistress		4.7 #	6.2
3.2		3.4	Years as senior teacher		3.2	2.3
4.5		3.4	Years as head of house and/or head of year		4.0	3.5
6.4		6.8	Years as head of department		5.9	6.2
(N = 163)		(N = 25)			(N = 187)	(N = 41)

\# t-test significant at 5 per cent level between male and female heads.
[1] *NB* Average refers only to those with relevant attribute.

The tendency was for women to be appointed to headship at an older age than men. It could be argued that the age difference was accounted for by time taken out for childbearing and rearing, but the fact that women spent on average three years more in teaching before achieving headship than their male counterparts suggests this explanation is incorrect. Trown and Needham (1981) in a survey carried out for the Equal Opportunities Commission, found in their sample of 1100 schools that headships were almost exclusively the province of men and *single* women. They point to career re-entry problems for women after childbirth, a problem they argue that is likely to become worse as falling rolls and public expenditure constraints take greater effect in the 1980s. Trown and Needham note that research has shown women with children prefer to return to teaching initially on a part-time basis, but for the reasons mentioned, such posts are becoming increasingly less common. In their view,

> would-be returners, who cannot obtain part-time teaching posts, have either to delay re-entry until they can manage a full-time position (thus lengthening the 'gap' in their teaching experience) or accept temporary supply teaching with its insecurity and irregular demands. The more delayed the re-entry the less time the teacher has to build up sufficient experience to make her eligible for promotion.

Interestingly, the researchers found that women with children were three times as likely as men to have been demoted en route to a headship. Men rarely experienced demotion after absence from teaching, even when they had worked outside the educational system.

The re-entry problem can therefore help to explain the female head's higher average age and longer length of service, although as the researchers note, married women were a minority of female heads. (Information on the marital status of the heads in the NFER research was not collected.) More recently, the introduction of maternity leave has allowed women the opportunity to leave teaching temporarily and return to the same post at a later date. However, Trown and Needham note from their survey that although greater numbers of women were taking maternity leave, many said they were unable to return to teaching when they wished, as adequate nursery facilities were often unavailable. Moreover, they state, 'most had chosen to be at home with their young children for a few years and felt that their right to make that choice, without giving up their career aspirations, should be defended'. (At present in the UK, it is necessary to return to one's school within approximately six months to obtain maximum benefits.) Trown and Needham's pessimistic conclusion is that if maternity leave is unable to provide a solution for most teachers and re-entry opportunities (both part-time and full-time) continue to decline, then 'the chances of women with families reaching headships would seem increasingly remote'.

Recent research into the selection of secondary heads has argued that the underlying concern of selectors is whether candidates – male or female – have a background of domestic harmony, rather that whether they are married or single. They do however note, 'many selectors have difficulty in conceiving of domestic arrangements where the women's career takes priority' (Morgan *et al.*, 1983).

The greater number of years in teaching and the longer period women had to spend as deputies suggested it was necessary to serve a longer 'apprenticeship' before achieving a headship. At present it appears necessary for *both* sexes to spend a longer period than before as a deputy, although interestingly the gap between the sexes has remained constant. Also, as previously mentioned, a higher proportion of women have served as acting heads, thereby offering proof to selectors that they had the necessary skills to cope with the range of duties and responsibilities associated with headship. As might be expected, the NFER data found there were proportionately far more male heads in coeducational schools and that a large proportion of females were heads of girl's schools in urban areas.

The differences in educational qualifications between the sexes is shown in Tables 2.8 and 2.9. Although on average women were less well qualified than men, a statistically significant difference was only found for 'old' heads and the possession of a first degree. For both groups, fewer women than men were graduates and they were more likely to possess a certificate of education. However, a higher proportion of the female heads were graduates compared with the national average, which showed only 65 per cent of female heads of maintained secondary schools had degrees (DES, 1983).

There were no statistically significant differences for highest level of qualification held by male and female heads in the NFER study (Table 2.9). Although further analysis showed a significant difference between new and 'old' *male* heads, with a greater proportion of the more recent appointments holding higher qualifications.

Table 2.8   Educational qualifications – gender differences

New Heads %			'Old' Heads %	
Male	*Female*		*Male*	*Female*
26	39	Certificate of education	16	29
93	79	First degree	96 *	85
63	58	Postgraduate certificate in education	68	51
25	30	Advanced diploma	11	7
35	21	Higher degree	22	20
N = 163	N = 24		N = 186	N = 41
N = 187			N = 227	

*Chi-square significant at 5 per cent level between male and female heads.
NB Percentages do not total 100% as more than one qualification can be held.

Table 2.9 Highest qualification held – gender differences

New Heads (%)			'Old' Heads (%)	
Male	*Female*		*Male*	*Female*
35	21	Higher degree (masters/doctorate)	22	20
12	21	Advanced diploma	8	5
38	42	Postgraduate certificate in education	51	41
14	12	First degree	15	24
1	4	Certificate of education	4	10
100%	100%		100%	100%
N = 163	N = 24		N = 186	N = 41
N = 187			N = 227	

Chi-square not significant between male and female heads for either group.

In terms of subject backgrounds and main teaching areas, the only statistically significant gender difference was found in English. Thirty-five per cent of females compared to nearly 20 per cent of male heads had a teaching background predominantly in English. Perhaps surprisingly, there were no other statistically significant differences in subject background.

Career preferences

Future career preferences for both groups of heads are listed in Table 2.10. Bearing in mind that more than one choice could be made, the main preference for both groups was to remain at their present school. The second most popular choice was to move to a different school. There were statistically significant differences in the first preference only with more experienced heads expressing a desire to stay in their current headship. There was no obvious reason for this difference and it could not be accounted for by a large number of 'old' heads having entered their second headships – in fact, only 7 per cent of the sample were currently in their second post. A statistically significant relationship was also found between the size of school and the career preference to remain at one's present school. Perhaps unsurprisingly, those with headships of large schools – approximately one-third of both groups were heads of schools with over 1000 pupils – were more likely to prefer to remain where they were, rather than seek a career move.

What did those interviewed regard as a reasonable period of time to be a head in any one institution? As might be expected, there was not complete

Table 2.10   Future career preferences

	Percentages	
	New Heads	*'Old' Heads*
Remain at present school*	57	66
Move to a different school	51	51
Become an HMI	13	7
Become a college or university lecturer	6	5
Take up an LEA advisory or admin. post	17	14
Leave the education system for employment in another field	13	13
Other (e.g. secondment, early retirement)	12	11
N =	188	228

*Chi-square significant at 5 per cent level between the two groups.
NB Percentages do not total 100%, as more than one preference could be chosen.

agreement, but by far the most common response was to suggest an optimum period of between four to ten years in any one school. No head suggested a period of less than four years and remaining in the same school for *more* than ten years was seen by some as having reached a situation of diminishing returns. As one head remarked, 'an individual can only give so much and after ten years in one school, you have probably given as much as you can'. Others suggested if heads remained in post for more than a decade, they would necessarily need retraining and re-enthusing and it was in everyone's interest to either 'pension heads off if they are past their prime' or find them alternative employment 'so as not to allow them to go stale' (for example secondments or job exchanges). A case study head expressed concern that it was difficult to inform heads when they had 'gone off the boil'. As a deputy he found, even when relationships between members of the senior management team were excellent, they were reluctant to criticize the head.

Several heads specifically stated they would remain at their schools until the job lost its creative appeal, they became bored or no longer derived satisfaction from their present posts; while others were happy to stay until retirement but felt, in due course, they would probably need a fresh challenge and the stimulus of change.

Heads clearly saw themselves as 'having a job to do' and several thought they would stay as long as it was necessary to change the school for the better. Others were more realistic and showed an awareness of the magnitude of the task ahead. One head remarked that his predecessor had been in post for 27 years, but he would remain at the school for no more than five. In the head's view, much needed changing at the school but there were limits on what could be achieved without a total change of staff. Others spoke of making an initial impression only, while leaving the remainder of the task to their successor.

Several heads, while agreeing career mobility and job movement was in the best interests of LEAs, schools and heads themselves, commented that after serving five years or so in their first headship, securing a second would not be easy. In their view, the reality was that those responsible for the selection and appointment of secondary heads would probably think they were too old to warrant serious consideration. There should be a greater preparedness on the part of the selectors, it was suggested, to consider applications from heads over the age of 50.

Applications for headship and the appointment process

The selection and appointment of secondary heads has, both in this country and abroad, aroused considerable interest in the 1980s. It could be argued the greater attention currently given to selection and appointment processes and procedures corresponds with the growing recognition – within the educational research field and elsewhere – of the relationship between school leadership and school effectiveness. Leadership selection procedures have come to be regarded as of key importance for this reason, as well as for the more obvious fact that many heads and principals are likely to remain in post for a long time. Put most simply, it is therefore thought vital to ensure the 'right' person is appointed in the first place.

In the United States, Baltzell and Dentler (1985) have summarized research and undertaken case studies into the process of selecting school principals as well as putting forward suggestions for improving practice; while in the United Kingdom two teacher associations have recently published discussion documents that include recommendations and suggestions to improve the selection of headteachers (Secondary Heads Association, 1983; National Association of Schoolmasters/Union of Women Teachers, 1985). The DES funded a major three-year project into the selection of secondary school heads – the POST project – and the research findings have recently been published (Morgan *et al.*, 1983).

Selection processes and appointment procedures were not a major focus of the NFER research, as it was felt the POST project would cover the area in considerable detail. This is indeed so, but while the POST team's observational study provides some fascinating insights into the process of selection, the reader is given little understanding of the experiences of individuals at the receiving end of the appointment process and their views, beliefs and actions are not given the importance they probably deserve.

Although appointment procedures and interview experiences were not part of our remit, some information was gained during the course of lengthy interviews with 47 newly appointed heads and 16 LEA officers. The picture of procedures they provided was one of considerable variety across LEAs (a point stressed by POST), but the uniformly black picture given by POST was not confirmed. The 'successful' new heads had experienced appointment procedures in a number of LEAs and while many castigated LEAs for their 'inadequacies' and lack of thought regarding the interview process, other LEAs (admittedly a minority) were referred to in more favourable terms. A considerable number of heads spoke of the importance of the selection process, and several commented that headship was now such a complex role that selectors did not always know which particular qualities they were seeking in candidates. An LEA officer made a similar point when he commented that selectors were faced with a dilemma and were often unsure whether they were looking for gifted educationists or, for example, first class managers of people and he added that currently heads were appointed on the slenderest of evidence.

Bearing in mind the previous section's discussion of the career paths of female heads, it is interesting to consider the POST team's findings on the position of women candidates. They report that officer perceptions 'can be summarized as initially welcoming, expecting a higher quality from them than from male candidates, and fearing lay selectors' doubts at the final stages'. The team also remarked that men consider applying for girls' schools' headships, while women very rarely apply for headships of boys' schools. They suggest a key factor for selectors in assessing female applicants' suitability was the ability to maintain discipline. It is interesting to note that in an analysis of 36 headships for coeducational schools, they found that only 11 per cent of the applicants were women. (This was, however, an improvement as Hilsum and Start's (1974) earlier research, based on 133 vacancies, found only approximately 5 per cent of the applications were received from women.) In the POST project, at the final interview, women accounted for 12 per cent of the candidates and of the 36 heads appointed, 11 per cent were women. The similarity of the proportions at each stage suggests there was little, if any, discrimination against women. However, the team's observational data did point to the differential treatment of female candidates and they suggest that in the selectors' eyes appointing a woman involved a greater risk than appointing a man.

By analysing the number of headships for maintained secondary schools advertized in 1980, the POST team calculated (although they do not give details) that the number of applicants varied from seven to 213 and was generally about 65. (With this average figure in mind, it is noteworthy that two of the 47 heads interviewed were successful with their first applications, while another was successful with his second!) As noted in the first section of this chapter, for a variety of reasons heads were selective in their applications, with some, for example, reluctant to move a considerable distance for family reasons, or due to the cost of moving home. Heads based in the north of England thought there was little point in applying for posts in the south, as the cost of housing was prohibitively high and relocation allowances far from generous or non-existent.

The head designate period

School visits prior to taking up post

After their appointment but before taking up post, all the new heads were able to visit their schools, usually to talk to the outgoing head and meet as many of the staff as possible. The number of days the heads designate were able to spend at the 'new' school varied from one to 20 days. However, nearly two-thirds were only able to spend between one and three days visiting the school. In general, the limited time spent at the school was either a deliberate choice on the part of the head designate, who often felt little could be gained from further visits, or more commonly, due to circumstances beyond their control. Many, for example, spoke of the continuing demands of their present schools (e.g. responsibility for timetable construction), or mentioned that geographical location or distance prevented frequent day visits. Some were more fortunate in that different end of term dates between education authorities allowed them the opportunity to spend several days or weeks at the 'new' school.

Visits to the school during this time were a very important part of the heads' preparation both in terms of obtaining information and establishing relationships with the staff, especially the senior members. It was also important, of course, for the staff to have an opportunity to meet the new head, ask questions and to see that the head designate was concerned enough about the school to make a number of visits prior to appointment, often at considerable personal cost.

Several heads stated the meetings with teachers were extremely useful in establishing staff expectations in advance, as well as ensuring they did not feel strangers or interlopers and knew how to get around the school. The visits also enabled the heads to gain initial impressions without the pressures of being the 'head' and having all attention concentrated on their reactions.

However, as many as one-third of the new heads surveyed made predominantly unfavourable comments about the value of school visits. Some said visits only provided them with background information, and that so much information within a short period was confusing and could lead to preconceived ideas about the school. Others felt the discussions with outgoing heads were of limited value with little useful information being gained. A case study head mentioned that he preferred not to return after his first visit, the retiring head had been at the school for over 20 years and the new head did not want to upset him in any way. It was best, he felt, to let his predecessor 'retire gracefully' and to keep out of the school until his departure. It is perhaps worth noting that several new heads, following on from heads who had been in post for a considerable time, were concerned with their predecessors' lack of any formal system of records or files ('Everything was kept in his head'). In these instances, time spent with the outgoing head should have been time well spent, but most remarked that it rarely was.

A small-scale research project into preparation for secondary headship by Dwyer (1984), similarly found many heads saw this period as a missed opportunity, with a number expressing negative comments about the unhelpful attitudes of LEAs and/or their predecessors. Dwyer's own view was that LEAs 'must encourage heads to spend time at the new school and in the new authority and pay expenses for travel and accommodation to enable them to do so'.

Information collected in the NFER project from a variety of sources clearly showed that the period before taking up appointment was not used to the best effect. More frequent visits to the school would enable the head designate to obtain sufficient background information about the school, its staff and pupils and thereby help minimize or reduce the numerous demands which often occur soon after the head takes up post. Many heads spoke of the 'endless queue' of individuals wishing to advance claims and express views on various matters. It is very important for things to go well at the outset as parents, pupils and teachers may perceive the new head to be a 'failure' if the initial appearance is one of chaos. Opportunities for greater familiarization with the school prior to taking up post could help reduce the chances of this possibility occurring.

Introduction to LEA prior to taking up post

It was also during the time found for school visits that heads designate had an opportunity informally to meet senior officers of the authority and familiarize themselves with LEA procedures. These introductions and visits, like those to the school, can be very important, especially for the 60 per cent or so of heads who are likely to be working in the LEA for the first time. During these visits the heads were often introduced to the various officers responsible for the different sections and they found this useful in 'putting faces to names'.

However, in order to be most effective these visits have to be carefully planned and thought must be given as to the best time for them. Some heads commented that their visits were virtually useless in some instances taking place over the lunch hour when few of the officers were available. Others said the introductions were far too cursory and superficial, or they took place very soon after appointment and hence much had been forgotten on taking up post several months later.

Whereas the majority (86 per cent) of local authorities surveyed said it was their policy to invite new secondary heads to County Hall (or its equivalent) for an introductory visit or induction day, only 26 per cent offered an induction programme or course of more than one day's duration. It was rare for the programme to take place in the head designate period and most occurred in the first term or year of headship. For this reason more detailed comments are found in Chapter 9, which examines LEA support in general.

An interesting account of how the time before taking up post can be used beneficially has recently been provided by a new head (Imison, 1985). This particular secondary head was able to design a seven week programme, which included spending eight days at the 'new' school, visiting 14 other comprehensive and eight feeder primary schools, and attending three conferences. Imison argues that heads designate should be given 'time, advice and a free hand to make one's own preparations to fit the new situations and the new role ahead'. As a head promoted from within the same authority the programme was possible with only the costs of a replacement at her previous school, plus her expenses. Indeed, some LEA officers interviewed as part of the NFER project, suggested a possibility worth further exploration was the establishment of a reciprocal relationship between authorities to cover a short period of preparation time for heads designate. Finally, a further suggestion made by some of the new heads was that, at the time of changeover, the outgoing head should be required to produce a full written report on the school. This it was thought would help ease the transition to headship.

Summary and discussion

Each year in England and Wales about 300 headships are advertized and data from the 1982/83 cohort showed that about 80 per cent of all secondary heads appointed were new heads. Their average age on appointment was 42, a slight increase in comparison to the sample of 'old' heads who all took up their first headship between 1975 and 1980. The difference seemed to be due to the fact that the new heads had spent, on average, about a year and a half longer as deputy heads than the 'old' heads. Most people had been deputy heads and a comparison between the two groups suggested it was becoming even less common to obtain a headship without spending about five to seven years at this level. Ninety per cent of the new heads' cohort had a first degree and a third had obtained masters degrees. An examination of the heads' teaching backgrounds indicated a higher proportion came from humanities, English and science in comparison with a DES sample of teachers, but why this should be so was not clear.

An interesting finding from the cohort was the small number of internal appointments. Only 10 per cent were appointed from deputy to head within their existing schools and many of these had already been acting heads. (Differences between internal and external appointments are further examined in Chapters 7 and 11.)

Women heads were seriously under-represented and accounted for only 13 per cent of the cohort. As might be expected, many were heads of girls' schools and therefore the proportion of women heads in mixed schools was very low. On average, women were three years older and had spent about one-and-a-half years longer as a deputy than the men before obtaining their first headship. The differences did not seem to be simply explained by time out for children, as the women had also taught an average of three years longer than the men.

During the head designate period – the time between appointment and actually taking up post – most people were only able to spend one to three days visiting their new school. These visits provided the new head with valuable information about the school by talking to the previous head, the deputies and as many other staff as possible. LEAs should recognize the importance of these early visits by providing more time and facilitating the release of heads designate from their present schools. The employing authority should also consider helping with expenses, both for these visits and removal costs. A further suggestion to improve the preparation of new heads is that LEAs should require all outgoing heads to produce a full written report on the school for their successors.

In 1982/83, 60 per cent of the new heads had moved to a different LEA to obtain their headship. If this is typical of most years, it has important consequences with regard to induction, as one of the most common difficulties mentioned by new heads was the lack of knowledge about LEA procedures. Most authorities invited new heads to the central and area offices to meet the senior officers, but the research showed this was often poorly organized. These visits could either occur during the head designate period or in the first term. LEAs need to plan the visits more thoroughly to ensure that heads have sufficient time to meet officers and that the process does not simply become a 'blur of faces' which are soon forgotten. In addition to the introductory visits, some LEAs organized a more substantial induction programme for new heads and these are discussed in Chapter 9.

CHAPTER 3
Preparation and Training for Headship

In the previous chapter the path to headship was explored largely in terms of quantitative data. This chapter examines the skills and knowledge heads need in their preparation for headship and how these needs are met. Almost all the heads felt their preparation had taken place both through job experience as they progressed through their career *and* by attendance at various management courses.

Skills, tasks and knowledge

Several attempts have been made to list the kinds of skills and knowledge that are needed to cope with the tasks and responsibilities associated with headship (e.g. Lyons, 1976; Jackson, 1976). More recently, the POST team (Morgan *et al.*, 1983) started with Robert Katz's (1974) three-fold classification of the 'Skills of an Effective Administrator' – technical, conceptual and human. For heads, the POST team felt a fourth category of 'external management' was necessary. The POST classification has become a frequent point of reference, but it is interesting to note it is not based on their own empirical research and the team devised a table of 'Managerial Tasks' because they were unable to find any LEAs with a written job description for secondary heads.

Another attempt at listing 'school leaders' professional development needs', based on discussions with administrators, heads and trainers, is provided by Clive Hopes (1981). In a paper prepared for an international workshop, Hopes lists 15 main 'areas' or needs and these, with examples, are shown in Table 3.1.

John Buckley (1985) provides a useful overview of these and other efforts at producing a comprehensive list of the skills and knowledge heads are thought to need. But it should be remembered that these are areas of knowledge and skills which other people think heads should have and, in general, these lists have not been produced by heads themselves. An exception is Anne Jones' (forthcoming) survey of 400 secondary heads who were presented with lists of tasks and skills and asked to indicate where they felt more training was required. Her research showed that motivating staff, team building, conflict resolution, strategic planning, staff appraisal and keeping up with what was

Table 3.1   Professional development needs of school leaders (from Hopes, 1981)

1 Personnel management	– allocating duties and tasks
– planning	– understanding the school as an
– recruiting	organization
– development and INSET	*9 Relating to governmental systems*
– appraisal	– reporting to regulatory system
– management of professional and	– reporting to regional, state, national
non-professional staff	system
	– negotiating with: regulatory system;
2 Interpersonal skills	other authorities
– communicating	– experience in the administration
– motivating	
– counselling	*10 Relating to the local environment*
– handling conflict	– community
– committees and chairmanship	– public relations
– group behaviour	– relating to professional groups
– group leadership	– parents
	– church
3 Self-management	– local industry
– managing stress	– culture
– management of one's own time	– press
– self-awareness	– politicians
– self-development	
	11 Knowledge of laws
4 Institutional planning	– law in relation to school
– assessing information from within	– personal rights
and outside school	– youth and social laws
– forecasting trends and needs	
– determining policies and priorities	*12 Educational leadership*
– institutional evaluation (organizing,	– supervision
reporting results, discussing results)	– advising
– determining policies, goals and	– methodology
values	– discipline
	– school events
5 Resource management	
– estimating budgetary control	*13 Relating to pupils/students*
– financial management	– dealing with individuals and groups
	– dealing with seriously disruptive
6 Curriculum skills	– dealing with seriously disturbed
– development of curriculum	
– management of curriculum	*14 School as a system in relation to other*
	environmental systems
7 Management of innovation	– system analysis
– creating innovations	
– reacting to innovations	*15 Developing a philosophy of headship*
– responding to innovations	– role of the head
– implementing	– styles of leadership
	– awareness of values in relation to
8 Organizational skills	managing
– devising internal management	– approaches to managing
structures	
– devising academic structures and	
record systems	

happening nationally were key concerns for heads.

The questionnaire to the experienced heads involved in the NFER study used an open-ended format rather than a checklist to obtain views on which headship skills and knowledge could be developed through training. The results are shown in Table 3.2 together with the number of heads who listed each topic. (As more than one area could be mentioned percentages have not been used.)

As an example of how to interpret Table 3.2, the first line shows that 118 of the 214 heads who responded to the question mentioned an aspect of 'curriculum'. But care has to be taken with the figures from this type of question, as it cannot be assumed that the other 96 heads who did not list 'curriculum' do not believe this to be an important area.

Table 3.2 shows that most of the areas mentioned were concerned with internal school factors, such as curriculum and timetabling, the management of staff and finance. It is interesting to note that relatively few heads mentioned innovation and the management of change. It is possible that the more experienced heads could have already introduced many of the changes that were of current concern for new heads.

The heads were also asked when training for such skills or knowledge could most usefully take place. Overwhelmingly, they felt that almost all of the areas should be initially covered *prior* to headship during the period as a deputy. But further training was also thought to be required after appointment and in the following years.

How are heads prepared for headship?

In order to obtain a measure of the level of preparation, both new and 'old' heads were asked to indicate on a five-point scale how well prepared they felt for headship. Table 3.3 shows the results of this self-assessment by both groups of heads.

While about half of each group rated themselves as well or very well prepared, it is important to recognize that one in five of the 'old' heads and about one in six of the new heads felt less than adequately prepared for headship.

In order to explore matters further, cross-tabulations were carried out between the heads' self-rating on the adequacy scale and a number of other variables. None of these analyses proved to be statistically significant. After completing the self-rating scale, the heads were asked to write down those areas in which they felt least prepared. The most frequently mentioned by the new heads in order of occurrence were: finance; the experience of becoming a head (the feeling of being in the 'hot seat' and fully comprehending that the 'buck stops here'); obtaining knowledge of LEA procedures and finding out 'who does what'; staff management, including staff development, appointments and dealing with incompetent staff; governors; and general administration. Similar areas were also mentioned by the 'old' heads and LEA officers as being those they thought new heads were least prepared for.

Table 3.2   Headship skills and knowledge
'In your opinion, which headship skills or knowledge can be acquired or developed by training?'

	Number of heads		Number of heads
Internal		*Management skills*	
Curriculum – development, analysis, planning	118	School organization and administration – office procedures	57
Timetabling	65	Management skills/ techniques (general)	37
Pastoral		Setting aims and objectives, establishing priorities	25
Pastoral care/organization	20		
Staff		School evaluation and assessment – organization development	21
Staff management – motivation, morale, incompetent staff	82		
		Communication	20
Interpersonal relations – counselling staff	32	Leadership	15
Interviewing skills	32	Delegation	15
Staff development/INSET	29	Chairing meetings	13
Staff appointments	17	Management of resources/ buildings	11
Change		Decision-making	10
Innovation and management of change	28		
		External	
Knowledge		LEA – knowledge of procedures – relationship with officers/advisers	46
Finance and capitation	53		
Head and the Law	26	School and community	17
Current/future educational issues	11	Governors	14
		Public relations – media	14
		Unions/professional associations	9

Data from random sample of 214 secondary heads with 3–8 years' experience (missing data 14)

Table 3.3 Adequacy of preparation
'Please circle on the scale below how well you feel you were prepared, prior to appointment, for the demands of headship.'

	Very poorly prepared	Less than adequately prepared	Adequately prepared	Well prepared	Very well prepared	N
			Percentages			
New heads	1	15	34	35	15	183
'Old' heads	3	17	34	34	12	221

Missing data: 5 New heads, 7 'Old' heads.
Chi-square not significant between the two groups.

As mentioned earlier, it is clear that preparation for headship occurred both through experience in school as a result of undertaking a range of previous posts, as well as through attendance at management courses. The next section uses both interview and survey data to examine what heads said they had learned from their previous experience, both in school and from various courses.

Most heads felt that they acquired various skills and knowledge from all their previous posts as they moved towards headship. As heads of department they began to obtain knowledge about curriculum development and planning and in order to run a department effectively, they also learned both organizational skills and staff management. If they had come through the head of year or head of house route, they had learned various aspects of pastoral care and, in addition to working with a team of form tutors, they also experienced contact with parents and numerous support agencies.

While all the experience gained as a class teacher, form tutor, head of department and head of year was seen to be beneficial, almost all the heads said that the most valuable experience was obtained during their period as a deputy head.

Many heads stressed the benefit of being part of a senior management team where members were fully involved in discussion and decision-making across all aspects of the school. A key point in preparation for headship was the breadth of experience as a deputy so that, for example, they had first-hand knowledge of timetabling and pastoral care. Also thought to have been of value was chairing various committees and working parties. Involvement in staff appointments – in terms of drawing up job descriptions, shortlisting and interviewing – was seen as important preparation for future headship. A smaller number of heads had been able to attend governors' meetings and had access to details about capitation and finance. For some, the role of head of upper or lower school had meant responsibility for a whole section of the school and provided a wide range of experience.

Clearly, the range of experience as a deputy was heavily dependent on the previous head's ability and willingness to delegate. The heads in the NFER study stressed the importance of being given responsibility and freedom to develop various aspects of the school in their previous posts as deputies. They wanted to be allowed to make decisions and feel that the head gave these their backing, some even saying how valuable it had been to learn from their mistakes.

As deputies, a great deal could be learned about headship from working with their previous heads. While there was no doubt about the value of a good head – 'if you have a good head while a deputy, you are made for headship' – several people pointed out that much could also be learned from poor heads – 'He was a disaster, so I learned what not to do.' It appeared that most heads did not deliberately prepare deputies for future headship, but some made it clear that they would give their full support and backing to the deputies' attempts to gain a headship. One of the case study heads said,

> At my last school the head saw me as a future head. Indeed, part of the application form for the job included a section stating that you would be expected to be here for at least four years as a deputy before moving on to another post. It was very much a training ground for heads and I think over the last eight years three, perhaps four, of the deputies became heads.

A number of other heads also referred to their previous schools as 'head teacher training grounds' and this appeared to be largely due to the heads' attitude and awareness of their role in preparing deputies for headship.

A strategy used by some heads as preparation for headship, was to rotate the deputies' responsibilities so that they experienced most aspects of school management; for example, several years on the curricular side followed by a period as the pastoral deputy. Three of the 16 case study heads had done this as deputies and found it particularly valuable.

The surveys of the new and 'old' heads provided information on the number of people who had deputized for their previous heads for a continuous period of two weeks or more. Twenty-nine per cent of the 'old' heads and 37 per cent of the new heads said they had stood in for their previous head. The average period of time was about 15 weeks and ranged from two weeks to a few cases of a year and a half, but most totalled under a term. For many of the heads, the time spent in deputizing or as acting head was extremely valuable in giving them their first experience of sitting in the 'hot seat'. As acting heads they were able to gain a wider experience of school management than they could as deputy heads. In particular, this meant far more contact with the governors, LEA officers, unions, support agencies and the community and possibly their first experience of professional isolation.

The questionnaire to the 'old' heads asked them to give details of any non-teaching experience which they considered to have been particularly useful in preparation for headship. The main out-of-school educational area mentioned was work for various teacher unions and professional associations, often as a member of the executive committee. A smaller number of heads had gained valuable experience as elected members of education committees which had provided an insight into local politics and decision-making. A number of heads also felt that their involvement as examiners for various exam boards had helped in assessment and syllabus design.

A wide range of answers were given about work outside education which was considered to have provided valuable experience for headship. The most commonly mentioned was bringing up one's own children, which allowed the heads to empathize with parents. Many of the 'old' heads had undertaken a period of compulsory National Service in the armed forces and spoke of the benefits obtained, particularly in terms of administration and specialized skills (e.g. interviewing).

The other main areas of non-teaching experience which the heads thought of value were work for the church in many different aspects, the youth service (e.g. youth club leader), marriage guidance work and other forms of counselling. A variety of experience in sports such as cricket, football and rugby was thought to have helped the heads in terms of team work and leadership. Those who had worked in industry and commerce said how important this was in giving them a wider perspective on society, while experience overseas was also valuable in gaining insights into different cultures and ways of life.

Management courses

During the last few years considerable interest has been shown in management training for heads and senior staff. (For useful collections of European papers, see Hegarty, 1983, and ATEE-NAHT, 1982. An historical overview of training for heads in England is given by Pennington and Bell, 1983.) Although in the United Kingdom attendance at a major course on educational management is not a statutory prerequisite for headship, it appears from the POST project that LEA selectors do consider this factor when shortlisting candidates. The information obtained in the current research from both groups of heads and the LEA officers showed that most people considered attendance at one or more courses to be an important form of preparation for headship.

The questionnaires to the heads with three to eight years' experience asked them to list the courses on school organization and management which they had attended in the last three years, as well as those attended *prior* to headship. The heads then rated the usefulness of each course, using a five-point scale ranging from 'no use' to 'extremely useful'. The results were very positive and only 5 per cent of all courses were rated of no use or little use. In general, the figures suggested that courses attended prior to headship were perceived as more useful than those attended after becoming a head.

More detailed information on management courses was obtained during the interviews with the 47 new heads. Only two had not been on a management course prior to headship. Both these heads had wanted to go, but had been too busy as deputies and had heads who did not encourage staff to attend courses. Most of the 47 heads had attended between one and three courses, while one head had been to six different courses. The courses were provided by a wide range of institutions and organizations. Eighteen heads had been on the one week DES COSMOS (Committee on Staffing and Management of Secondary Schools) course and all spoke very highly of it. LEA officers stressed the advantages of mixing heads, deputies and LEA officers on COSMOS courses. The curriculum and timetabling aspects and particularly the curriculum notation scheme used, were thought to be highly valuable. The case studies on curriculum planning with falling rolls were seen as very helpful. The HMIs' lectures and group leadership were praised by several LEA officers and, as one pointed out, 'HMI have a different set of jokes from us!'

Also given very high praise by heads were the lengthier courses run by the North West Educational Management Centre at Padgate and the six-week Inner London Education Authority (ILEA) course. About half the heads had been on short LEA courses such as 'The Role of the Deputy Head' or 'Timetabling' and 'Interviewing Skills'. A variety of universities and polytechnics also provided courses, most of which were thought to be of value in preparation for headship. Courses on the curriculum and timetabling were the most frequently attended.

The points made by both 'old' and new heads about the aspects which they felt particularly useful largely confirmed what is already known about in-service courses in general. Thus, many heads stressed the value of residential components during a course, as these provided an important break from the everyday pressures of school and enhanced the valuable informal contact between the participants. Time and again, the importance of informal discussions was mentioned. Input from experienced heads and other practitioners was particularly welcomed. The course had to be well-organized with good speakers and group leaders. Some heads preferred all the course members to be from secondary schools and thought that a mixture of new and experienced heads worked well. There was disagreement about the value of speakers from industry and other non-educational areas; while some heads welcomed this, others felt there was little common ground.

A range of techniques was mentioned as being of value and these included: in-tray exercises, simulations, role play, case studies, small group work and video-feedback.

Some courses were criticized as being badly organized and poorly led. It seemed that Doyle and Ponder's (1977) 'practicality ethic' of teachers also applied to heads, who wanted courses to be of practical relevance to their school and not idealized and heavily theoretical. For this reason, tasks or projects which had to be carried out in their own school were seen as highly valuable, although these were more likely to occur on longer courses. (Heads' views on LEA induction courses which may include a 'management' component are considered in detail in Chapter 9.)

Management course provision and LEA views

The survey of LEA officers asked them to list and comment on those courses which they thought were of value to their heads and deputies. DES courses were mentioned the most frequently, with 55 per cent of the LEAs listing COSMOS, and 26 per cent the DES regional courses. Courses provided and run by the LEA advisers and officers themselves were listed by 45 per cent of the authorities. Many of these were related specifically to LEA problems and policies. Their value was seen in terms of sharing experience, ideas and the demonstration of good practice by the heads and deputies from schools in the authority. In one LEA all the secondary heads and deputies attended the management course, which was run by heads and advisers in four two-day blocks. Another authority ran a course which included opening each secondary school in turn for visits by senior staff from other schools, which provided 'frank and fruitful discussions and forged useful links'.

A large county authority had run its own management course for heads since 1976. The course for 10 to 15 secondary heads commenced with a residential session of two days, followed by nine one-day meetings throughout the year and then concluded with another two days in residence. The course was run by the LEA advisers and concentrated on interpersonal skills, an evaluation of the current situation in the head's school and problem-solving of various issues of concern to the participants. The chief adviser spent a day in each school, talking with small groups of staff and students. Each head was asked to prepare a plan for the next two to three years and this was discussed in the school by the head and various advisers. After the course a brief report about progress was originally requested annually from the head, but this had now become a bi-annual event.

One of the case study heads had attended this in his first year and greatly appreciated the course. It had helped create an instant peer group, as he had met 14 other heads from the authority and formed impressions about which ones to contact about particular issues. However, he found part of the course included an expectation for change when he would have preferred a longer settling-in period.

As well as building good relationships between the heads, the course also helped to establish a feeling of trust between the heads and the advisers. Most of the secondary heads had been on the course and the LEA was currently contemplating sending complete senior management teams from several schools on a residential course.

The LEA survey provided details on the groups of authorities who worked with regional providers (Padgate, Regional Headship Unit at Woolley Hall and WISH – the Wessex Inservice Scheme for Secondary Heads). All the authorities involved praised the schemes, seeing them as valuable in exchanging views across LEAs, encouraging good group discussions and providing study of a range of topics including an in-depth project relevant to each participant's own school. The length of these courses (up to six weeks) allowed 'fruitful relations to be built up with the other participants, which often continued after the course had finished'.

Various long-term award-bearing courses such as an MEd and Diploma in Educational Management were mentioned by 17 per cent of the LEAs. These courses were seen to be of value in that they were intellectually demanding and provided refreshment through contact with the latest books and articles. If they involved a one-year secondment, the substantial period away from the pressure of school allowed the person to reflect on their practice. One LEA had a scheme whereby 17 deputies from half the secondary schools in the LEA attended a Diploma in Educational Management course for one day/week for two years, which meant that a detailed study of real problems in school could be undertaken. Short non-award bearing courses provided by institutions of higher education, usually one week in length, were only mentioned by 12 per cent of the authorities.

Industrial providers of management courses such as IBM, Rank Xerox, ICI and the Industrial Society were listed by 9 per cent of the LEA officers. The value of these courses was seen in meeting other types of managers and gaining a wider perspective and insight from industry, and from some courses 'the opportunity to develop interpersonal skills often overlooked in education'.

The new national initiative

In 1979/80 the DES funded a one-year study based at the University of Birmingham to survey the extent and nature of courses and other forms of professional development available to heads and senior staff (Hughes, Carter and Fidler, 1981). The survey gave details of the types, number of courses and people attending them and showed the considerable variety of provision. The report suggested that a major national initiative was required to increase and improve senior management training and that a School Management Unit should be established to 'stimulate and support such development'. Many of the recommendations seemed to have been considered favourably by the DES and in 1983 Circular 3/83 gave details of a new initiative. Two million pounds was made available to LEAs for the first year of the scheme. The money was to be used to provide release for heads and deputies to attend either a 20-day basic course or a one-term training opportunity (OTTO). Both types of course were provided by about 20 DES approved institutions of higher education. The programmes were seen to have the following goals: to improve individual management skills, to provide professional and personal development and, for the OTTO courses, to enable 'graduates' to contribute to the staffing and organization of the 20-day basic courses and LEA INSET provision. The DES have continued to show their support for senior management training in Circulars 4/84 and 3/85 which maintained the funding of the scheme.

The NFER survey of all LEAs in England and Wales took place in March 1984 and included several questions which provided details of the LEAs' initial reactions to the 3/83 scheme. Table 3.4 shows the number of heads and deputies who had attended 3/83 courses in the first year of scheme.

Table 3.4 Number of heads and deputies attending DES 3/83 courses up to July 1984

	20-day	Number of LEAs	OTTO	Number of LEAs
Secondary heads	105	22	79	37
Secondary deputies	286	41	44	20

Data from 80 LEAs

Over 500 senior staff had either been on a 20-day basic course or on an OTTO course for one term. Twelve of the 80 LEAs in the survey had not sent any heads or deputies on a 3/83 course. Some of these authorities found it difficult to find an appropriate course or an accessible provider. The figures in Table 3.4 indicate that many LEAs preferred to send deputies on the 20-day courses and heads on the OTTO courses.

The LEAs were asked which criteria were used to select participants; what plans they had to use them after completing the courses; and what were their initial views and opinions of the scheme. The following information is drawn from the 80 LEAs who returned completed questionnaires.

While many of the authorities welcomed the new scheme, very few did so without qualifying their response with some form of critical comment. The most common criticism, mentioned by a quarter of the respondents, concerned the scheme's hasty implementation and inadequate planning. Some negative reference was made to the courses themselves, 12 local authorities seeing them as limited, inflexible and of poor quality. As might be expected, a number of LEAs were keen to obtain feedback on course quality before encouraging other senior staff to attend.

Only three authorities mentioned the difficulties they had experienced in attracting applicants, which seemed to be related to the uncertainties of senior staff and LEAs concerning the purpose of the courses. The above criticisms were most forcibly summarized by one chief adviser, who referred to the scheme as 'an exercise launched without adequate rationale, pre-planning of content and time-scales, or (apparently) careful impartial analysis of "good" providers at a period of the year when most LEAs in this region had already agreed their secondments. Quality seems variable. A good example of mismanagement.'

Several LEAs stated there was a need for the providers to be more aware of their requirements and they were critical of the initial lack of consultation. The relevance of some course components was criticized, as was the expertise of some course tutors; as one authority stated, 'It would be most useful if the courses could be tutored by existing, credible heads'. Some of the providers were seen as reluctant to address the issue of appropriate teaching methods and there was a desire from several LEAs to minimize formal lecturing, to use course tutors as facilitators and enablers, and place a greater emphasis on experiential learning.

Senior staff were clearly seen to benefit from spending a term in the company of heads and deputies from other authorities. However, what seemed of crucial importance to several LEAs was what happened when participants returned to their schools. It was therefore essential that effective follow-up procedures were established to ensure that potential benefits were realized. This was more likely to occur if senior staff pursued topics that were relevant to identified LEA or school needs. Although mentioned by only a few authorities, additional benefits were seen to be gained by deputy heads and senior staff within the participants' schools, who gained valuable managerial experience during the head's attendance at the OTTO courses. The importance of this act was highlighted in our interviews with newly appointed heads who, as earlier noted, stressed the value of a period as acting head.

Many of the above LEA criticisms of both basic and OTTO courses could apply to in-service courses in general; indeed other research has shown that teachers commonly criticize the relevance of content, credibility and competence of course leaders, and the methods of presentation. Clearly, this raises questions of how needs can be diagnosed, the kinds of credibility course leaders require and how course content can be made more relevant to participants' schools. Some 3/83 courses appeared to have made more progress than others in addressing these issues.

The additional training grant was certainly welcomed, although five LEAs said that its effect should not be overestimated as the funds were merely 'a drop in the ocean' and insufficient to meet demand. One county explained that if they were to rely solely on 3/83 funding, it would take ten years to cater for their heads alone. Another thought the detailed and retrospective claim system was a retrograde step, as it had meant setting up new, centralized procedures. The question of virement was raised by a few authorities, who would have preferred to use the additional moneys to develop or continue their own management initiatives. Some LEAs, either individually or on a regional basis, had developed school management programmes to a greater extent than others, and these authorities were still considering how to make best use of the new initiative. The situation was complicated by the fact that some regional units were initially not recognized as providers of 3/83 courses.

Other criticisms concerned the difficulties of finding adequate cover for absent staff and this was not helped by the time-structure of the OTTO programme. Such programmes reflected the terms of institutions of higher education and several authorities commented that they would have preferred a closer correspondence to the school term. Clearly, geographical factors were also important and a number of LEAs mentioned the problem of distance from the nearest course providers and the fact that any residential costs incurred were not met under the new training grant.

In selecting participants for 20-day basic courses, the criterion most frequently mentioned by LEAs was length of service or experience. However, there were interesting variations; some authorities chose senior staff within their first three years in post, while others tried to provide a mixture by including those relatively new together with those who had had more extensive management experience. Other LEAs specifically excluded senior staff close to retirement, while several saw the value of the courses as providing necessary 'refreshment'.

Other important selection criteria for basic courses included the individual's professional need, the needs of the school, promotion potential and an expressed interest to take part. A few authorities saw these courses as for deputy heads only. Also mentioned by some of the LEAs was the ability of basic course participants to train or influence others in the authority. This last criterion, as was to be expected, was far more important concerning selection for the one-term programmes. The OTTO participants, who were often expected to perform a training function on their return, were required to be good practitioners, acceptable to colleagues and of known standing in the authority. Other selection criteria were similar to those mentioned for basic courses, although an important additional consideration was the existence of effective senior staff to ensure the smooth running of the school in the prolonged absence of participants. Several small LEAs said they had no need to use selection criteria, as they intended that all senior staff would ultimately be involved in such programmes.

An analysis of LEA plans to make use of 3/83 participants showed that 43 authorities intended to use OTTO 'graduates' for INSET provision, with a further nine stating that a decision had not yet been made. Fourteen LEAs commented that they had no plans to utilize course participants and, interestingly, four said they did not subscribe to the 'training the trainers' concept or the 'cascade model' underpinning the initiative. One chief adviser saw the strategy of utilizing staff for INSET provision within the LEA as undesirable, quoting that 'a prophet is without honour in his own land'. Another LEA, although using senior staff informally, found that heads were reluctant to be designated as 'trainers'. It was also felt to be unrealistic to ask heads to run a course and yet at the same time maintain responsibility for their school. Surprisingly, few authorities referred to the fact that the subsequent release of trainers would have to be funded from LEA resources. Finally, one authority found this question rather difficult to answer, as their sole participant had been recruited by HMI!

The points made above reflect the LEAs reactions to the start of the new scheme and some of their criticisms clearly relate to 'teething problems'. Although this section has largely concentrated on the negative side, it is important to stress that most LEAs welcomed the initiative and that the number of heads and deputies attending courses funded under DES Circulars 4/84 and 3/85 is likely to be higher than the figures given in Table 3.4.

In addition to the funding for senior staff to attend management courses, the DES also established the National Development Centre for School Management Training (NDC), directed by Ray Bolam and based at the University of Bristol. The role of the NDC is to establish a resource bank of materials and set up an information network, undertake the evaluation of some of the courses, develop new training materials, disseminate findings and offer support to LEAs.

In its first year the NDC was mainly concerned with the new programmes of school management which resulted from 3/83 funding. But as a consequence of what the team learned about educational management and the relevance of industrial approaches, their emphasis shifted from course development and management training towards the broader perspective of management development. External training courses are seen as only one component of management development and other aspects may include: self development, action learning, team building, organization development, job rotation and action research. These may take place in the school and could involve various forms of consultancy and support. In order to explore the feasibility of these ideas, the NDC is currently working with 52 pilot schools and eight LEAs. Each LEA and school will produce a management development policy and programme in collaboration with the NDC, which will produce guideline materials. After this pilot work, the eventual aim is to make the materials and the information gained about management development available to other LEAs and schools (Bolam, 1986).

Information from the NDC shows that the number of institutions providing 20-day and OTTO courses increased in 1985 and the number of senior staff (primary and secondary) attending the courses was likely to be double the 1983/84 figures. The NDC's analysis of new course submissions showed a significant change towards school improvement and involving participants in experiential learning. There was also a move away from the topic centred course to one which focused on management needs, as identified by the participants themselves. Greater use was also being made of industrial and other non-educational managers and consultants (Bolam *et al.*, 1985).

The use of ideas drawn from industrial management is still somewhat contentious, as can be seen from several articles in the education press and the responses these provoked (for example, see Barker, 1982; Trethowan, 1983; Gray and Waitt, 1983; Wood, 1983; Fielding, 1984; Maw *et al.*, 1984). As mentioned earlier, the heads in the surveys also disagreed about the relevance of industrial management to education. Most were against wholesale borrowing of 'industrial' methods, but felt that some aspects could be used beneficially. The small number of heads who had actually been on industrial or commercial management courses had found a considerable amount of the course interesting and useful. Two of the 16 case study heads had been on one-week courses run by large industrial companies for their managers. Both heads had found it a worthwhile experience and spoke highly of the courses. A few of the heads in the surveys had been able to attend the general management course at Henley and had found this extremely valuable. For one, the experience had led to a new understanding of both himself and headship. Mixing with managers from industry and commerce had helped overcome the isolation and parochialism found in education.

Heller (1982) gives details of how one LEA integrated various industrial approaches into their management development scheme for heads. This started in 1973/74 and has been refined over the years to encompass Organization Development (OD) methods involving heads, advisers and industrial trainers. A useful summary of industrial methods and their relevance to education has recently been provided by Everard (1982 and 1986). It is important to note that, as Everard makes clear, there is not *one* industrial model of management training, but considerable diversity. Many of the points he raises have important consequences for management development in education and one of his recommendations is particularly relevant to the current form and content of courses, namely that 'the participative, experiential, practical approach, grounded in the actual problems faced by the participants in their daily work, is usually more effective than the didactic, generalized approach delivered by theoreticians without recent experience of management'. At least one of the 3/83 courses (Pert and Weeks, 1985) used an action learning approach based on the work of Revans (1980). An evaluation of the course showed that the participants (heads and advisers) spoke very highly of their experience. By working on real problems in their own jobs and discussing these with the group, most of the course members felt they had made progress (Ballinger, 1985).

The greatest problem facing heads who have been on any course is how to implement that which has been learned on the course – this is what the Americans, using an analogy from space travel, have graphically called 'the re-entry problem'. The directors of the 20-day 3/83 course which used an action learning approach were very aware of this problem and the evaluation suggested that the active group participation had helped members transfer learning to their jobs.

Summary and discussion

While most heads felt well prepared, it is important to note that 16 per cent of the new and 20 per cent of the 'old' heads rated themselves as less than adequately or very poorly prepared prior to their appointment. By drawing on the data presented in this chapter, a number of suggestions can be made to improve the preparation for headship.

There was general agreement that although various skills were learned from all previous posts, the most valuable experience was gained as a deputy head. But the research also showed the majority of previous heads had not deliberately prepared deputies for headship. Heads need to recognize that they can play a key role by working as a team with the senior staff and fully involving them in whole school planning and decision-making. It is important to delegate confidently and give real responsibility and authority to deputies, allowing them, where possible, to learn from their mistakes. Many new heads felt well prepared because of the breadth of experience gained as a deputy and this indicates that far more attention needs to be paid to the possibility of job rotation for senior staff. The kinds of experience which heads saw as particularly valuable preparation as a deputy included chairing meetings and working parties, involvement in job interviews and governors' meetings, managing major innovations and making contact with parent and community groups, HMI and LEA officers and advisers. Constructive criticism of the deputies' performance by the head was seen as an important source of feedback. A few heads held regular career discussions with their senior staff and encouraged them to improve their qualifications, attend relevant management courses, visit other schools and to keep up to date with educational documents and current trends.

The move from deputy to head was difficult for many people. Despite having been told about various aspects and having worked with heads, the initial experience of being a head and sitting in the 'hot seat' still came as a shock. It is difficult to prepare deputies for this aspect, as it obviously needs to be experienced firsthand. This can be achieved, to some extent, by working as an acting head or deputizing for the head. But only a third of new heads had stood in for their previous heads for a continuous period of more than two weeks. This was a valuable learning experience and it is hoped that as more heads undertake the OTTO courses their deputies will gain from running the school in their absence.

Most heads had attended at least one management course and this was seen as an important form of preparation for headship by both heads themselves and LEA officers. The surveys and interviews revealed a wide variety of courses, the majority of which were rated as 'useful' or 'very useful'. Heads stressed the value of residential components and the importance of informal contacts with other members of the course. Most wanted courses of practical relevance and welcomed project work based on their own schools. COSMOS courses were seen as particularly valuable by most heads and officers, while LEA courses were seen as a useful forum for heads, deputies and officers to share experiences and ideas. Heads were divided on the usefulness of input from industrialists, but the small number of heads who had attended industrial management courses found them to be valuable and that many of the aspects were applicable to secondary schools.

The positive benefits of experiential learning have been shown in an industrial and commercial context. A few educational courses have tried this approach and the initial reactions have been highly favourable. It would seem it has much to recommend it, as concerns directly relevant to each individual are discussed in a supportive group environment.

The LEA survey showed that authorities had welcomed the DES initiative on management training and most of their criticisms related to the hasty implementation and inadequate planning and consultation of the first courses. About 500 secondary heads and deputies had attended either 20-day or OTTO courses during the first year of the scheme and most authorities said they were planning to use the 'graduates' to develop local schemes for senior staff.

Data from heads were presented in Table 3.2 and show which skills and knowledge they felt could be acquired and developed by training. This, together with other information given in the chapter, could be used by trainers as a guide to the content of courses for senior staff.

Laplant (1981) describes a US programme which attempted to overcome the 're-entry' problem and used a similar approach to that of experiential learning groups. Over 50 principals were trained as 'facilitators' during a two-week course. Groups of between six to ten principals then met with a facilitator at least once a month for the two-year programme. The groups provided a supportive atmosphere and developed a climate of trust and mutual assistance as principals shared their concerns and helped with the problems that each member faced. During the first year, the groups concentrated on the personal, professional development of each member, focusing on many of the skills that are currently found in most courses for heads. Most course planners appear to assume that if they can 'improve' the head this will automatically be translated into an improvement in the school. While this may happen, there is no guarantee that such improvement will necessarily occur. To increase the likelihood that some improvement will be made in the school, in the second year of the Ohio scheme each principal designed, implemented and evaluated a school improvement project based on the needs identified by the staff. The support group of principals was used to provide assistance and encouragement to each other as they engaged in both the professional development and school improvement phases.

The Ohio scheme appears to be a structured version of what a number of heads in this country already do on an informal basis. Heads who have met on a COSMOS, LEA or other course, attempt to continue meeting informally after the course has finished. (Further details about informal support groups are given in Chapter 8.)

Recently the Far West Laboratory in California has introduced a professional development programme which pairs principals who observe each other's practice. The Peer-Assisted Leadership programme, lasting a year, gives heads the opportunity to analyse and reflect on their own leadership behaviour and that of a peer. (For further details of this particular training technique see Barnett, 1985.)

Evaluating the effectiveness of management programmes has proved to be particularly difficult. While numerous course evaluations have obtained feedback on the participants' levels of satisfaction and their likes and dislikes, the crucial question of whether it makes any difference within the school remains largely unanswered. But this is true of all INSET, not just programmes for heads – it is very difficult to establish a causal link between something that happened to a person on a course and a change that occurred in the school some time later.

Anne O'Shea (1983) reports on the evaluation of a training programme for secondary principals in Northern Ireland which was perceived very favourably. Follow-up interviews about one term after attending the course showed that in general it was far too early to see tangible results in the schools, but that in terms of 'personal development, broadening of ideas, sowing seeds and general raising of awareness' much had been achieved.

The work of Mats Ekholm (1983) probably provides the most detailed attempt yet at evaluation. He examined the effects of the Swedish compulsory training programme for heads, but even this lengthy piece of research found it hard to detect much real change in the schools.

Although various attempts at evaluation have produced little evidence to show that training courses have measurable effects on schools, the data presented in this chapter showed that heads and LEA officers considered most courses to be extremely useful and the national initiative to be particularly welcomed. It is important to stress, as the National Development Centre has, that management development encompasses far more than just training courses. This chapter has indicated which skills and knowledge heads believe are important and shown how adequately prepared they felt when they began their headship. A series of suggestions about how to improve the preparation of heads is given in the recommendations in Chapter 12.

CHAPTER 4
Relations with the Senior Management Team

A new manager entering any kind of organization, whether a school or a commercial concern, inherits a management structure and a group of individuals with differing abilities, interests and attitudes. It would appear that all the schools in the surveys had senior management teams and, clearly, the relationships between the new head and the members of the team were of considerable importance in determining both how the head settled in and the kinds of changes they were able to implement. The senior management teams always consisted of the head and deputies but in some larger schools also included senior teachers, so that the size of the team varied from three to about six people.

Deputy heads' responsibilities

An early study by Burnham (1964) of 277 deputy heads in eight LEAs found that in most cases no clearly defined role existed. Instead, the single deputy in each school was only allowed to undertake tasks delegated by the head, which often meant minor technical or clerical duties. Comprehensive reorganization considerably increased the size of schools and the DES decided in 1971 that schools of Group 10 size and above could, at the LEA's discretion, employ three deputy heads. In 1972 LEAs were additionally allowed to designate three people as senior teachers in schools of Group 10 and above. The increase in school size, coupled with the ability to appoint more than one deputy, led to a reassessment of the roles of deputies and senior teachers.

A small-scale survey by Todd and Dennison (1978) of 37 deputies in 11 comprehensives (which were each entitled to four deputies) provided evidence of a continuum of job definition. At one end, there were very clear divisions of role, usually curriculum/pastoral, while at the opposite end a policy decision had been made not to divide the roles and deputies shared responsibility for all tasks. Todd and Dennison argued that the situation had changed from Burnham's time and that most deputies now had clear roles and were part of a team. 'What has emerged markedly is the existence of policy and management teams, comprising deputy headteachers and occasionally other senior teachers, under the chairmanship of the headteacher.' More recently,

Matthew and Tong (1982) have discussed the role of the deputy head and point to the notion of partnership at the senior management level based on a shared responsibility for all that happens in the school, rather than a strict curricular and pastoral division.

An analysis of the NFER data showed that most of the deputy heads in the 47 schools from the cohort had clearly defined roles and responsibilities. The three main divisions were: the curriculum and timetable; pastoral care; and administration (which included staff cover, resources and building maintenance). Other areas of responsibility included examinations, staff development and INSET, and primary/secondary liaison.

It was interesting to note that in most schools the traditional roles of boys' and girls' welfare and discipline were still allocated to a male and female deputy respectively. In one of the case study schools the new female head, who believed strongly in reducing forms of sex differentiation, upset the second deputy by removing 'boys' discipline' from his responsibility. He was so angry that he took out a grievance procedure against the head, which was only resolved after discussions with a senior LEA officer and the deputy being given new responsibilities as Head of Upper School and Exams Officer. In another of the case studies, the head stressed to the staff that a newly appointed woman was the second deputy and not simply a senior mistress in charge of girls' welfare. But it seemed that, because the previous holder of this post, who had just retired, had seen this as her main duty, a number of the staff found it difficult to adjust to the new deputy's role.

Newly appointed deputies

An obvious advantage for new heads was to be able to appoint a new deputy or senior master/mistress. This situation usually arose with the retirement of one or more deputies. The questionnaire survey showed that 51 per cent of the 188 new heads had been able to appoint at least one deputy during the first two years of their headship. Sixty per cent of these appointments were external and 40 per cent were internal promotions of a teacher already at the school. From the interviews it seemed that, given a choice, most new heads preferred to appoint a outsider to bring 'fresh blood' into the school. This was a recurrent theme: the new heads wanted people who thought in similar ways to themselves and with whom they could discuss ideas and plans for the school. Several heads felt that the best possible senior management team was one that contained a balance of both new and old staff. With such a team there was a reasonable chance of benefiting from continuity and in-depth knowledge of the school and its history, while also ensuring that new ideas did not emanate from the head alone.

The national survey also showed that 39 per cent of the new heads were unable in their first two years to appoint any new senior staff, i.e. senior teachers, senior master/mistresses or deputy heads. In the 16 case studies, four heads were not able to appoint a new member of the senior management team, another four were able to appoint two new senior staff, while the remaining eight heads appointed one new member of the team.

The following section uses material from the case studies to illustrate the effects of not being able to recruit new senior staff.

Two of the heads inherited schools where all the deputies had been at the school for a considerable length of time and were close to retirement. Most had only taught in the one school and in one case had given 'almost a hundred years of loyal service between the three of them', to quote the new head. It is interesting to compare the two schools, as different outcomes occurred in each.

At the first school, the new head found that relations with the senior management team were friendly and relaxed and better than he had initially hoped. On arrival, the head had asked each of the deputies to write down their roles and responsibilities but, as he put it, 'I was none the wiser' – they did not seem to have clearly allocated duties. This stemmed from the previous head, who was described by the deputies as very traditional and very grammar school orientated. He had been successful at getting what he wanted by obtaining the agreement of the three deputies to give policies a democratic gloss before taking them to the staff. Clearly, after years of this sort of working relationship, the deputies, who were used to being told what to do, accepted the new head's ideas with no sign of opposition. The problems for the new head arose from the ill health of the deputies: 'none are shirkers, they are simply old and not fit and need considerable time off.' In addition, few new ideas came from the deputies and they were not used to delegation or making decisions, which meant that the new head felt he was having to do everything himself. But the important thing was that they were prepared to 'give the changes a go'.

The new head in the second school inherited a different situation. The previous head had delegated a great deal and had given the three deputies freedom to operate as they wished. During his last few years, he had been a very sick man, following a car crash, and the first deputy had virtually run the school. All the deputies had great respect for the previous head, 'an academic, cultured gentleman and a first class teacher'. The three deputies mentioned their academic background and that they had taught at A-level when the school was a grammar school. Because of this, they were somewhat scornful of the new head's 'non-academic' craft background. At the beginning, the new head felt that relations were amicable on the surface, but they were not able to work very well as a team. Once he started to discuss and institute change, things became more problematic. By the end of the first year, the head said the deputies responded to his ideas by either stating that they would not work, or employing behind the scenes manipulation to try and make sure that they would not work. Because of this, the head stopped discussing things with the deputies and worked directly with a number of heads of department and a newly appointed senior teacher, all of whom welcomed the changes he wished to introduce.

The new head also took control of the timetable from the first deputy, who had produced the same one year after year. He found a number of anomalies and felt that the first deputy had favoured a few people, including the deputies, with very light teaching loads. (Most deputies seem to teach about 50 per cent of a timetable, but in the 16 case studies class contact varied from 25 to 83 per cent.) The new head made changes in the timetable in order to distribute the teaching more evenly and to enable staff from the lower school, on a separate site, to teach in the upper school. Interviews with a number of teachers in the lower school showed how much they welcomed the opportunity, which in the past the first deputy had said was not possible to timetable.

Not surprisingly, the three deputies were very unhappy with the new situation. They disliked the increase in their teaching load and felt alienated and completely left out of things. As an illustration of this, they said that the first and second deputies had previously opened all the mail and directed it to the relevant person, a task now undertaken by the new head. After about 18 months, the deputies asked to see the head and expressed their concerns. He listened and took notes and told them that he thought his ideas were being subverted. The deputies denied this and said they were loyal to the school but admitted their ideas of what was good for the school differed from those of the new head. This meeting did not solve the problem and the deputies felt at a loss about what to do next. In the end, the deputies informed the governors of their worries and at a later meeting the governors voted for an LEA inquiry into 'low morale'. The first deputy, who was seen by many as the 'real architect' behind the school, announced his retirement just before the Assistant Director and other senior officers were due to visit the school. After interviewing the head, the senior management team and heads of department, the LEA officers produced a fairly neutral report. The head felt this had helped and together with a redrafting of the deputies' roles, the management team was now working more cooperatively.

In contrast to the two previous case studies, one head was able to appoint two deputies in his first year, so that all members of the senior management team were new. The head was very happy with the new appointments and felt able to relax and speak freely, as they were 'more of my generation and on the same wavelength as myself'. This provided the head with considerable stimulation and a dynamic team approach to innovaion, but he recognized the danger of a 'them and us' situation developing.

The possible gap between the senior management team and the rest of the staff was recognized by most of the heads and they particularly valued senior staff who had an 'ear to the ground'. It was very important for the deputies to be in the staffroom and maintain contact with staff feelings.

Senior management team meetings

Data from the 47 interviews showed that in most schools an informal meeting of the head and deputies occurred each morning. A more structured meeting of several hours was usually timetabled once or, in some cases, twice a week.

In some of the case studies, the heads kept a note of points they wished to mention at the weekly meeting and used this to produce the agenda. At two of the case study schools, the deputies felt that the agenda should be drawn up jointly beforehand. They were unhappy that the heads simply added the points raised by the deputies to the end of the agenda, because in most cases time did not permit full discussion. Several of the schools had no agenda at all and some of the deputies expressed concern about the ad hoc nature of the meetings.

Interviews with the heads and deputies and observation of some meetings showed a number of similarities across the 16 schools. In most meetings, it was common practice to go through the diary of events for the forthcoming week before moving on to other points. This was often followed by an exchange of information and reporting back on various meetings. Issues such as staffing, capitation, suspensions, additions and deletions to the roll were weekly agenda headings in one of the case studies. The meetings had two main functions: the first was one of providing information and the second was the floating and discussion of ideas before decision-making. Most of the heads and deputies interviewed were happy with the meetings as a means of information giving. But a clearly recognized danger was 'getting bogged down with trivia' and some of the deputies felt that the meetings were not as efficient as they would have liked. At one school all three deputies were critical of the meetings and attributed some of the blame to the poor chairing by the head, who they said 'butterflies from one thing to another'.

In two other schools, the deputies were unhappy because they felt that the meetings were dominated by the head. The meetings were used as a sounding board for the head's ideas or simply to provide information. Despite some negative comments, in most of the case study schools the deputies thought that their senior management meetings were very good and that there was genuine discussion in a relaxed and open manner.

Delegation

One of the areas explored with the case study heads on our second visit after they had been in post for a year, was that of delegation. Most of the new heads had found it difficult to delegate at first. An obvious factor determining the extent of delegation was the quality of the senior management team. Three of the 16 heads said they had no difficulty in delegating because they felt they had outstanding deputies. In one case the young first deputy had successfully run the school as acting head during the previous year.

A variety of factors seemed to explain the difficulties the other heads had experienced. In some instances the deputies were not used to delegation, as the previous head had run a 'one-man band' and they were reluctant to take on responsibility. The new head in one small school had to work without a deputy for his first 18 months and the stress was further increased as he attempted to maintain a heavy teaching load. Most of the heads realized they had to overcome their feelings that it was quicker and easier to do the jobs themselves. During the early stages this was compounded by the fact that the new heads wanted to be involved in all aspects and find out everything about the schools. 'In theory, I am happy to delegate things but not yet: I don't want to let go of the reins. At present I am still chairperson of the curriculum and pastoral committees.'

At the beginning of the first year there was also a reluctance to delegate because the heads did not know the strengths and weaknesses of the staff. As they learned more about the school and the staff, all the heads began to delegate a variety of tasks. Once delegated, the degree of monitoring by the head varied depending both on the person undertaking it and the task. The heads expected to be kept informed, and one of the functions of the senior management meetings already mentioned was that of reporting back. A close link exists between delegation and effective communication and because of the frequency of these meetings, it was easier to monitor the work of the deputies than that of the heads of department and heads of year. Most of the heads tried to let their staff get on with the delegated task but found it quite difficult to do so.

Probably the main factor concerning the reluctance to delegate, as mentioned earlier, was the ability of the person undertaking the task. Several of the new heads in the case studies gave examples of difficulties they had experienced having delegated a task. For example:

> I did the initial curriculum plan and talked it through with the deputy and then let him get on with it. I said, come along to me if there are any serious problems. But the timetable was a botched job and the result has been very unsatisfactory. So I cursed myself and said, perhaps I should have monitored it more closely. In fact, he did a similar thing with capitation and in the end I had to do it. His attitude, like that of several others at the school, is 'It'll be all right on the day – or the day after!'

Charles Handy (1981) eloquently summarizes the vital link between delegation and trust:

> True delegation, effective delegation, is delegation with trust and with only the necessary minimum of controls. But trust is hard to give, for:
>
> 1   to give trust, the superior has to have confidence in the subordinate to do the job...
> 2   Like a leap into the dark, trust must be given if it is to be received. This is not as trite as it may sound. If a superior wishes to get the benefits from trust, he must initiate the process, give trust and release control and then sit back and wait. If proved wrong, he can withdraw the trust and replace the control.
> 3   Trust is a fragile commodity. Like glass, once shattered, it is never the same again...
> 4   Trust must be reciprocated. It is no good the superior trusting his subordinates if they do not trust him.

The areas mentioned by the 228 'old' heads as those which they did *not* delegate, are shown below, in order of frequency.

Areas not delegated by heads

1   Staff management
    e.g. staff discipline
2   Staff appointments
3   Liaison with external agencies
    e.g. LEA, governors
4   Figurehead and public relations
    e.g. media, PTA
5   Finance
    e.g. allocation of resources, capitation
6   Policy
    e.g. aims and objectives, long-term plans
7   Curriculum
    e.g. overview, consultation, curriculum development
8   Ultimate sanctions for pupils
    e.g. suspension

Information collected from the case studies and interviews with 47 new heads showed a very close match with those above, suggesting that these areas are retained by most heads and seen as their ultimate responsibilities. It also appears that the areas are reasonably stable over time, as a survey of 315 headteachers by Bernbaum (1976) produced similar results with regard to those tasks which heads did not delegate.

Strengths and weaknesses of the senior management team

During the new heads' first year they became aware of the strengths and weaknesses of their senior staff. This type of knowledge was particularly important, as the head relied upon the senior management team, both to obtain information and guidance and to implement new policies. A less effective member of the senior team could have a considerable impact on the new head and the whole school. Data from the surveys of both the new and 'old' heads provide an indication of the number of heads who considered they had a weak member of the senior management team.

Reference to Appendix 1 shows that this was a problem for most heads and 'coping with a weak member of the senior management team' was one of the highest rated difficulties. Although the figures suggest the problem was more serious for the 'old' heads, the differences between the 'old' and new heads were not statistically significant. The fact that nearly a fifth of the new heads and a quarter of the 'old' heads marked this a 'very serious' problem was confirmed in the case studies and the interviews with new heads, where some form of difficulty with a member of the senior management team was mentioned by 20 of the 47 heads.

The following difficulties were those most frequently mentioned by the new heads. Senior staff in some schools were defensive about their areas of responsibility and displayed rigidity and narrow interpretation of their tasks. Alternatively, the new head could encounter a situation where there were no clear job descriptions and an overlap of roles. In other cases, examples were given where the new head felt that the deputies had had no management training in dealing with comprehensive schools and could make only minor contributions to pastoral care or the curriculum.

A number of senior staff were felt by the heads to be promoted beyond their ability and unable to cope. Some were also near the end of their careers and suffering from what the Americans have termed 'burnout'. Where this occurred it put extra pressure on the head and the rest of the senior management team, who had to 'carry' or 'patch around' the person concerned. Obvious difficulties also occurred where members of the management team did not get on with each other and 'personality clashes' arose, sometimes casting the head in the role of referee. New heads clearly needed the element of trust in their relationships with the senior staff and this had a major effect on their feelings of professional isolation. The situation for one head was obviously particularly difficult and he wrote in his questionnaire, 'Trustworthiness has been the greatest problem. Some members of the senior management team have proved totally disloyal. I would have appreciated some warning as to these characteristics.'

The very positive responses from heads occurred where most of the problems outlined above were absent and the group was seen to be functioning well as a team. Where heads praised their deputies and senior staff, they usually spoke of them as being reliable, dependable and efficient. They also valued people who were open and frank and did not 'sit on the fence' but spoke up and told the head when they did not agree with something. The majority of new heads provided mixed responses in discussing their relationships with the senior management team – while some deputies and senior teachers were praised, others in the team were felt to be a problem. The most detailed information was provided by the 16 case studies and the following section uses quotations from two of the new heads to illustrate both the positive and negative points made above. The extracts are lengthy in order to provide details of the context in an attempt to illustrate the head's perspective on relations with senior staff.

The first deputy handles the administration and was acting head for a year, but doesn't want a headship. We have a little joke which is that she runs the school while I play at being head. I rely very heavily on her. She is fully behind me and I couldn't get greater support. She has been here since the school opened and could take early retirement but is not going to, and I am very pleased about that. I am afraid of losing her, at the moment the school would sink without her. She works very hard and picks up a lot of the work of the other two deputies. In fact, I am very disappointed with both of them. I don't think the second deputy is really capable of doing the curriculum job. I have to write most of the papers for him and check everything he does. He is a charming man but he really can't cope. The heads of department are coming straight to me instead of going to him first. I have insisted that he has regular meetings with the heads of department. Soon after I arrived I asked him for a breakdown of the whole school curriculum. He gave me half a page – this was useless. I made him head of lower school but the staff said it was the worst year ever, so I have taken him off that. I have realized that you can't wait for people to leave, you have to work with what you've got, so now I detail things to him one point at a time with a deadline. I will probably have to take over the chair of the curriculum committee because he is useless and the staff all know it. The pastoral deputy works quite hard but seems to go round in circles. He does a lot of home visiting and talks to the staff but finds it very hard to work with the heads of year. We have long chats about it. I went to one of the heads of year meetings and they absolutely pulled him apart because he hadn't prepared himself well enough beforehand. Afterwards I threw the book at him and he agreed that he hadn't been well prepared. He has upset the heads of year and some of the form tutors and just doesn't seem to know how to go about things. The senior management team is certainly not as I would want it. I would never have appointed the second and third deputies as neither, I think, is really up to the job.

In the second school, the head was fortunate to be able to appoint two new deputies, but was very unhappy with the existing deputy:

I am totally confident in the two deputies that I have appointed. I am absolutely delighted with them. The first deputy is certainly not a 'yes man' and will stand up to me. I delegate anything to him, he is honest and I know that he will do things in the way that I want. I have gained more confidence with the other new deputy and I respect his ability. I can give him anything that fits within his pastoral job, but he can flare up, get very angry and then cool down rapidly, so I am a bit wary about giving him anything that will upset him. I think the second deputy tends to be indiscreet and I find I am not able to be as open as I would like. I don't believe I've got 100 per cent commitment from him, although it is much improved since last year. He is a poor organizer but the problem is that he thinks he is very good. We had a row once when he called in the police and I told him that he should not do that without consulting me. He got extremely angry and phoned the union, asking whether he had the authority to call in the police without my permission. Later, however, he apologized. I get on superbly with two of the deputies but with the other one, I simply exist. He sends me memos, saying 'This is the end of the line'.

It seems likely that the situation outlined above was relieved at the beginning of the new head's third year when the second deputy was due to take a year's secondment for a Masters course. He was very pleased with this and felt that it would improve his chances of obtaining a headship. In another of the case studies, after a certain amount of tension, the first deputy was also given a year's secondment for a higher degree and later obtained a headship. Secondment would thus appear to be one strategy which might be used to relieve difficult situations temporarily.

Another common strategy used by the new heads to overcome weaknesses in the senior management team was to redefine the responsibilities of the group members. For example, one of the case study heads spoke of the first deputy at the school whom he thought had been promoted beyond her level. Although she tried hard and was well meaning, the staff did not have a very high regard for her and occasionally she annoyed the staff by using her rank. The head had recently made her coordinator of the school's special educational needs project and she was greatly enjoying this new role. Some of her previous responsibilities had been taken over by other senior staff and the head, and there had been an overall improvement.

While changing the responsibilities of the senior staff was a useful mechanism to motivate and generate new interests, it had to be done with great tact and care. It is worth noting that in two of the 16 case study schools deputies took out grievance procedures against the new heads because they were unhappy with the way their tasks had been reallocated.

Interestingly, in the four case study schools where divisions had occurred between the senior management team and the new head, many of the teachers interviewed were clearly aware of this fact and expressed concern. Such conflict was felt to be detrimental to the school; as one teacher said, 'We need to have the whole hierarchy as one to achieve what we want at the school'.

Unsuccessful internal candidates for headship

An area of potential difficulty for the new head could arise when one or more of the existing deputies had unsuccessfully applied for the headship. The survey data suggested that this was not a very serious problem for most new heads and it seemed that, after some initial 'coldness', the deputies accepted the situation quite well and in some schools very amicable relationships were established. 'The potential tension never materialized. The first deputy is utterly loyal and reliable and in fact we have become friends as well as colleagues.'

In many cases it seemed that the unsuccessful candidates initially expressed their resentment by opposing or not wholeheartedly accepting the changes suggested by the head. In some cases a confrontation occurred between the head and the deputy, after which the situation was resolved, or an agreement was reached, with the new head giving full support to the deputy's applications for headships elsewhere.

Interviews with the 47 new heads brought to light two examples where particular difficulties had occurred. In the first example a deputy had been led to believe he would be offered the job, and when unsuccessful wrote a bitter letter to the Director of Education, sending copies to the new head and the school's governors. The head designate during one of his visits to the school spent a whole day with the deputy, but nothing was resolved. In fact, the problem had still not been settled six months later but, as the new head explained, the unsuccessful deputy was not popular and his application had received little support from the staff, so at least the problem was not as bad as it could have been.

In the other example, there was a younger first deputy who had been acting head for a term and obviously thought he had done a good job. On the deputy's own admission, the problem was largely one of envy but matters were gradually being resolved. The new head was very surprised that he had not been informed by the LEA that the deputy had applied for the headship and had not even been shortlisted.

Although serious problems rarely occurred with unsuccessful internal candidates, the examples given above show how important it is that LEA officers provide the new head with full details about the situation prior to their taking up post. In addition, LEA officers need to give serious consideration to the amount of counselling given to unsuccessful deputies, particularly when high expectations were held.

Summary and discussion

The information presented in this chapter has shown the particular importance of the relationship between the new head and the senior staff. The case studies illustrated the situation where all the deputies had been at the school for a considerable length of time. New heads in this position found that it was sometimes difficult to introduce change without the full support of their senior management team. About half the cohort of new heads were able to appoint at least one new deputy during their first two years in post. This provided a valuable impetus as the head was usually able to appoint someone who shared their philosophy of comprehensive schooling. Many heads spoke of the need for an injection of 'new blood' which provided another source of ideas and support for the heads' plans. Some heads saw a mix of both new and experienced deputies as the ideal combination in the senior management team, as it provided a balance between innovation and stability. In most cases, deputies were able to act as a link between the head and the staff. New heads particularly relied on their deputies to provide valuable feedback on staff attitudes and feelings. Some heads were clearly aware of the danger of drawing the deputies towards them and creating a large gap between the senior management team and the rest of the staff.

Most deputies saw the head informally each morning before school started and the whole senior management team usually met once a week. While it is probably best to retain the informality of these meetings, they certainly need a structure. Many had an agenda but this should be constructed by all the senior management team and not just the head. Time limits should be set for items such as the diary of forthcoming events and other routine matters, as discussions of these frequently leaves insufficient time for more substantial topics. In some cases it may be advisable to allocate a whole meeting to one major theme. The case studies showed that senior management team meetings appear to function quite well for information giving, but both heads and deputies were less happy about the meetings in terms of discussion and decision-making. It is important for heads to encourage the participation of each member of the group and not to over-dominate the meetings. It seems that some need to improve their skills with regard to organizing and chairing meetings. (Useful advice is given by Lindelow, 1981.)

Most of the heads in the research favoured a team approach to school management and where positive comments were made about the deputies they usually referred to how well they worked as a team in terms of joint planning and decision-making. For this to function effectively the head had to delegate clearly defined areas of responsibility to the senior staff. While many new heads found it difficult at first, they began to delegate more confidently during the first year, although this largely depended on the ability of their deputies. The research showed that most heads did not delegate the links with agencies such as the LEA, governors, PTA and the media. These seem to relate largely to the 'figurehead' and 'gatekeeper' roles of the head. Internal control was maintained over school policy, long-term planning and the curriculum. The management of resources in terms of staff (e.g. appointments and discipline) and finance was also not usually delegated by the heads. Data from 47 schools showed that most senior staff had tasks which were usually divided into curricular, pastoral and administrative responsibilities. As mentioned in the previous chapter, full responsibility for an area, together with involvement in whole school planning and job rotation, provided deputies with a range of experience and acted as an important form of preparation for headship.

The survey data showed that coping with a weak member of the senior management team was a very serious problem for almost a fifth of new heads and a quarter of the 'old' heads. Heads found this a particularly difficult situation and either tried to work around the person concerned or redefined their responsibilities in an attempt to capitalize on their strengths. In some cases the weak deputy was being 'carried' by the head and the rest of the senior management team and this produced extra work for an already hard-pressed group. Early retirement was a possibility for those near the end of their career, although in some schools the person would not accept this solution. The case studies showed situations where the deputies disagreed with the new heads' ideas or found it difficult to adjust to the change in leadership style from that of the previous head. The rest of the staff were usually aware of any strong disagreement among the senior management team and saw this as detrimental to the effective working of the school. Heads obviously need to be alert to potential conflict between themselves and the deputies and to difficulties that exist between members of the senior management team, and to minimize these wherever possible.

Serious difficulties between a new head and a deputy who had unsuccessfully applied for the headship were surprisingly rare. (It appears that some LEAs do not encourage deputies to apply for the headship of their existing school.) The research suggests that in almost every case where such a situation had occurred, the new head and the deputy were able to resolve matters amicably within the first term. Most deputies acted in a very professional manner and accepted the new head or were able to obtain a headship elsewhere with full support from the new head. It is, however, extremely important for the LEA to provide the new head as soon as possible with details concerning internal applicants and adequate counselling for the unsuccessful deputy.

LEAs need to think about management development by working with the whole senior management team and not just individual members. A few authorities have started to develop this approach which seems to have considerable potential for school improvement.

CHAPTER 5
'Can They Walk on Water?'
Teachers' Reactions to New Heads

The arrival of a new head is a significant event in any school's history, not only because of its relative infrequency (for example, 11 of the 16 case study heads were replacing others who had been in post for ten years or more), but also because it provides an opportunity for new relationships to be established between the incoming head and the staff. Heads taking up appointment in a school are likely to face an organizational structure and social system which has been temporarily suspended on their arrival and can therefore take advantage of this 'to manoeuvre and reshape the structural patterns of the social system' (Carlson, 1962).

With the previous head's departure, many of the conflicts and divisions found within the 'old' organizational structure are likely to disappear or at least be held in abeyance. The majority of new heads, therefore, will enter a situation where many relationships have to be established anew, and to a considerable extent participants' reputations have, once more, to be made. Even though relationships have to start afresh there is, within schools, a history of relations between heads and their staff. In seven of the 16 case study schools relations between teachers and the previous head left a lot to be desired and in four of these they were particularly poor. To some extent, it was advantageous for new heads to be aware of this historical context, and several case study heads made deliberate attempts to gain an understanding of both their predecessor's style and the quality of the relationships enjoyed with staff.

The informal power structure of the school is likely to be affected by the arrival of the new head, so that those with established interests under the old regime potentially have the most to lose, whilst other less powerful parties or individuals have most to gain. For those working within the organization, the head's initial period of incumbency is therefore crucial and is an interesting example of the process of negotiation and impression-management. The head's first month or even first term in post is invariably an extremely busy one, with many individuals wishing to make their views known at the earliest opportunity. As a deputy head interviewed said, 'a new head is bombarded in the beginning from all areas' and this was all the more likely given the case study heads' strong beliefs in accessibility and availability to staff. Such beliefs ensured no shortage of teachers willing to express views and state claims.

These initial contacts did, however, provide an excellent opportunity for new heads to gain a better understanding of the organizations they were to manage. Indeed, some heads tried, albeit with varying degreees of success, to see members of the teaching staff individually and informally to elicit views on such matters as the school and their role in it.

It is the overall aim of this chapter to draw upon interview data from the 16 case study schools, in order to consider the situation largely from the teachers' perspective. The following questions will be discussed: 1) What is it like to be a teacher in a school with a new head and what expectations are commonly held by both parties? 2) What in the teachers' view constitutes a 'good head'? 3) What sort of problems and difficulties are generated by the actions of heads themselves?

Expectations and realities

The arrival of a new head can be a difficult time for both the teaching staff and the new heads themselves. It is often a time of apprehension and fear of the unknown with high expectations being held by both parties. In all 16 case study schools, teachers commented that the initial reaction of the staff had generally been very welcoming and responsive. This was true even for those schools with a previous history of poor relations between heads and teachers. There was an air of expectancy and many staff were excited and optimistic, looking to the head for a fresh start and knowing that the new head would want to introduce changes. Some heads found they had 'a hard act to follow', but were nevertheless given a sincere welcome. Others were seen as the school's new champion or saviour. In fact, the number of biblical references was noticeable, with comments occasionally being made about how the staff wanted a 'second coming' or 'a Moses figure to lead them out of the wilderness'. Some heads even commented that the expectations the teaching staff had of them were so great they felt on occasions as though they were expected to be super-human. One head said, 'I think the staff here had unrealistic expectations of me and wanted someone who could "walk on water". We are all mortal and there was no magic solution. I had to disabuse them of this early on.'

Although new heads were 'welcomed with open arms on arrival' by the vast majority of teachers, and there was an initial fund of goodwill, this had often been dissipated at a later stage. In seven of the 16 schools a large number of teachers commented that their expectations were too high or, in retrospect, unrealistic. It had proved virtually impossible to please everyone and some teachers felt disappointed, by the end of the second year, that the new heads had not been able to match what they had said they would do.

In general most teachers received the heads favourably and responded to their enthusiasm. They were prepared to 'give them a chance' and there was an expectation that new heads 'would want to make their mark'. The vast majority of teachers interviewed in all 16 schools expected changes to take place and there was a general recognition of the need for change; what was more problematic, and is briefly discussed later and in more detail in Chapter 7, was the speed and timing of the change process.

Teachers at one school referred to the head's first year as one of optimism, whereas by the end of the second year, the staff were fed up as their workload had increased considerably and yet they felt this had not been sufficiently recognized. In a similar manner new heads often had very high expectations of their staff, and occasionally these were seen by teachers as unreasonable.

It was not uncommon for teachers to welcome new heads as their arrival provided an opportunity for workloads to be more evenly or fairly distributed, slackness identified and culprits rebuked. In two case study schools, the new heads had redistributed teachers' workloads more equitably and this had proved to be very popular with junior staff, some of whom thought this was long overdue. Similarly, in several schools, staff were impressed with the new head's timetabling abilities which had enabled some staff, especially junior staff, to teach classes and offer options which, they had been informed in the past, were simply impossible to timetable. Before, the timetable had been seen as sacrosanct and staff appreciated the greater flexibility and equity resulting from the new head's timetabling skills.

By the time of the researcher's third visit, some teachers mentioned that the head's 'honeymoon period' was over, or specified an earlier time when it had ceased. The notion of a honeymoon period – i.e. a time when staff are less critical, more amenable to change and the new head is allowed more freedom of action – was specifically explored with the 16 heads during the final school visit. Thirteen of the 16 heads agreed they were given a honeymoon period by the staff, although there was less agreement over how long it lasted. One head thought it lasted only a few days, while another said it went on for 18 months or so! Several heads made reference to a specific incident (for example, a union dispute, the introduction of a particular innovation or the appointment of a member of staff) from which time the honeymoon period ceased. One head saw the honeymoon period coming to an end on a more staggered basis, ending more quickly with some staff than with others. The heads were aware that the honeymoon period was finite, the euphoria of having a new head wore off and the staff became less forgiving and more critical. The honeymoon period, according to another head, was a period when 'positions were established' and it was likely to be brought to an abrupt end if heads had failed to consult their staff, introduced changes very rapidly or 'went in with both feet'. Several heads thought that the period ceased when teachers realized that the changes made did not necessarily coincide with the directions in which the teachers desired to go. Also, by the later part of the first year and the beginning of the second, the new heads had often encountered the more entrenched attitudes of some members of staff.

The three heads who did not see themselves as experiencing a honeymoon period thought this was the case for two reasons. One head, promoted internally from a deputy headship, was obviously already familiar to this staff. In addition, as a result of being short of a deputy head for an initial period, the new head had, more or less, to continue in that role. The other two heads did not see their staff as very supportive in their initial period in post, but rather, as relations developed over time, greater support had been forthcoming.

What constitutes a 'good' head?

While there has been no shortage of research into pupils' perceptions of teachers (e.g. McKelvey and Kyriacou, 1985), studies requesting teachers to evaluate or comment on headteachers appear to be much less common. One large-scale US study used rating scales and asked teachers to evaluate the qualities of high school principals (Blanchard, 1981). Seventeen qualities were identified by the researcher as characterizing good educational administration and management. These included, for example: professional preparation and growth; balance between administration and supervision; stimulating intellectual attitude; approachability; new ideas; curricular knowledge; fairness; relations with parents; sense of proportion and humour; self-reliance and confidence. Over 250,000 high school teachers were asked to rate their principals on a ten-point scale for each of the qualities. Blanchard states that for the 17 qualities there was an average rating of 7.7 out of ten, which in his view, 'testifies to the fact that secondary school teachers believe their principals are executing their major tasks in a highly commendable manner'.

The NFER research, however, did not approach the issue of what constitutes a 'good' head, by presenting teachers with a set list of qualities and seeking levels of agreement; instead senior staff were asked, during the course of an interview, to reflect upon the strengths and weaknesses of the new head. Other teachers were also invited, after discussing the staff's general reaction to the arrival of the new head, to compare the new head with their previous head and to give their personal reactions and impressions. By drawing on the comments of nearly 300 teachers, it is possible to construct a composite picture of what, from the teachers' viewpoint, went to make up a 'good' head and Table 5.1 records desirable and undesirable personal traits and characteristics.

There was considerable consensus concerning desirable personal characteristics of heads and it is noticeable that many of the features identified were what might be termed desirable traits in humans per se, and not just in secondary heads.

The qualities shown in the table were all derived from teachers' comments and if an opposite, undesirable feature has not been listed this was because it was not specifically mentioned during the interviews. Some of the more equivocal issues associated with headship styles are pursued in detail in Chapter 11. The next section focuses on difficulties identified by teachers as having arisen from the actions and inactions of heads.

Difficulties resulting from heads' actions

Teachers were asked to comment on the staff's general reaction to the new head, to state if there had been any adverse reaction and to give examples, if

Table 5.1   Teachers' views of heads

Personal characteristics and traits

Desirable	*Undesirable*
'Looks the part'	
Dynamic and enthusiastic	Quiet and unassuming
	Uninspiring; lacks charisma
Committed and hardworking	
A sense of purpose	
A motivator	
Unruffled, unflappable, implacable	Unpredictable, impetuous
Confident	Lacks confidence
Credible	Lacks credibility
Courageous	
Tactful	Thick-skinned, tactless
Patient	Impatient
Articulate and vocal	Verbose
Intelligent and full of ideas	A plodder, poor memory
Well-versed in educational thought	
Polite, charming	Discourteous
Sociable	Unsociable; poor with people
Outgoing and affable	Unfriendly
Sense of humour	No sense of humour
Loyal, humane and sensitive	Insensitive; shouts at pupils; uncaring
Trustworthy and honest	Untrustworthy, devious and deceitful
Admits errors	
Open-minded; flexible	Holds set views
Puts interests of school above others	Careerist

relevant, of difficulties or problems that had been caused specifically by the new head's actions. It is proposed to focus only on examples of difficulties which occurred in a number of schools and were mentioned by several staff in each. It is hoped that by examining teachers' negative comments the research will highlight issues of which new heads should be particularly aware.

Staff appointments

The most common difficulty, mentioned in 14 of the 16 case study schools, was associated with staff appointments, especially internal promotions. A number of separate issues were raised by those interviewed. Internal candidates not shortlisted for internal or external posts were often seen as 'hard done by' or 'having a bad deal' by the rest of the staff. Many teachers commented that appointments had been badly handled: internal applicants should at least be interviewed and heads should make deliberate attempts to have 'quiet chats to inform those unsuccessful that they were not quite what was wanted'. In one school, for example, it was generally agreed that an internal appointment had been poorly handled; the relevant head of department had not been consulted, and a teacher not considered for the post was informed of this fact by the successful, more junior teacher. The unsuccessful applicant was upset by this and many staff thought it was the head's responsibility to have informed the teacher of the situation.

Some heads thought that they did not have sufficient time to interview all internal applicants or that it was hypocritical to shortlist those who clearly had little chance of success. This may be so. However, it should be noted that the perceived 'poor' treatment of internal candidates had a deleterious effect not only on the individuals concerned, but also on the staff as a whole. As a case study head later realized, 'It might make them feel better if they were all shortlisted'.

A related cause for complaint came from those teachers who had been informed by the previous head that a particular scale post was theirs, or perhaps harder to accept, where an internal candidate was specifically asked by the head to put in a formal application and then was unsuccessful. In a number of schools, posts had been 'promised' by the previous head and some staff were particularly upset when they neither obtained such posts, nor were they even shortlisted by the new head. One teacher was particularly angry because he felt all three internal candidates interviewed had less experience than himself for a particular post.

Those responsible for making appointments have always had to face the problem of rewarding experience while at the same time ensuring talent is recognized and promoted. In at least four schools, a number of teachers believed that experience and length of service were not sufficiently recognized by the new head. Comments were made about how points were allocated to 'like-minded' individuals or to young whizz-kids, or that 'the head wants to bring in her own people', and in one school there was some disquiet over the rapid promotion of the new head's appointments. Some teachers clearly believed in the importance of reward for long service, whilst others thought on occasions that the best person had not been appointed. In one school, for example, there was virtual unanimity amongst the staff that the wrong person had been internally promoted. The head felt he had received poor advice from the deputy on this particular appointment and suggested all new heads 'are allowed one mistake – that was mine!'

Other difficulties were caused by heads not openly advertizing posts, or being inconsistent by requesting formal applications for some positions but not others. In some of the six schools where certain appointments were 'just announced', comments were made that the new heads' appointment policies were similar to their predecessors, and the unions and staff associations had made successful representations concerning the advertizing of future posts to the governors, the LEA or the heads themselves. Elsewhere, many staff commented that at least with the new head, points were internally advertized rather than being given out secretly, while others were more sceptical, believing the appointments procedure to be a sham. On one occasion the researcher was shown a job description by the head, who stated the internal appointment was genuinely an open competition. However, at a later stage, after the details had been attached to the staffroom noticeboard, comments were made by staff that the whole affair was a charade and that the job was 'lined up for the head's and deputies' favourites'. The mistrust appeared to be symptomatic of this particular staff's disappointment with the new head.

Clearly, the appointment and promotion of staff, always a delicate undertaking, was even more so at a time of restricted career mobility. At times it was virtually impossible for the heads not to offend some teachers and for many appointments, noticeably those to be filled internally within the school, they were in a 'no win situation' unless there was an obvious and agreed upon favourite candidate. The appointment and promotion of staff was the issue most likely to generate adverse reaction and examples have been given where teachers felt aggrieved by the head's actions with resulting deleterious effects on individual and/or general staff morale.

However, although the appointment of staff was always fraught with difficulties, there were actions that could be taken to minimize adverse reaction. The examples given have shown that those responsible for making appointments should be aware of the need for, amongst other things, fairness, consistency, courtesy, consultation and openness. A recognition of these factors may help alleviate potential difficulties.

Consultation and communication

Another issue, raised in 13 case study schools, concerned the areas of consultation and communication. A large number of teachers pointed to examples of occasions when the new head had made little or no attempt to consult the staff. On some matters they felt they had been presented with a fait accompli. Some thought there was less consultation than hitherto, while others made reference to working party recommendations being ignored or not discussed sufficiently. The issue of communication and consultation is further considered in Chapter 11, but it is worth noting here that teachers in at least five schools thought there were too many meetings and/or memos. A teacher in one school had worked out there were 75 meetings in the head's first year and several felt that a situation of diminishing returns had set in. In general, staff were pleased to be involved in the decision-making process, but there needed to be an end product – otherwise disillusionment was likely. A teacher said, 'We have so many meetings, yet little seems to be achieved'. There was a danger of some matters being over-discussed.

Similarly, a heavy reliance on memos was severely criticized and the increased use of bureaucratic procedures and the reduction of personal contact were mentioned by teachers. In one school the point was made that ill-feeling had been generated as the head had used a written communication to *all* teachers commenting on staff lateness, when what was needed, it was suggested, was face-to-face contact with the few offending individuals. Teachers in another school also said it was wrong to blame all staff for the faults of individual teachers. In general terms, however, staff appreciated being kept informed by the head, but there was a need to ensure the right balance between written and other forms of communication.

Discipline

In exactly half of the case study schools, teachers made a reference to disciplinary procedures. Many teachers in these schools saw the new head as 'too soft' or 'too lenient' and claimed that staff did not get the disciplinary back-up they desired or deserved. Several commented that pupils saw the new head as weak and confused kindness with weakness. One case study head said in his first year he was very aware of teachers 'deliberately pushing disciplinary matters through to the top' to see how much back-up they could expect, especially concerning pupil suspensions. In only a few schools was it readily admitted that the head 'backs us up to the hilt on the disciplinary front'. An ironic situation was found in one school when the all new senior management team complained to the staff about the general decline in standards of discipline, whereas the majority of staff saw the new head and deputies themselves as largely the cause of the problem! Needless to say, the teachers resented and felt angered by such comments.

Favouritism

In just under half of the case study schools adverse reaction amongst staff had been caused by the head's alleged favouritism. Some subject departments felt devalued, while others were seen as being favoured and gained additional resources. A few heads were seen by teachers as a 'man's man' and showed preference for appointing men or unattached women, while other heads (of both sexes) were seen as favouring women. In some of these schools it was thought the head had encouraged divisions amongst staff along the lines of age (young *v.* old), or length of time at the school ('old-timers' *v.* the new head's appointments). Staff turnover at these schools was noticeably higher than at others.

Support for staff

In five schools, a number of teachers suggested that the new head favoured pupils or parents and gave insufficient support or attention to individual teachers or the staff as a whole. (In only two of these schools was there an overlap between this and lack of disciplinary support referred to earlier.)

These heads were often seen as too approachable or friendly to the pupils. It was felt important to teach, to be seen with pupils and to be able to relate to them, but too great a familiarity could only lead to the pupils taking advantage. According to one teacher, the head's open-door policy had backfired, as he had lost the pupils' respect and was seen as an 'easy touch'; while others in the same school were angered that their accessibility to the head was limited by 'the constantly engaged sign on the office door and the queue of pupils outside!' Teachers welcomed the head's interest in pupils, but in several schools expressed concern that a similar interest in staff was not clearly demonstrated. Some teachers suggested a little more time spent with staff would reap considerable benefits.

The importance of establishing personal, face-to-face contact at all levels was recognized by a scale 2 teacher who said,

> the head was in the school at least a term before some staff met him. I made a move to meet him in the first week, by introducing myself at a meeting. If you were senior staff, you had contact with the head, but you didn't if you were rank and file. One teacher told me that the head still hadn't spoken to her after one term. She said that he was approaching her one day in the corridor and he was smiling, so she thought – 'Aha! At long last recognition!' – but it transpired that the smile was for the sixth formers behind her!

Some heads were seen as giving preference to parents and were seen as having gone too far in wooing them. Examples were given of occasions when parents had complained and the head had immediately taken the parents' side, often to the detriment of the staff.

Implied criticisms

In five of the case studies, adverse reactions had been generated by the new heads' constant reference to their 'old' school and the implied criticism of the 'new' school and its staff. Frequent reference to the need for change, accompanied by comments as to how well arrangements worked at the head's last school, upset many teachers. New heads, it was said, should not give the impression that nothing of value was currently on offer. It was considered important to acknowledge existing good practices and procedures, and to leave unchanged those that were working well. Similarly, heads should be more aware that what worked at their 'old' schools need not necessarily work in the different context of the 'new'.

Although the vast majority of teachers expected the new head to introduce change, too many changes too quickly often caused upset and some staff equated change with criticism. The vexed issue of how new heads manage change and the reactions of teachers to the change process are further explored in Chapter 7.

The first staff meeting was a crucial time and was often regarded with some trepidation by both new heads *and* their staff. At least four of the case study heads did not conduct their first staff meeting as well as they would have liked and unintentionally upset a large number of staff. Teachers commented how a bad impression had been given during the meeting by, for example, heads outlining plans for the school, stating they were not impressed with what they had seen or making constant reference to how things operated at their last school. At least one case study head was pleased with the first staff meeting and thought he had managed to overcome the tendency to allude to his previous school by presenting the teachers with a gift. He said at the time of the first interview,

> We arranged to have a staff meeting on the day before term started. Here, I introduced myself and my new deputy head (I was involved in his appointment). I have a good memory for faces and names and I greeted a fair few of the staff by name. This helped a lot. I also broke the ice by bringing a present for the staffroom. It was a brass bell. I told the staff to ring the bell if I mentioned my old school more than twice!

The difficulties mentioned so far resulting from the heads' actions were raised by a number of teachers in at least a quarter of the case study schools. Other actions which resulted in negative comment by some staff, but which were not as common as those mentioned hitherto, included for example: lack of feedback on papers requested by the head, use of Christian names in front of pupils, indecisiveness and too close an adherence to 'the rule book'.

Summary and discussion

The information in this chapter has been drawn from interviews with about 300 teachers to examine their views on the new heads in the 16 case studies. The themes which emerged provide useful pointers for those taking up their first headship.

A new head needs to be aware of the relations between the staff and the previous head. While this may seem an obvious point, the NFER study indicated that historical factors are an important influence on the way the school operates and yet many new heads seem to assume that they are starting with a clean slate. Heads need to obtain as much knowledge as possible about the situation which existed prior to their arrival and to take this into consideration when making their plans for the future.

The arrival of a new head produces an air of anticipation for staff, pupils and parents. During the initial months heads found queues of people waiting to see them, each wanting to state their case, for example heads of department arguing for more staff and equipment. The research showed that many staff had very high expectations of the new head but these proved to be unrealistic and most heads were not able to live up to them. This is clearly a problem and new heads need to establish some short-term objectives and show that they can achieve them. An example which proved popular with staff was to get the school redecorated or to obtain various building improvements. The new head has to maintain a balance between plans which are long-term and difficult to achieve, yet act as a motivating and uniting force for the school and other smaller scale objectives which can be achieved fairly easily. In several of the case studies, the teachers' expectations had dropped to a very low level by the end of the head's second year, because as far as staff were concerned, the heads had little to show for their actions.

Most of the case study heads felt they had been given a 'honeymoon period' when the staff were more receptive and less critical. However, the length of this varied considerably and often seemed to be ended by a specific incident. New heads should assume they will be given a honeymoon period, which could last from one term to a year, and decide how best to use this time, e.g. by establishing the groundwork for major changes.

Table 5.1 summarizes teachers' views on the qualities of the 'good' head and identifies some of the aspects which they did not like. The data given in this chapter also highlighted a number of problem areas of which the new head needs to be aware. The most common difficulty appeared to be related to staff appointments and particularly, internal posts. Heads must act consistently by advertizing each post, interviewing all internal applicants, and being courteous and tactful in informing unsuccessful candidates. This proved to be a very sensitive area and heads have to face the difficulty of rewarding experience on one hand and encouraging the rising talent of younger staff on the other.

Teachers welcomed attempts to improve communication but consultation was a more complex issue. They wanted some degree of consultation about major issues and needed to see the head genuinely take account of their views before making a final decision. But they did not want to be consulted on everything and fully recognized that the head had the final say.

In many of the schools, the staff wanted the new head to take a firm line on pupil discipline. Several of the heads were criticized for being too lenient and not giving sufficient support to teachers by appearing to side with pupils on some occasions. This was linked to another issue where staff felt that some new heads were 'over-friendly' with the pupils and had not maintained the appropriate social distance. New heads have to demonstrate their support for staff if they wish to obtain the maximum involvement of teachers and gain their confidence.

Heads must take considerable care not to show undue favouritism to particular groups or individuals. A number of teachers expressed critical comments about heads who they felt had given preferential treatment to certain departments, individuals or younger staff. In most cases it seemed the heads were unaware that their actions had upset some staff. The new head has to be particularly careful to demonstrate fairness and consistency.

A source of annoyance for many teachers was the tendency for new heads continually to praise what had happened at their previous school. This was often interpreted as criticism of the new school, whether intended or not, and irritated the staff. New heads must acknowledge the school's good points as well as suggesting areas for change and must not automatically assume that because something worked well at their last school it can be transferred wholesale to the new situation.

The first full staff meeting is an important time for the new head as the impression they create appears to have a powerful effect on the staff. While it is necessary to provide an outline of future plans, it is too early to give a detailed blueprint and this suggests that everything is wrong with the school. The head needs to show a strong commitment to the staff and a belief that jointly they can improve the school.

Much of this chapter has dealt with the adverse reactions of teachers and consequently the emphasis has been rather negative. In conclusion, however, it should be noted that in the majority of schools, overall teacher reaction to the new heads was positive or very positive. In only four of the 16 schools could the general reaction be described as mostly negative. Many teachers made favourable comments concerning the heads' first two years in post and spoke in terms of the school and its staff having gained a new sense of direction, a purpose, a feeling of teamwork and of being a much more cohesive unit than was the case previously. In some schools, teachers referred to an overall increase in staff morale and this and other staff-related issues are discussed in the next chapter.

CHAPTER 6
Staff-Related Difficulties and Morale

A new head entering a school inherits an organization and its resources – without doubt the single most important of which is its staff. For any organization to operate at all people are needed: 'It is their presence, their willingness and their efforts which enable the organization to discharge the task expected of it. The focus of management is very much on the membership of the organization' (Paisey, 1984). A vital factor in ensuring the effectiveness of any organization is therefore the management of human resources and, as Batchelor (1981) has observed, 'nowhere is this factor more crucial than in our schools, where the kind of education that children receive is so heavily dependent on the quality of the performance of teachers who staff them'. For Batchelor, quality is defined in terms not only of teachers' knowledge and skills but also, most importantly, 'their dedication to teaching and the strength of their motivation to attain high levels of performance'.

The previous chapter examined, from the teachers' viewpoint, a number of factors relating to organizational membership and performance. This chapter uses data from the heads' perspective to focus on two overlapping areas – namely, staff-related difficulties faced by heads in their early years and the maintenance and development of staff morale.

Staff-related difficulties

In order to gain a overview of difficulties facing new heads, the two groups surveyed were asked to indicate, using a five-point scale, the problematical nature of various staff-related areas during their first two years in post. In this chapter the five-point scale has been collapsed into three to simplify the presentation of data for both groups of heads. Table 6.1 shows the eight areas most frequently seen by the new heads as problematic. (The results are reported in full in Appendix 1.)

The most problematic area for both groups of heads surveyed related to the previous head's allocation of points. This was perceived as a more serious problem by the heads of larger schools. Analysis of open-ended responses showed that the problem focused on a number of factors. Concern was

Table 6.1 Staff difficulties facing the new head in the first two years of headship

	New Heads (%)			'Old' Heads (%)		
	Very serious or serious problem	Moderate or minor problem	Not a problem	Very serious or serious problem	Moderate or minor problem	Not a problem
Issues arising from previous head's allocation of points	54	33	13	56	30	14
Persuading members of staff to accept new ideas	47	47	6	50	47	4
Coping with a weak member of the senior management team	38	36	26	46	26	28
Dismissal/redeployment of incompetent staff	37	32	31	41	30	28
Dealing with poor staff morale	36	51	13	31	52	17
Promoting staff professional development/INSET	30	60	10	31	57	12
Staff reductions as a result of falling rolls	36	34	30	–	–	–
LEA restrictions on staff recruitment*	42	42	16	21	51	28
	N = 188			N = 228		

*Chi-square on the above 3-point scale and the original 5-point scale (Appendix 1) significant at 5 per cent level.

expressed over the manner in which points had previously been allocated and the fact that it appeared little could be done to alter existing staffing structures. Comments were made about imbalances across subject departments, 'top-heavy' structures and how some previous heads had 'given away points like confetti or sweets'. It was suggested that points had often been allocated as reward for long service or 'in order to keep staff quiet rather than to promote a positive structure'.

In some instances, points were awarded to staff who held no specific responsibilities or whose responsibilities no longer existed. Such allocations it was felt, were no longer deserved and it had often proved difficult to produce suitable job descriptions in keeping with staffs' abilities and salaries. Perhaps more importantly, it often meant very good teachers were unable to be rewarded and younger staff, more receptive to new ideas, saw their chances of advancement blocked. It also meant some teachers were seen as overpaid for their efforts while other, more junior and more committed staff, were underpaid for theirs. The resulting effects on staff morale and staff development were obvious and several heads commented that in times of restricted teacher mobility the system was too inflexible, points were difficult to reallocate and there was insufficient room for manoeuvre. Many heads, for example, wished to modify the school's curriculum and pastoral system, but found they could not offer promotion to staff who took on additional responsibilities. Only one head in the surveys was fortunate enough to be able to report that some staff restructuring had proved possible as his predecessor had left 12 points unallocated. (Another reported that although seven points had been left available, the new head felt the points had been allocated without really knowing the staff concerned.)

A few heads commented that on arrival they had been approached by staff concerning promises of promotion made by the previous head. Also in a few schools, departments had come to regard points as 'departmental property' and staff were disappointed when the new head made it plain that this arrangement would no longer apply.

A large number of the heads surveyed perceived 'persuading members of staff to accept new ideas' to be a serious problem. In fact, it was 'not a problem' for, approximately, only one out of every 20 heads. Comments were frequently made that too many teachers, especially senior teachers, had remained at the same school for too long and in some instances general apathy had set in. Many were seen as too old and insufficiently experienced or qualified to move elsewhere. Others, it was claimed, were often unaware of recent issues and developments within education.

Some heads thought the discussion and introduction of new ideas was often interpreted by older staff as focusing on existing weaknesses, or neglecting that which previously existed within the school, and as such were resented (see Chapter 5). Many stable, senior staff had to be persuaded that 'curriculum development, organizational change and course planning were not only essential for a changing world but also professionally invigorating, satisfying and potentially invaluable for career development'. Another noted, 'the most serious issue has been to break out of a very well established dull routine with staff who have been here a long time and feel that everything is very good as it is'.

Issues relating to innovation and change are further considered in Chapter 7, but it is worth noting here that nearly a third of the 47 new heads interviewed in their first year, referred specifically to inertia within the school, largely caused by the lack of movement at middle-management level. Related to this was the fact that many of the more able junior staff were leaving, as promotional opportunities were often not available within the school. Matters were made worse in those schools with falling rolls where new heads were often not permitted to replace staff.

Other staff-related areas seen as particularly problematic were 'dealing with poor staff morale', 'dealing with staff professional development/INSET' and 'coping with a weak member of the senior management team'. The latter issue has been discussed in Chapter 4, while an analysis of the other two areas is found later in this chapter.

For approximately three out of every ten heads surveyed 'dismissal/ redeployment of incompetent staff' had not proved problematic, whereas for about four out of ten, it had been perceived as a 'very serious' or 'serious' problem. Of course, regardless of the size of a school's staff, it merely required one teacher to be seen as inadequate to constitute a major nuisance for any school manager. Heads said dismissal proceedings against incompetent staff would be taken only as a last resort when all other alternatives had been exhausted.

In those schools with ineffective and/or incompetent teachers, heads made considerable efforts to provide various forms of support. Several heads stated that in an attempt to overcome particular weaknesses, the advisory service had been brought in or INSET suggested. Some heads spoke of personal interviews which attempted to resolve problems, while others tried to redefine job responsibilities to achieve greater effectiveness and ensure the school was 'getting the best out of them'.

Another means of overcoming or alleviating this problem, especially at middle management level, was to 'work around' the individuals concerned. For example, a case study head with a very poor head of department was able, as a result of an adviser's visit, to obtain additional points which were used to create a second-in-charge of the department. Extra resources had also been obtained for the department. The head now gave copies of all documents directly to departmental members and had expressd a desire to attend departmental meetings 'when they thought they were ready for me to come'. The problem had been further reduced as a result of the new deputy head's teaching commitment in this department. The head remarked however, at the time of the researcher's third visit, that this particular ineffective head of department had expressed a desire to take early retirement, and this was mentioned by several heads as the least painful way of removing incompetent or 'burnt out' teachers.

Early retirement is, however, an option not always available for heads and, as one head put it, 'all the will in the world is sometimes not enough to get around the dilemma of inadequate teachers'. There comes a time when disciplinary or dismissal proceedings must be instituted. This is more likely to take place when attempts to shield or protect incompetent teachers prove increasingly difficult or when parental complaints become a major concern. Heads were reluctant to enter into dismissal proceedings against staff members for a number of reasons, not least because they were seen as very stressful for all parties and extremely time-consuming. What is more, a few thought it was almost impossible to remove incompetent teachers and that some LEAs were reluctant to grasp this particular nettle.

An example of disciplinary proceedings being instituted against a teacher was found in one of the 16 case study schools, where a member of staff, for no legitimate reason, had been frequently absent (e.g. in one term the teacher had attended school for only three days). The new head had tried, unsuccessfully in the first instance, to get the LEA 'to do something about this particular matter', which he felt was detrimental to pupils and had placed an additional burden on a hard working staff. The LEA's notes for heads on staff discipline stated they were not prepared to take action over frequent absenteeism, but they did on the head's insistence approach the teacher, seeking approval to contact her doctor. (It was later discovered the teacher was registered with two doctors.) The new head said it had been necessary to find out as much as possible about disciplinary proceedings and he had issued the teacher with a formal written warning and then a final warning, with copies being sent on both occasions to the authority. The head had spent a lot of time on this particular matter and felt he had received little assistance from either the LEA or the local branch of his professional association. The head insisted the authority took immediate action and the teacher was eventually summoned to a meeting with a senior officer at the LEA office. At this point and much to the relief of the head, the teacher offered her resignation. At the time of the researcher's second visit to the school, the head remarked that this particular incident had proved to be the single most serious problem he had faced since taking up appointment.

'Staff reductions as a result of falling rolls' was seen as a 'very serious' or 'serious' problem for 36 per cent of the new heads' cohort. (Data on this particular issue were not available for the sample of experienced heads.) Due to a fall in pupil numbers, many schools had to reduce the number of staff and this was achieved predominantly through voluntary redeployment and early retirement. In some schools, however, these reductions had a significant effect on the curriculum, with several heads commenting on the difficulties of its maintenance, let alone its development or diversification. Comments were made that some teachers were having to teach their second subjects or teach in areas for which they were not trained or qualified, while other heads expressed more general concern as to how they were to utilize remaining staff to best effect.

In ten of the 16 case study schools, staff reductions had been necessary because of falling rolls and in some instances these had proved extremely difficult to implement. In one school, for example, the head had managed, through various means, to 'lose' nearly 9 per cent of staff, but on his own admission had been left with a very difficult situation. There was a surplus of 0.5 of a teacher in each of two interrelated subject areas and until this matter had been resolved, decision-making and timetabling were proving to be extremely difficult. The head remarked he had had regular conversations with the LEA's staffing officer on this issue and explained the staffing situation to the individual teachers in the relevant departments. The head had also informed one of the departmental heads that she was to be redeployed. This particular incident occurred during the researcher's third visit to the school, and the head explained the decision to nominate a teacher for redeployment had been the most difficult he had had to make in the first two years of headship. The head of department had not taken the decision very well, but in the view of a senior teacher it had been taken in the best interests of the school, rather than in terms of, for example, seniority or length of service. The senior teacher also remarked that although the head was the best person in the school to make decisions regarding redeployment, heads in general were not LEA employers and perhaps it would therefore be more appropriate if staffing officers were primarily responsible for informing teachers of decisions made.

In another case study school, the head had been asked by the LEA to nominate staff for redeployment, but had refused and insisted that if teachers were to leave, then the task of selecting individual teachers was the staffing officer's responsibility. In the past, because of a number of difficulties faced, the school had been allowed a generous pupil–teacher ratio: it was now intended, however, to redeploy nearly 20 per cent of staff. The head strongly believed he had to resist LEA attempts to reduce staffing levels, partly to demonstrate *his* commitment to the school because the staff had had a particularly difficult relationship with the previous head and the authority. In the end, the staffing officer was forced to make the decision and selected a small number of teachers for redeployment, although the situation had not been fully resolved at the end of the new head's second year.

The staff and staffing issues considered so far have all been seen as serious problems by at least three of every ten heads involved in the surveys. It is worth noting that there was a statistically significant difference between the two groups of heads concerning 'LEA restrictions on staff recruitment'. Whereas 42 per cent of new heads mentioned this as a 'very serious' or 'serious' problem, it was mentioned by only 21 per cent of 'old' heads. Similarly, there was a statistically significant difference on the 'internal' issue 'dealing with a contracting education budget', with over one-third of new heads compared to only 22 per cent of the more experienced heads seeing it as a 'very serious' or 'serious' problem (see Appendix 1). The differences between the two groups of heads surveyed probably reflect changed demographic and financial circumstances. It will be recalled the 'old' heads with between three and eight years' experience, were asked to consider how serious a problem these issues were in their first two years of headship; the question therefore referred to the years 1975–1980, whereas the new heads' survey referred to 1982–1984. The situation had clearly become more problematic over this period.

For the new heads 'LEA restrictions on the recruitment of staff' was a major issue and comments were made about the limitations imposed by redeployment and 'ring-fence' policies and how, as a result of staffing decisions being made at a very late stage, it became increasingly difficult to make appropriate plans for the forthcoming academic year. In some authorities, schools were not permitted to advertize for staff until after the closing date for teacher resignations, and heads therefore felt they were left with the weakest candidates or probationers, or it proved necessary to appoint teachers on a temporary basis and readvertize with a later start date. Such unsatisfactory staff recruitment arrangements have also been referred to in the HMI document *The New Teacher in School* (1982). A useful overview of staffing issues within the context of falling school rolls is provided by Walsh *et al.* (1984).

In conclusion, it is worth noting the staff-related issue that was generally seen as least problematic. Reference to Appendix 1 shows that 'dealing with staff unions and professional associations' was perceived by the least number of heads – both new and 'old' – to be a 'very serious' problem. Furthermore, the rating scale shows that very nearly a third of both groups of heads did not see this area as a problem. A cross-tabulation of the data showed a slight tendency for the heads of larger schools to perceive dealing with unions as a more serious problem than the heads of medium or small schools.

In a few of the schools where dealing with unions and professional associations was a very serious problem, heads made reference to small groups of activists who, in their view, tried to cause maximum disruption and saw heads as 'the enemy' or 'symbols of authority'. In three of the case study schools, the new heads felt that dealing with teacher unions and professional associations had been problematic, although to be more accurate, in two cases the problem centred on specific union representatives.

At the time of the researcher's third visit, most teacher unions were involved in a national dispute and the new heads were being extremely careful not to take actions which could be interpreted as undermining the unions' sanctions. This was made more difficult by the fact that conditions of service for teachers was such an ill-defined area. One head went as far as ringing a union's national headquarters to ensure his actions concerning lunchtime supervision of pupils could not be interpreted by the staff as 'unsupportive'. Another referred to an incident which, in the head's view, rather abruptly marked the end of his 'honeymoon period'. A letter sent to parents had been interpreted by the unions as critical of their 'industrial' action. Similarly, several case study heads referred to a heightened awareness of professional isolation and the uncomfortable feeling of being 'the meat in the sandwich' during times of 'industrial' action. (See Chapter 8 for a more detailed discussion.)

The DES have recently funded research into problems in staff management/ employment relations – to include union issues and the impact of labour law on the role of the head – with a view to producing training materials appropriate for the in-service training of heads (Lyons and Stenning, 1986; McQueeney,

1985). It is also worth noting that a prolonged dispute between teacher unions and their employers can have significant effects on the overall morale of teachers. It is to the general notion of staff morale that attention is now given.

Staff morale

Staff morale is a complex notion, having several dimensions including those related to leadership, group effectiveness and individual motivation. It usually refers to groups and includes 'feelings, thoughts and actions which relate to group cohesion, survival, improvement and development' (Williams, 1984). The morale of teachers within schools, either collectively or individually, is rarely static, and will rise or fall for a number of reasons. A fall in staff morale for example, may be attributed to either local or national factors, such as the possibility of school closure or a protracted union dispute over conditions of service. Leadership, however, is a major factor affecting staff morale as leaders influence it directly or through their effects on individuals and groups. For example, morale in some case study schools had risen and was, according to the majority of teachers interviewed, largely a consequence of a change in leader.

It is the intention of the second part of this chapter to use data, derived from the survey of heads with three to eight years' experience, to discuss two questions. Firstly, to what extent and for which reasons did the 'old' heads perceive staff morale to be a problem in their schools? And secondly, which strategies had they successfully employed in attempting to improve the overall morale of their staff?

Is it a problem?

As earlier stated, both groups of heads surveyed were asked to consider how serious a problem 'dealing with poor staff morale' was during their first two years of headship (see Table 6.1). The data showed that just under a third of 'old' heads and over a third of new heads perceived this as a 'very serious' problem. Further analysis showed that there was a significant relationship between the size of school and severity of the problem. The heads of larger schools tended to report that 'dealing with poor staff morale' was a more serious problem than it was for heads of smaller schools.

The experienced heads were also asked if staff morale in their schools had been adversely affected by poor career prospects, limited staff development or INSET, and the increased demands on the job of the teacher. Over four out of ten 'old' heads referred to limited career prospects as definitely affecting staff morale, with approximately another 30 per cent seeing this as a partial problem. References were made to LEA 'ring-fence' policies, unadvertized vacancies and the severe competition for most scale posts. Falling rolls had resulted in fewer opportunities and an increasing number of staff, it was suggested, had reconciled themselves to staying in their present positions. Other heads commented that reward for energy or initiative was reduced, thus causing increased resentment of any 'passengers' and in some cases there was a 'reluctance to do more than 9 to 4', or to participate in extracurricular activities.

Limited opportunity for in-service training or staff development was identified by only a quarter of the 'old' heads as a problem; indeed, many made positive references to INSET, stating that opportunities were readily available. Others qualified their enthusiasm by noting there was little connection between in-service training and career development. For some, morale was seen to be adversely affected by a shortage of supply teachers to cover for colleagues involved in INSET, or by the LEA's refusal to pay accommodation expenses or for 'out-of-county' courses. Reference to Table 6.1 shows, however, that *'promoting* staff professional development/INSET' in their first two years was a 'very serious' or 'serious' problem for as many as three out of ten heads. Only approximately one in ten heads said this was 'not a problem'. This suggests that new heads experience difficulties in persuading some staff to attend various forms of INSET, even though opportunities are available.

Two-thirds of experienced heads referred to increased demands on the job of the teacher as a problem adversely affecting staff morale. References were made for example, to the increased accountability of teachers and the greater demands put on them as a result of curriculum development; new forms of assessment and reporting; community involvement; parents' evenings; pastoral care; multicultural and non-sexist educational initiatives; mixed ability teaching; and attempts to change teaching methods, improve the overall quality of education and raise the achievements of all pupils.

The greater level of professionalism demanded of teachers had, in the view of many heads, been accompanied by additional administrative work; larger classes, less time for preparation and marking and a shortage of resources and support staff. Teachers were also expected, far more than hitherto, to be much more than professional educators and to undertake tasks which were peripheral to their main role. 'We have to be everything to everybody for up to 15 hours a day' was the view of one head, while the head of an urban comprehensive said, 'the sheer pressure of work has to be experienced to be understood and appreciated. The surprise is that staff morale is kept up when teachers play the parts of counsellor, parent, social worker, probationer, policeman, educator, etc.'

Comments were also sought on other factors affecting staff morale. Many points were raised by the 'old' heads, but the following were most frequently mentioned. It was thought to be increasingly difficult, in the light of financial restraints, to maintain a satisfactory working environment. Often there was a shortage of resources, equipment and materials, inadequate services and a need for building repairs and maintenance. Insufficient capitation and poor facilities accompanied by the more obvious physical deterioration of schools, it was claimed, was having an adverse effect on the morale of both staff *and* pupils. Morale was also being affected by high rates of local unemployment and the resulting disillusionment with education of many pupils and parents.

In addition, staff morale was seen to be adversely affected by the general consequences of falling rolls – notably the reorganization, amalgamation or closure of secondary schools and the accompanying possibilities of teacher redeployment. Similarly, many references were made to the poor esteem in which teachers were held, especially by the media, and the general loss of confidence, by others, in the profession. As a head commented, 'there seems to be little said or written that puts the profession in a favourable light'. The lack of respect for the profession together with the lack of recognition of the role of the teacher affected the self-confidence of staff and had led, it was suggested, to a combination of low status and low pay.

How can morale be improved

Many of the issues raised so far are clearly beyond the ability of most individual heads to alter in any meaningful way, yet reference has been made to the fact that leadership is frequently a major factor affecting morale. It is therefore intended to consider the strategies the experienced heads stated they had used in attempting to raise the morale of their staff. An analysis of the strategies described showed they fell under five main headings: discipline; staff development; school organization; qualities of headship and general morale boosting.

The automatic and effective support of heads in all matters relating to pupil discipline was seen as an important factor affecting staff morale in general. Heads stressed the significance of personal support in all disciplinary matters, and as was shown in the previous chapter, a number of case study heads had been criticized by teachers for the lack of such support. References were made by experienced heads to basic changes in school organization and supervision, the introduction of systems of pastoral care and other ways in which it was felt discipline could be maintained and improved.

The importance of developing human potential has been stressed by many organizational theorists who argue such development is beneficial not only for individuals, but also for organizations, as people constitute any organization's most important resource. Many heads made reference to staff development as a morale-raising strategy. Staff development programmes had been encouraged and professional tutors appointed. In some schools, interviews with all staff were held annually by heads (occasionally by deputies and heads of department) in order to discuss the school, the member of staff and their career. Some gave advice on job applications and interview techniques and one head said teachers were shown the reference written for them when they had applied elsewhere. Several made reference to the desirability of internal promotions if possible, the need to reward worthy staff and the necessity to interview *all* applicants for internal appointments (see Chapter 5).

Regularly changing staff responsibilities to add variety and help promotion was also frequently mentioned. It was felt to be important to give teachers as broad and varied experience as possible and job rotation, job sharing and staff involvement in the more rewarding and interesting aspects of school administration were stressed.

Making maximum use of INSET was a means of maintaining morale and staff were encouraged to attend more substantive courses and to apply for secondment. One head suggested secondment had a greater effect on morale than other measures as it enabled points to be allocated elsewhere, albeit temporarily. Similarly, school-based INSET and occasional staff weekends were mentioned as helping 'to pull the school together', while other heads encouraged staff to offer *their* services on LEA courses. Finally, teacher exchanges and visits to other schools were mentioned, with one head claiming that visits to other schools and departments was the best form of INSET available.

Other strategies used to improve staff morale centred on the organization of the school. There was a need, it was suggested, for efficient and realistic communication systems and consultative procedures. Staff needed to be kept fully informed through personal communications, information bulletins and the publication of the minutes of all meetings. Staff should be involved in decision-making and responsibility should be delegated when possible. Opportunities should be created to permit staff to meet and discuss problems in an open way allowing negative views to surface and be freely discussed. Participation and involvement in policy-making can be facilitated by the setting-up of consultation groups and working parties and it was felt important to ensure that young and relatively inexperienced teachers were involved in such forums. For example, one head wrote of the need to run an 'open school' where staff were informed of normally 'sensitive' matters affecting capitation, the allocation of points and promotion criteria and to extend consultative arrangements. Another thought morale could be raised by employing 'whatever generates a real sense of participation, shared responsibility, mutual respect and shared aims'.

Institutional stagnation could also be avoided, it was claimed, by the school's involvement in curricular initiatives, especially those that had received favourable comments from outside. Care had to be taken, however, to recognize the increased demands on the role of teachers and to give support whenever possible. For example, opportunities were made where possible to increase non-contact time, provide classroom materials, close early half-termly for departmental meetings and to remove or replace unsatisfactory teachers. Other heads spoke of their generosity concerning casual time off for teachers (and the resulting positive effect this had on general staff attendance!) and attempted to meet all expenses for 'out of hours' activities.

The restructuring of the points system (to upgrade pastoral posts, for example) and continuous efforts to maximize the school's establishment were also mentioned. Some heads thought it helpful to widen the base of the organizational pyramid by gradually changing the balance of points and spreading scale posts among as many staff as possible (for example, one scale 4 post could be converted into three scale 2 posts).

Another strategy employed by heads was increasingly to involve the governors in the school by, for example, encouraging visits to various departments, or conversely by inviting heads of department to address governors' meetings. Invitations were also made to others to visit the school (e.g. chairperson of education committee or Her Majesty's Inspectorate) and LEA advisers were encouraged to be used where possible to obtain resources.

There are a number of similarities between some of the strategies documented so far and many of the points made by teachers and referred to in the previous chapter. Nowhere is this more apparent than with the fourth of the five areas – strategies employed relating to the qualities of headship. Many 'old' heads made reference to facets of headship that the case study school teachers identified as constituting 'good' heads. For example, reference was made for the need: to be accessible and visible ('do not be an absentee head or a Howard Hughes!'); to operate an open-door policy ('give priority to staff and be prepared to listen'); to deal with people personally ('preferably on a day-to-day basis and not via bits of paper'); to teach ('include the most difficult pupils'); to visit and observe others teach; to express an appreciation of staff achievements ('praise people at all possible times and avoid blanket criticism', 'it's vital to make people feel important'); and to be seen as 'on their side' and 'to be fighting as best we can to improve their lot' (e.g. to ensure staff are aware that problems are brought to the notice of governors and the LEA).

Other qualities in heads mentioned and seen as improving morale included: consistency, calmness, courteousness, confidence, clear leadership, humour, hard work and a preparedness to take at least an equal share in extra duties while avoiding the delegation of onerous ones. It was also felt important to be an enabler ('try to meet all staff requests'), not to prejudge issues, to participate in fun activities, to look for and encourage good practice and to refer to the school as 'ours' and not 'mine'.

Finally, reference was made by experienced heads to a whole package of strategies used to boost morale generally. For example, positive moves being made in the public relations area to improve the school's image and using the local press to publicize the achievements of both pupils and staff. Greater community and parental involvement was encouraged and attempts made to increase pride in staff and pupils (e.g. by feeding back favourable comments from visitors). Maximum efforts were made to effect repairs, encourage LEA expenditure and improve staff facilities and give staff welfare a high priority. The experienced heads also suggested morale could be raised by staff participation in school productions (e.g. musicals) and fund-raising campaigns. Lastly, it was felt social functions, sporting activities and the formation of staffroom associations were also useful as general morale boosters.

Summary and discussion

This chapter has concentrated on the types of difficulty new heads faced with regard to the staff and staffing of their schools. Many of the heads wanted to restructure the curriculum and organization of the school and partly tried to do so through the allocation of scale points. However, they often found this particularly difficult because of the way the previous head had distributed points. As far as the new heads were concerned, some teachers were holding extra points which were hard to justify. This meant few free points were available and new heads also found it hard to move them to different departments. The research suggests that heads have limited opportunities to use scale points to encourage new developments and if points become available their reallocation must be carefully considered.

Many heads thought that persuading staff to accept new ideas was problematic and spoke about inertia within the schools which was often located at the middle management level. The heads of department played a crucial role in implementing any curricular changes and heads were concerned about staff who had little experience in other schools or adopted a narrow subject perspective. New heads adopted a variety of strategies to encourage heads of department which included: a curricular review, visits to other schools, working with LEA subject advisers and INSET.

A problem for some heads, which took up large amounts of time and energy in the most severe cases, was dealing with incompetent teachers. Several methods were used to help the teacher and these included: classroom observation, advice from the head, head of department and LEA adviser, extra resources, and changes to the teacher's timetable or job responsibilities. If all these avenues of help failed, the heads were forced to take out dismissal procedures or seek early retirement for the teacher. Although the number of instances was fairly low, the research indicated that new heads were poorly prepared for handling these disciplinary proceedings. This is an area which needs to be covered on management courses, as some heads found they received little help with this particular matter.

The management of redeployment due to falling rolls was very stressful for heads and staff. Thirty-six per cent of the new heads cohort reported this as a 'serious' or 'very serious' problem, while for a fortunate 30 per cent it was not a problem at all. Some new heads were also affected by LEA restrictions on recruitment as authorities tried to control the number of teachers employed. The dual problems of having to reduce the number of staff and not being able to recruit from a wide field caused new heads considerable difficulty. Heads need to develop their interviewing procedures and counselling skills and more training in personnel management is required to equip them for these complex tasks.

Prolonged industrial action by the teacher unions meant that heads had to 'walk a tightrope'. While they generally sympathized with the teachers, they also had to keep the schools running. For many heads the dispute highlighted how much they relied on teachers' goodwill and the need to clarify conditions of service. Although the unrest raised a number of difficulties, the majority of heads, both new and 'old', did not find 'dealing with the unions' to be a great problem. The case studies illustrated situations where the new heads had experienced difficulties in trying to work with particular union officials.

About a third of the heads considered staff morale to be a 'serious' or 'very serious' problem; although it should be noted that the surveys took place before the prolonged industrial action by the teacher unions. Many heads believed morale had been adversely affected by limited career prospects and the increased demands on teachers. Although a number of external factors affect the situation, effective leadership can do much to improve staff morale, motivation and commitment. This chapter has outlined a number of strategies which heads can use to sustain and improve morale.

CHAPTER 7
The Management of Change

Innovation was a major concern for almost all of the new heads. For some, it had been made clear at their interviews or soon after by either the LEA officers or school governors, that various changes were seen as necessary. From interviews with new heads it appeared that many arrived at the school with an image of an 'ideal' school which then had to be tempered with reality before deciding on which changes to make and when to make them.

The first section of this chapter outlines the major findings from previous research on educational innovation with particular reference to the role of the principal or head. The rest of the chapter provides information on the changes taking place in the survey schools, while the head's involvement in innovation is examined by using more detailed data from the case studies.

The following section draws on Fullan's review of recent research in North America to provide an outline of the change process and some of the major factors involved (Fullan, 1982). Most research on innovation divides the process into three broad phases:

1 Initiation
   - the period during which a decision is made to proceed with a change and plans are formulated and developed.
2 Implementation
   - a crucial stage when teachers are asked to begin the innovation. For curricular changes in secondary schools it is the time when the innovation is timetabled and put into practice.
3 Incorporation
   - the final stage when the innovative practice becomes a routine part of the school. Alternatively, the change may disappear, either by way of a decision to discard it or simply through attrition.

The time-scale for the whole process is lengthy and it may take three to five years to cover the process from initiation to incorporation. What happens at one stage strongly affects subsequent stages, but new factors appear at each stage and it is possible to return to earlier phases at various points in the process which does not necessarily follow a straight line.

Initiation

Educational adoption never occurs without an advocate. In the United States, the chief district administrator and central office staff play an important part and numerous studies show their importance as sources of advocacy and support in adopting new programmes at the district level. At the school level, principals and heads play a similar role in deciding whether to adopt a particular innovation. By the same token, administrators and heads can be equally powerful at blocking changes they do not like.

In the US, the large-scale Rand study of various Federal funded educational innovations (Berman and McLaughlin, 1975) found two types of contrasting motivations which characterized the initiation phase. They called these 'Opportunism' and 'Problem-solving'. Projects generated by opportunism seemed to be a response to the available funds and were characterized by a lack of interest and commitment from the level of district administrators to classroom teachers. As a result, little in the way of serious change was ever attempted – or occurred. The problem-solving motive emerged primarily in response to locally identified needs and was associated with strong commitment. The Federal funds were seen as a way to support the local solution. The Rand study found four general patterns with regard to project planning:

a) Top-down strategies
   – plans were made almost entirely by central officers.
b) Grassroots planning
   – plans were devised by teachers with little involvement by district officers.
c) No planning by anyone.
d) Collaborative planning
   – plans were made with input from district personnel and teachers – all participants were treated as partners.

Top-down methods gave 'indifferent implementation' and 'spotty continuation' – they usually met with indifference or resistance from teachers, who felt it was 'not theirs'. The grassroots approach was only a little more successful. These projects had a high initial teacher commitment, but without support from district administrators this waned and, in general, grassroots projects disappeared as completely as top-down projects. The collaborative model was the necessary style for both short- and long-term success. 'Who' originated the project did not matter – 'how' the planning was carried out was important and only the collaborative strategy made for success.

More recent research has shown that the matter is not quite so straightforward and, in a later paper, Fullan (1985) suggests that the most effective strategy will depend on the particular change to be introduced. For major school-wide changes, a combination of top-down and bottom-up approaches to planning is needed.

Implementation

This is the most important and complex phase in the innovation process. Many attempts at change have concentrated on producing curriculum materials and devising plans in a way which ignores the fact that what people do, or do not do, is the crucial variable. As Fullan (1982) points out, 'This neglect is understandable, because people are much more unpredictable and difficult to deal with than things. Unfortunately, they are also much more essential for success.'

Fullan outlines a large number of factors which affect success or failure at the implementation stage and these include the following:

Need   As mentioned earlier, the Rand study showed that many innovations are attempted without a careful examination of whether or not they address a perceived need. If teachers do not see a need for the change, they are unlikely to implement it.

Clarity   Even when there is agreement that some kind of change is needed, it is not always clear what teachers are expected to do differently. Problems relating to clarity have been found in virtually every study of change. Lack of clarity – diffuse goals and unspecified means – represents a major problem at the implementation stage.

Complexity   This refers to the difficulty and extent of change required. It is interesting to note that several US studies have found that the projects attempting major changes accomplished more than those aimed at minor changes – the more tried for, the more achieved. Simple changes are easier to carry out, but they may not make much of a difference.

Mutual adaptation   Many studies of change have used a 'fidelity' model, that is, unless the change was implemented as the designer had intended, it was considered to have failed. This type of view led to attempts to produce 'teacher-proof' curricular packages. The Rand study found that successful implementation was characterized by a process they called 'mutual adaptation', which involved a modification of both the project itself *and* changes in the institution and individual participants.

History of innovation attempts   The importance of an LEA's, district's or school's history of innovation affects implementation. The more the teachers or others have had negative experiences with previous attempts at innovation, the more cynical or apathetic they will be about the next change, regardless of its merit.

LEA or district support   Individual teachers and heads can bring about change in a school without the support of central administrators, but LEA- or district-wide change will not happen. Most of the research shows that support from central administration is critical for change in district practice. But it also shows that support or endorsement in general has little influence on change in practice. Teachers and others will not take change seriously unless senior administrators and advisers *demonstrate through actions* that they should.

Staff development and INSET Since the essence of educational change consists in learning new ways of thinking, new skills, knowledge and attitudes, etc., it follows that INSET is one of the most important factors relating to change in practice. But there is now considerable evidence to show that pre-implementation training, in which even intensive sessions are used, does not work. One-shot workshops prior to and even during implementation are not very helpful. The reason is that most INSET is not designed to provide the continuous, interactive, cumulative learning necessary to develop new concepts, skills and behaviours. Failure to realize that there is a need for INSET *during implementation* is a common problem. No matter how much advance staff development occurs, it is only when people actually try to implement new approaches that they realize the problems and need support and training. The initial stages of any significant change always involve anxiety and uncertainty, and support and interaction at the implementation stage are vital, while continuous planning meetings are necessary *throughout* the project.

Incorporation

Many of the factors mentioned already which affect implementation also affect the final stage of incorporation, e.g. the level of interest and support by district administrators or heads.

Continuation of a project is usually seen as a clear yes/no decision by the school or district. However, the Rand project found that it was not so straightforward. In fact, parts of the project were continued and incorporated. This could occur at the classroom level where some elements of the project were assimilated into a teacher's regular routine. At the district level, the data suggested that superintendants weighed four general concerns in reaching decisions about whether to continue funding projects: the project's perceived success during implementation, the importance of the educational needs served, the resources required, and the organizational-political forces inhibiting or promoting the innovation.

The role of the head in change

In the UK, relatively few studies have focused on the role of the head in change. Most of the research has taken the form of case studies of individual secondary schools and the part played by the head has been considered as only one aspect of the work (e.g. Bell, 1979; Waddilove, 1981; Gilbert, 1981; Bailey, 1982; Nicholls, 1983; and Burgess, 1983). A few studies have used interviews or questionnaires to look at heads and innovation across a number of schools (e.g. Dickinson, 1975; Hughes, 1975; McGeown, 1979; and Collier, 1982). Dickinson's study, although small-scale and limited to one LEA, revealed some interesting findings with regard to the current NFER project. He found that heads were the main originators of the innovations which were introduced to answer a perceived need in the schools. Each of the 15 headteachers spoke of all the innovations as being highly successful, but as Dickinson points out, 'real measures of evaluation in terms of learning outcomes, or understanding, appeared to be irrelevant, providing the innovation was successfully brought about'. The current NFER project found similar results, indicating a tendency for heads to see an innovation as successful once it had been implemented.

While a full review of the literature is not possible, the next section outlines some of the work from North America, where the most detailed research on principals and innovation has been carried out. Although this work provides important insights, care must be taken to avoid a simple application of these findings to different cultural contexts.

Fullan (1982) provides an excellent summary and stresses that 'change is only one small part of the forces competing for the principal's attention and usually not the most compelling one'.

Wolcott's (1973) pioneering ethnographic study of one elementary principal, together with Morris *et al.*'s (1981) research in eight elementary and six high schools where the principals were shadowed for up to 12 days over a two-year period, showed that most time was taken up with one-to-one personal interactions, meetings and phone calls. The main role of the principal seemed to be one of maintaining stability and little attention was given to programme changes.

The Rand project, although not a direct study of the role of the principal, found that one-third of the teachers surveyed thought their principal functioned largely as an administrator who was uninvolved in change. In successful projects it was found that the principals gave active support to the innovations. This was confirmed in case studies of the Teacher Corps projects (Reinhard *et al.*, 1980, and Rosenblum and Jastrzab, 1980). The most successful projects had principals who were intensely involved in the initial stages – what was done at this stage by the principal drastically affected later success or failure of the project. Active involvement by principals was important, but active did not always mean direct – in some cases the principals delegated day-to-day responsibility. As long as the principal was involved and interested in getting feedback and the staff were aware of the principal's commitment to the innovation, the project did not suffer.

A major study of innovation, the DESSI project (Dissemination Efforts Supporting School Improvement: Crandall and Loucks, 1983 and Huberman and Miles, 1984) looked at 61 innovations in 146 sites, and conducted case studies at 12 sites. In the summary of their findings, Crandall and Loucks report that 'Forceful leadership is the factor that contributes most directly and surely to major effective changes in classroom practice that become firmly incorporated into everyday routines'. The leadership could come from a central officer administrator or an influential principal: 'When the involvement is enlightened, forceful, resourceful and long lasting, highly significant changes are carried out.' From this it appears that the principals played a major role in change. But in the case studies reported by Huberman and Miles, we find that the prime advocates for change in ten of the 12 sites were central office administrators who often reached directly into the schools to implement the innovation, thereby leaving the principals to play a secondary role. In 11 sites, central office administrators were the key personnel in making the decision to adopt the innovation and 'principals had to get into line'. 'The principals were often as much the targets or consumers of the projects as were the teachers so initial commitment was not always high.'

The principal's role in innovation was examined by Hall *et al.* (1984) in their work with 29 elementary principals. They identified three types of change facilitator style which they termed Initiators, Managers and Responders.

Initiators had clear, decisive long-range policies and goals which transcended but included implementation of current innovations. Decisions were made in relation to these goals and in terms of what they believed to be best for the students. These principals had high expectations for students, teachers and themselves, which they conveyed through frequent contact with teachers. Initiators reinterpreted district programmes to suit the needs of the school.

Managers demonstrated responsive behaviours to situations but also initiated actions to support changes suggested by the central office. They defended staff from what they felt were excessive demands and provided basic support to facilitate teachers' use of an innovation, but did not move beyond the basics of what was imposed.

Responders placed a heavy emphasis on allowing teachers and others the opportunity to take the lead. They saw the principal's main role as maintaining the smooth running of the school by concentrating on administrative tasks. Teachers were viewed as professionals who were able to work with little guidance from the principal. They stressed the personal side of their relationships with staff and before making decisions, tried to allow everyone an opportunity to express their views. In most cases, the decisions were in response to immediate circumstances rather than in terms of long-range goals. This seemed to be due in part to their desire to please others and in part to their more limited vision of how the school and staff should change in the future.

The three styles were found in a number of studies by the team of researchers and, independently, Thomas (1978) identified three very similar roles for principals in managing innovations. Hall and his colleagues found that there was more quality and quantity of change in those schools with 'Initiator' style principals than in schools with 'Manager' and 'Responder' principals.

Fullan (1982) summarizes his review of the research by saying, 'A large percentage of principals (at least half) operate mainly as administrators and as ad hoc crisis managers. These principals are not effective in helping to bring about changes in their schools. Those principals who do become involved in change do so either as direct instructional leaders or as facilitative instructional leaders. Both styles of leadership can be effective.'

Most of the work in North America has been conducted at the elementary level and although similarities exist between elementary and secondary schools, far more research is needed on the role of the secondary principal or head. Hall and his colleagues at the University of Texas, having previously worked with elementary principals, have recently begun a study of change at the high school level. They found that most of the changes originated from outside the school and local school administrators (which included principals) were the impetus for only a quarter of the changes. Interviews with staff presented 'a clear picture of the teacher being primarily a *recipient* of change rather than an *initiator* of change'. Teachers reacted positively to most of the changes and showed a greater commitment to those changes which were originated by teachers. The researchers concluded, 'In relation to school change, there seems to be a common assumption that teachers are quite resistant to change. These data do not support that assumption' (Rutherford and Murphy, 1985).

Other members of the team (Huling-Austin *et al.*, 1985) looked at the role of the principal in 18 high schools. They found a number of different decision-making and committee structures but

> the connecting link in all these patterns, however, is the principal, especially in terms of change. The principal may only say yes or no to change, may only provide sanction and support, or may be actively involved in some way. Yet in every instance the principal was a key figure... if only by virtue of his/her role as primary facilitator or in establishing goals for the school.

Nine of the selected schools were 'active' in change and nine were 'typical'. A high number of the principals in the active schools had an 'initiator' style, which was also found to be the most effective in the previous work with elementary schools.

The NFER study

Details of the head's role in the management of change were obtained from the case studies, while the surveys of both new and 'old' heads sought information on the types of changes being made. The more experienced heads were only asked to list the major changes introduced in the 1982/83 school year, while the new heads were asked to provide details of changes introduced during their first two years as well as those planned for the future. Tables 7.1 and 7.2 show the most common curricular and organizational changes, as mentioned by both groups of heads.

Only 10 per cent of the new heads and 9 per cent of the more experienced heads said no major changes had been introduced during the period. The main reasons given were the amalgamation, reorganization or closure of the school; staffing cuts resulting from falling rolls; or for the 'old' heads, a period of consolidation following considerable change.

As an example of how to interpret Table 7.1, the first line shows that various types of vocational preparation courses had been introduced in 26 per cent of

Table 7.1 Curricular changes introduced by new and 'old' heads (1982–84)

	New Heads		3–8 Year Heads
	Introduced in first two years %	Planned %	Introduced (1982–83) %
Most frequently mentioned changes			
Vocational preparation e.g. City and Guilds courses (yrs 4–6)	26	22	19
Computers and information technology	21	12	13
Personal and social education plus careers	18	9	10
Remedial education plus special needs	13	4	2
Craft, design and technology plus control technology	10	4	9
Active tutorial work/timetabled form tutor period	9	4	8
Courses for less able	7	5	9
Modern languages	8	2	5
Creative studies (music, drama)	6	2	4
Humanities and social science	5	2	5
TVEI (Technical and Vocational Education Initiative)	4	2	–
Science and integrated science	2	2	3
General change to core curriculum	9	4	10
General change to option pattern	23	5	6
No major changes	10	10	9
	N = 185		N = 206

Missing data: 3 new heads, 22 'old' heads

Table 7.2   Organizational changes introduced by new and 'old' heads (1982–84)

Most frequently mentioned	New Heads		3–8 Year Heads
	Introduced in first two years	Planned	Introduced (1982–83)
	%	%	%
Communication/consultation (e.g. staff briefings)	41	1	5
Senior management team (e.g. change of role/meetings)	25	1	–
Pastoral system (general change)	23	4	–
Parent-teacher association (e.g. parent evenings)	22	2	2
School day (number and length of teaching periods)	15	7	8
Liaison with feeder schools	15	3	2
Staff development/INSET	15	2	3
Job specifications	13	1	–
School reports to parents	13	4	3
Assessment/homework policy	12	6	2
Assemblies	11	–	–
Subject setting introduced	11	1	–
School uniform (introduced or emphasized)	10	–	–
Mixed-ability teaching across subjects	8	4	3
Profiling	7	8	2
School building improvements/changes	7	4	–
House to year system	7	1	5
Discipline system altered	7	1	–
Community initiatives (e.g. youth club)	5	10	1
Staff handbook	4	2	–
Capitation system for departments changed	4	–	–
Form tutors move up with class	4	–	1
Faculty system introduced	4	1	1
School prospectus	4	–	–
Banding introduced	4	1	4
Mixed-ability form tutor groups	4	1	2
Corporal punishment abolished	4	1	1
Links with further education colleges	3	1	4
No major changes	10	10	9
	N = 185		N = 206

Missing data: 3 new heads, 22 'old' heads

the new heads' schools and a further 22 per cent of schools had plans to introduce them in the next years. Nineteen per cent of the more experienced heads had introduced this type of change in the year 1982/83. As can be seen from the table, many of the curricular changes being introduced by the new heads were similar to those being implemented by the more experienced heads. The most obvious difference is that for many items the proportion of new heads introducing a particular change was higher than of 'old' heads. This indicates that more curricular change was going on in the new heads' schools, but of course it may be that the three to eight year heads have already brought in some of the changes in their first few years, e.g. a general change to the option patterns. However, this has to be speculation, as the 'old' heads were only asked to list those changes being introduced in 1982/83 in order to provide a 'snapshot' of innovation at that time. It appears that some curricular changes, such as vocational preparation and courses for the less able were being implemented in both the new and 'old' heads' schools because they were currently 'in vogue'.

An examination of the organizational changes in Table 7.2 shows much clearer differences between the two groups, with few changes being made by the 'old' heads. The case studies confirm that organizational changes were made by most new heads during their first years and it is reasonable to speculate that many of the 'old' heads would have already instituted a number of these changes. While most organizational changes were made within two years, the table indicates that some more complex changes were often left for a few years. An example of this was a change in the school day, where altering the length and number of teaching periods can have a major effect on all departments, as can new methods of assessment, such as profiling. Various community initiatives were seen as fairly long-term ventures and could not be achieved in a short period of time.

The most detailed information on innovation is provided by the 16 case studies, where the types of changes being introduced closely mirror those shown in Tables 7.1 and 7.2. Close study of the changes showed patterns in the types of innovation made by the new heads. Organizational changes made soon after the new head's arrival were frequently concerned with communication and consultation. For example, regular meetings for heads of department, heads of year, departmental and full staff meetings were planned in most of the case study schools. Daily or weekly staff briefings by the heads were established in eight of the 16 schools and a weekly bulletin was introduced in six schools.

Another group of early changes was concerned with promoting the school's image, something of particular concern to the new heads, especially where the community had a low opinion of the school or in areas where the roll was falling. Changes in this category were building improvements, the introduction of school uniform, improved liaison with the feeder primary schools, new school reports and a newsletter for pupils and parents. A more controversial change was the abolition of corporal punishment which took place in four of the 16 schools. Most of the new heads were aware of the need for good 'public relations' and publicity, and had established links with the local newspapers and a variety of community groups (see Chapter 10).

Curricular changes which affected the timetable could not be implemented until the beginning of the case study heads' second year in September 1983, but a considerable amount of preparatory work was undertaken in the preceding year. This usually took the form of a curriculum review, where each department was required to set out its aims, objectives, schemes of work and, in some cases, methods of assessment. Twelve of the case study schools undertook full-scale reviews during the new head's first year. In three cases the request for such a review came from the LEA and in one other school it was required for a forthcoming inspection by the HMI. The heads in these schools welcomed these outside requests as a means of involving staff and persuading heads of department to evaluate existing practice. In the other schools where the heads instituted the reviews themselves, they met a mixed reception, with a few heads of department delaying as long as possible – 'it's like trying to get blood out of a stone' – while others welcomed the opportunity for a full-scale review.

The strategies used by the heads to introduce change were similar across the case studies. In addition to the curricular reviews, the heads discussed the proposed changes with their senior management teams and the relevant heads of department or heads of year, and produced discussion papers. A number of working parties were usually set up if the changes were cross-curricular or affected large numbers of staff. The aim of the working parties was to involve teachers in the consultation and planning process. In some cases they were required to seek information about the topic, sometimes by visiting other schools, and produce a short report with recommendations. These were usually further discussed by the senior management team and the relevant committee (e.g. heads of department or heads of year) and then put to a full staff meeting. Once a decision had been made, a different type of working party was often established, whose purpose was to produce curricular materials for the new course. A variety of working parties was found in all the case study schools. However, industrial action by the teacher unions during the period of the research meant that many meetings had to be cancelled and this particularly affected material production groups.

The curricular changes in the case study schools were very similar to those shown in the surveys (e.g. various vocational and technical courses, and courses for the less able). Seven of the schools had introduced a timetabled form tutor period in the new head's second year and a further five schools planned to do so in the future. Seven of the 16 schools were also introducing personal and social education courses for their fourth- and fifth-year students.

Of the several hundred changes – both major and minor – mentioned across the 16 schools, it was noticeable that only a handful did not appear to originate from the new heads themselves. The LEA initiated some of these, either in reponse to national schemes (e.g. TVEI and the Lower Attainers Project) or to local schemes such as profiling. Surprisingly, very few changes originated from the teachers in the schools, although school reports in one school and integrated science and integrated humanities in other schools were introduced in this way.

It was clear that the new heads were the major initiators of the changes; but once the decision to adopt a change had been made, day to day responsibility was usually delegated either to a deputy head or a head of department. In some schools the heads tried to chair several of the working parties, but found that it became too time-consuming or that their presence inhibited some junior members of staff. In most cases, they maintained a watching brief, requesting regular feedback from the chairperson of the group and occasionally sitting in on some meetings. One of the new heads said, 'The mark of a good head is to be able to facilitate things and then withdraw, but I find a problem in getting involved in too many things at once'. It was noticeable that most deputy heads were heavily involved in the change process, both during the initial discussion and planning stages and during implementation. The new heads to a considerable extent relied on their deputies to support the changes.

In the next section the case study heads' views about change are summarized and this is followed by an examination of the teachers' perceptions.

Heads' views on change

A problem of central concern to the new heads was the pace and timing of change. The majority felt it was best not to introduce major changes during the first year. But it was necessary to start planning and laying the groundwork for change almost immediately. Some of the heads arrived with the intention of waiting a year in order to settle in and have a 'good look' at what was required. However, this was not always possible, and several heads remarked that so many things were 'wrong' that they could not afford to wait that long.

Several of the heads deliberately chose to make early changes which they called 'cosmetic', in non-controversial areas and recognized the importance of being seen by staff as someone who could get things done. A common example of this concerned various building improvements. A balance had to be kept between making an impact, but not approaching things 'like a bull in a china shop'. Two of the heads said that ideally they should have moved a little slower but specifically referred to the children and felt they would suffer if the changes were left too long.

The heads recognized that some staff expected them to make changes and this was especially so where the previous head had been in post a considerable length of time. In 11 of the 16 schools the previous head had been in post for over ten years and in six of these, for more than 20 years. However, in some of the schools it proved harder for the majority of staff to accept some of the head's proposed changes. 'The changes I am trying to introduce are simply to make the school a very normal comprehensive, but the staff think some of the ideas are way out.'

As mentioned earlier, the heads established various committees and working parties in order to try to involve the staff. All the heads spoke about the importance of staff participation and consultation, but also stressed that they reserved the right to make the final decision. Wherever possible it was important for the head to try to carry out the recommendations of a working party. Some heads found they had not clearly specified the brief of the working party and what would happen to their recommendations. In one case, the working party's suggestions for changes in the school report were overturned at a full staff meeting. Several of the heads found it much harder than they expected to get the staff involved in discussions about change. One of the heads wrote an outline paper on the aims and objectives for the school, but he was disappointed when it went through 'on the nod with no discussion'.

Timing proved difficult for some of the heads. In order to introduce a curricular change for the beginning of the school year in September, one of the heads said it was necessary to have made a clear decision by the previous Christmas to allow two terms to prepare the staff and any teaching materials. Another head, with help from the LEA, had set up a residential conference for the staff in July 1983. About 30 of the 80 teachers attended the conference and most felt it to have been worthwhile. However, in retrospect, the head realized that he should have held it much earlier, as it was too late to affect the next year's timetable and the enthusiasm generated was lost over the summer holidays.

In-service training was an important factor in helping to prepare teachers for change. Heads used both school-based and course-based INSET to 'gear up' for the forthcoming innovations. One of the heads was able to use annual LEA closure days to provide some school-based INSET for staff preparing for integrated science and integrated humanities. This head was clearly in favour of INSET and pointed out that 45 teachers had been on 95 courses in his first term. Although heads used INSET as a means of facilitating change, it was noticeable that most took place *before* the change was implemented.

Many of the heads felt it was important to demonstrate a personal commitment to the changes they were proposing. This was illustrated by one head attending an LEA course on active tutorial work with some of his staff. Another method used by several of the heads was to teach on some of the new courses, such as personal and social education.

In the later interviews the heads were asked how the various changes were progressing. It was very noticeable that all the heads felt that most of the changes which had been implemented were going well. If they had experienced a strongly negative reaction to a proposed innovation, the usual strategy was to postpone the introduction of the change. But this seemed to have happened quite rarely and the most noticeable examples concerned mixed-ability teaching in two schools. Although all the heads felt the changes were going well, three heads felt that 'real change' (by which they meant changes in the way that teachers and pupils interacted in the classroom – the 'quality of learning') would take much longer to achieve.

Towards the end of their second year, the new heads were asked in both the case studies and the questionnaires whether they felt they had been able to introduce all the changes they wanted to at that point in their headship. The results from the survey showed that 60 per cent felt they had *not* been able to achieve all the desired changes. The reasons for this varied considerably and included: industrial action by the teacher unions, financial restrictions and falling rolls, 'no other change agents in the senior management team apart from me', and obstructive staff in key positions – 'I am waiting for two staff to retire next year, they have Paleolithic attitudes'. (It is interesting to note that Doyle and Ponder (1972) called one group of resistant teachers 'stone age obstructionists'.) The survey data show that one of the most frequently mentioned difficulties for heads was 'persuading members of staff to accept new ideas' (Appendix 1). About half the new and more experienced heads rated this a 'serious' or 'very serious' problem. In addition, about a third of the 47 new heads interviewed spoke about problems of inertia with some of the middle management. While some inertia and resistance to accepting new ideas obviously occurs in most schools, it must be stressed that so far we have only dealt with the heads' perceptions and information presented in a later section suggests that perhaps teachers are not quite as resistant to change as is commonly believed.

How fast major changes could be introduced during the first two years was a factor that concerned most new heads. Some heads decided to move cautiously, but realized that this could also cause problems: 'I had a clear programme before starting and concentrated during year one almost exclusively on getting to know the staff, buildings and matters of discipline. I'm glad I didn't venture very far into curriculum areas, as I now realize I would have made a lot of mistakes. Unfortunately, my priority list has probably given some staff the impression that I am only interested in toilets and ties!'

Half the 16 case study heads felt they had managed to introduce all the changes they had wanted to by the time of the researcher's third visit towards the end of the second year. As with the survey data, the reasons the heads gave for not being able to introduce all the changes varied across the case study schools. For the head of one of the smaller schools, it was simply that he did not have a deputy head for about a year and had taken on all the deputy's functions himself, so that he felt totally exhausted. The main restriction for one head was his three elderly deputies, whom he believed were blocking his proposed changes (see Chapter 4 for further details). Where the heads felt they had brought in all the changes they wanted, they spoke about the necessity for a period of consolidation as the introduction of change had been very time-consuming and the teachers were exhausted.

Teachers' views on change

When the teachers were asked about the changes taking place in the 16 case study schools, the most noticeable finding was that virtually every one expected the new head to introduce change. The only exception occurred in the school with an internal appointment, where the head had previously been a deputy. About a third of the teachers interviewed at this school said they did not expect the new head to introduce major changes because 'he had been part of the senior management team and did not appear to be radically opposed to things under the previous head'. In all the other schools there was a clear expectation that the arrival of a new head meant change was most likely.

The second general finding was that the vast majority of teachers interviewed felt that most of the changes were needed. The only changes that were seen as unnecessary were those termed 'change for change's sake'. An example of this was the new head's instruction that teachers' initials on the timetable were to be changed from their first and last names to the initial letters of their surname. The teachers at this school believed this was being done because it had happened at the head's last school – what advantages the change brought were not clear.

The fact that almost all teachers expected change and thought most were needed, suggests the traditional belief that teachers are simply opposed to change per se, has been overstated. The research indicates that it was the way in which changes were introduced which upset some teachers, not necessarily the changes themselves.

The teachers' comments about the changes in the case study schools showed that the overall reaction was largely favourable in six schools, largely negative in four schools and mixed in the remaining six schools. An analysis of main reasons for this indicated that teachers were happy when the head did not come in like a new broom and sweep everything away: 'He didn't come in like a whirlwind. We expected change, the feelings were of the anticipation of summer after experiencing a hell of a winter.' (At this school, very little change had taken place under the previous head.)

A further point stressed by teachers, and already mentioned in Chapter 5, was the need for the new head to recognize the good things that had happened previously at the school. Considerable change was seen to imply that nothing undertaken previously was any good. Teachers also wanted to be involved and able to express their views about the proposed changes and see the head respond to these. Positive comments were made about heads who encouraged INSET and school visits and provided the necessary resources for an innovation.

It was difficult to please all the teachers about the pace of change. There was some indication that younger staff wanted more rapid change than their older colleagues, but this was by no means a clear-cut distinction. Staff have different concerns at different points in their career (Hall and Loucks, 1978). While change can be very threatening for some staff, for others it is highly motivating: 'He made haste slowly at first, but once the changes started, then wow! It was like having to hang on to a canoe as it was going over the waterfall. But it has been very challenging and I like that.'

In the four schools where overall reaction to change was negative, the speed of change provided the main reason. Interestingly enough, in two schools the pace was felt to be too slow, while in the two others, the pace was too fast. In those where the pace was too slow, teachers said, 'We've talked a lot but done little'. Lots of papers were produced and numerous staff working parties had made their recommendations, but nothing further had happened. In one of the schools the teachers believed there was a desperate need for change, but felt they were not going anywhere and they wanted leadership and direction. The staff had high expectations of the new head initially, but towards the end of the second year they had become very disillusioned. In the other two schools, where the pace was seen as too fast, teachers said, 'Nothing is the same, the school has been turned upside down, there is too much change too quickly'. It was noticeable that the turnover of staff in these two schools was particularly high (42 per cent and 30 per cent) over a two-year period. Teachers who did not like the way changes were introduced and who were able to leave or take early retirement, did so. For a point of comparison, in three-quarters of the 188 cohort schools the staff turnover in the new head's first two years was under 10 per cent.

Various reasons were provided in the six schools where staff reaction to change was mixed. For some staff, their high expectations of the new head were not fulfilled, while elsewhere middle managers (heads of department and year) felt they simply rubber-stamped decisions already made by the senior management team. For some staff, there were too many working parties and meetings, and many spoke of the increase in the amount of paper circulating in the schools.

Two case studies

The staff reaction to change in the 16 schools showed one school where almost all the teachers interviewed felt the head had 'got it right' and, at the other extreme, a school where most of the reaction was negative. By focusing in more detail on these schools, some guidelines for the management of change can be obtained. Table 7.3 shows the changes introduced at the two schools.

In common with most of the other case studies, during the first year the heads of School A and School B initiated curricular reviews, established regular meetings of middle management and set up a number of working parties open to any member of staff. Similar curricular, pastoral and organizational changes were introduced or planned at both schools, namely: integrated science, integrated humanities, a timetabled form tutor period and a change to the school day in terms of the length of each teaching period. School A also had two government funded pilot projects, the Technical and Vocational Education Initiative (TVEI) and the Lower Attaining Pupil's Programme (LAPP). In School B major changes were the abolition of corporal punishment and a move towards mixed-ability teaching. Although many of the changes were similar for both schools, they differed in the rate of innovation. In School B all the major changes were implemented in September 1983 at the beginning of the new head's second year, whereas in the other school a number of the main changes had planned start dates of September 1984 and even 1985. While most of the staff in School A appeared to have accepted the changes, considerable difficulties were found in School B.

Table 7.3   Changes introduced in two case studies

	Curricular	Pastoral	Organizational	Other
School A 11–18 Comprehensive 950 pupils 60 teachers Staff turnover in new head's first 2 years 4/60 (7%)	*General Studies (Year 6) programme *Vocational courses (Year 6) *Work experience (Year 5) (200 pupils) *TVEI (Yr 4+) *Computing courses (extended) *Low attainers course (Year 4/5) Integrated (Year 4) Science (Sept '84) Integrated (Year 1/2) Humanities (Sept '85)	Form tutor period (20 mins) (for all year groups Sept 1984) Combining Personal and Social Education, Careers and form tutor period (Sept 1985) (Year 4 & 5)	#Heads of year and head meetings *Annexe (Years 4 & 5) phased out *Remedial Department (improved/more integrated) *Consortium arrangement (Year 6) School day (35 to 40 period/wk) (September 1984)	#School reports #Finance/capitation system altered #School image/PR #Building improvements *Visits to feeder schools (Interface group set up) Community education (1986+)

Key: # Introduced in first year
  * Introduced at beginning of second year (September 1983)

Table 7.3 Changes introduced in two case studies (continued)

	Curricular	Pastoral	Organizational	Other
School B 13–18 Comprehensive 1350 pupils 80 teachers Staff turnover in new head's first two years 24/80 (30%)	*Common Core (6 subject areas) *Computing (Reduced to Year 5 only) *Integrated Science (Yr 3) *Integrated Humanities (including Peace Studies) (Yrs 4/5) *SMILE Maths (initially for Yr 3 then roll through)	* Tutorial period on timetable (1½ hours per week ATW) (Years 3/4) #Discipline System (Backup changed)	*Head of faculty meetings *School day (from 6 to 3 × 1½ hr periods) *Banding to mixed ability teaching (first two years i.e. Years 3/4)	#Corporal punishment abolished. #Use of teachers' Christian names * Community involvement increased * Playgroup using school rooms

Key: # Introduced in first year
* Introduced at beginning of second year (September 1983)

School A

The previous head had retired after being in post since the school opened in 1960. He had a very relaxed, informal style and was generally well thought of by the staff. He avoided conflict and compromised whenever possible. Some teachers saw him as 'too casual' and he was described by the LEA officer interviewed as 'more of a shepherd than one who leads from the front'. Most of the staff thought change was needed, as things were too complacent and the school, although a caring institution, was in rut.

The new head described his style as operating in an open way, approachable, leading from the front and not being office-bound. He was on first name terms with the teachers and felt that relations with the staff were paramount. Unlike his predecessor, he involved the senior management in everything and they fully supported the new initiatives.

The teachers interviewed saw the new head as tactful, open and accessible, very friendly, having a sense of humour, incredibly hard working, very determined, intolerant of slackness and good at public relations. They felt he considered their views and then made a decision. He had given the school a sense of direction, and was seen as having a similar philosophy to the previous head but a much wider grasp of educational issues.

With regard to innovation, the new head stressed it was important to get to know the staff and that decisions about innovation had to be reached by consultation. It was best to introduce only superficial change initially, while preparing the ground for more fundamental change. As head, he 'sowed the seeds' initially with senior staff who had to be united, and then discussed the plans with middle management and all interested parties so that there were few, if any 'surprises' when the decision to adopt the innovation was presented. He said,

> There are no strategies for introducing change that will work in all situations. You must know the previous head and the way he operated, and you must be very careful not to create disaffection amongst the staff. I do not advocate a steamroller approach – a management technique deliberately used by some heads – as this can be counterproductive, and in times of little teacher mobility it means that you can be harbouring a lot of resentment on the part of your staff and in the long term, this is not in the pupils' interest. I prefer to wait and ensure that the staff are on my side, try to get them to see the need for change and get them to think that the ideas are theirs. By introducing lots of change rapidly, it can look good on paper or on your curriculum vitae, but at the end of the day it's the people that suffer and the staff commitment will not be there, and it can't therefore be good for the development of the school. You need to create the right kind of atmosphere and get staff involved in things like INSET, then the changes will gather momentum and people will begin to approach you with new ideas.

In their interviews, the staff said they had been a little anxious and concerned that the new head might bring in sweeping changes very quickly, and all were happy that this had not happened. The majority of teachers were pleased to have been involved in the discussion of change and the decision-making process and their reaction to the new head and the changes was very favourable, as can be seen in the following quotations:

> He has done things very gradually and made some fairly big changes without people realizing. He hasn't upset anyone. He did not say at the outset that we are going to do this and so on; he has done it through discussion and consultation.

> We are looking at one step at a time. This is important so that people don't feel threatened.

> Before, we were never really asked to discuss matters. The new head will involve us in discussions which will produce a result. The senior teachers here, at first felt immature, as green as grass. It was a new experience for us, and felt like going from second gear to fourth, so that our early discussions were at a very poor level.

> We feel we are a team going somewhere with a good leader.

School B

The previous head, who retired, had taught in the area all his life, having been head of the boys' grammar school which was merged with the girls' grammar to form the comprehensive school in the mid-1960s. He was described as 'traditional', 'authoritarian', 'very autocratic', 'ex-army and very efficient', 'a competent and business-like manager', who knew exactly which way he would go. He was not seen as an innovator – 'very conservative, played it safe' – but had done a good job in bringing the two schools together. He would listen to staff but was very obstinate: 'a fat cat boss'. Over his last three to four years he became ill and morose, and running a large comprehensive became too much for him. It seems that the first deputy basically ran the school during this time.

The new head had previously been a deputy for four years at a very innovative school and spent five years as head of department at another progressive school. He described his style of headship as 'charismatic', or 'consultative' but also 'manipulative at times'. Teachers felt the new head was approachable and would listen, but was not at all open to their views. Many saw him as devious and did not trust him, some even called him a liar. Although he said he wanted democracy and consultation, the staff felt this was not the case in practice: 'he sees himself as a great democrat and then behaves in a very autocratic way'. The staff, and apparently the pupils, saw him as 'soft on discipline'.

The relations between the new head and the first deputy were quite good and she felt he certainly listened and considered her opinions. However, relations between the second deputy and the head were very poor and the deputy had taken out a grievance procedure against the head. (This concerned the removal of his role as head of resources and the job being given to another teacher, without consultation.)

The first deputy felt changes were needed and agreed with most of the things the new head had tried to introduce, but she disagreed with the way these had been done. The second deputy was not in favour of most of the changes introduced by the new head and certainly was opposed to the methods used: 'He just came in and swept things away.'

The head had felt that ideally he should wait a year before introducing change, but then he believed he had to start straight away to achieve anything in five years, so he was going like 'a bat out of hell'. 'I found that so many things had to be started at this school that I couldn't be democratic. I had to provide the institution with a philosophy and the institution needed a wallop. I had to hit them when they were down.'

At the beginning of his second year, he felt that he had brought in all the changes he wanted and could relax the hard leadership line and move step by step. He said that a difficulty for a new head was 'seeing the consequences of your actions. It is hard for the staff to adjust to these changes. I think your objectives are not as important as your methods.' However, it seemed to be the head's *methods* that the staff largely objected to.

The head was the initiator of all the changes and had not acted as a facilitator for other people's ideas within the school, nor taken on any external (national or local) initiatives. With regard to delegation and consultation, he set up a working party on the school day chaired by the second deputy, and also a working party on active tutorial work (ATW – Baldwin and Wells, 1979) chaired by the first deputy. The head said he wanted to move to a 3 x 1½-hour period day. The working party did not recommend this and were unable to find any schools which operated such a system. (They had even contacted the DES to obtain the names of schools but the DES could not provide any.) The other working party recommended that ATW should be timetabled for one 50-minute period. These recommendations were discussed by senior and middle management and at staff meetings and in general the staff seemed in agreement. However, the head overruled both working parties and introduced the three-period day with one-and-a-half hours' ATW on a Friday afternoon.

The teachers were clearly upset by the way the head had handled matters and their anger bubbled over at a Staff Association meeting, when they voted overwhelmingly in favour of a resolution expressing their concern about poor discipline and the 'inconsistent and ambiguous leadership' of the head. (This came very close to a total vote of no confidence.) The governors were informed and a small sub-committee interviewed the head and a few teachers representing the Staff Association. The sub-committee recommended that the LEA advisers should carry out a major review. This took place at the beginning of the head's second year and all staff were interviewed by a small team of advisers, who produced a finely balanced report. The general reaction to the report was positive, with most teachers seeing it as rather brief but reasonably fair.

At the beginning, the majority of staff seemed optimistic but during the first two years the head appeared to have alienated almost all the staff, whose views ranged from extreme anger to general unhappiness. All the teachers interviewed recognized that changes were needed at the school and they expected the new head to introduce these, but over half stated there had been too many changes, too quickly. 'Change was like a tidal wave, we felt we were drowning, it was hard to keep our heads above water.' 'We're not a bolshy staff. It's a lovely staff here but we felt threatened by all the rapid changes.' They felt the new head had a blueprint for the school and he had ignored their views and imposed his own, saying that it *would* work because it did at his last school. But, in general, it was not the changes themselves that generated the adverse response from teachers, it was the ruthless way the head had imposed them. One of the senior staff summed it up as follows:

One of his great strengths is that he is full of ideas but this is part of his weakness: his ideas are not thought out clearly. He is trying to employ management techniques but he can't put them into operation successfully. He is good on theory but is poor on the practical applications. He doesn't really know how to move people in the direction that he wants.

When the head was interviewed towards the end of his second year, he said:

I think most of the changes are going better than I hoped and I am glad I did them all early. I think you have to hit people hard - you mustn't allow them to dig in their heels. They had to cooperate to keep their sanity. We can now modify things to the demands of the teachers. I would certainly do it again the same way: even though it means going through all the trouble we had, I would still do it.

If I'd done what the staff recommended, it wouldn't have gone far enough.

When asked if he had deliberately used conflict as a strategy to achieve change, he replied:

I haven't got this at a conscious level and I don't know whether I deliberately engineered confrontation.

I think staff are glad that the advisers' visit and the report are all over. It gave them more exposure than they wanted, but it has flushed things out and that is good.

To what extent the two heads had been successful in implementing change was difficult to assess fully, as the research was not designed to look inside classrooms, nor to follow the case studies beyond the end of the second year. What is overwhelmingly clear is that the staff in the two schools responded very differently to the new heads and the innovations. This could be partly explained by the fact that the nationally-funded programmes introduced in School A (TVEI and LAPP) brought welcomed additional resources and affected relatively few teachers, while two of the changes in School B were more wide-ranging. The move towards mixed-ability teaching and the abolition of corporal punishment affected all the staff in School B and were seen by some as particularly threatening. However, the teachers' reactions were probably better explained by the heads' different approaches to the management of change. The head of School A took considerable trouble to ensure the cooperation and involvement of staff, while the head of School B believed strongly that very rapid change, largely through imposition, was necessary to achieve his goals.

Case studies of change in more experienced heads' schools

In order to obtain information about how more experienced heads introduced change, short case studies were undertaken in four schools where the heads had been in post between three and eight years. From an analysis of the 228 questionnaires completed by the 'old' heads, it was decided to focus on a change that affected large numbers of teachers and this ruled out innovations being introduced into a single subject area or year group. Finally, a change in form tutor work was chosen and four schools which had introduced a systematic programme for all year groups in September 1982 were contacted. The schools were visited in May and June 1983, towards the end of the first

Table 7.4   Pastoral changes introduced in four schools by more experienced heads

School	Content	Time Allocated
1	Active Tutorial Work	Part of 25-minute morning registration time
2	List of weekly topics for each year (variety of sources)	Part of 20-minute morning registration time
3	Materials developed by school working party (variety of sources)	1 × 55-minute period on 25-period/week timetable
4	Active Tutorial Work	1 × 40-minute period on 41-period/week timetable

year of the innovation, and interviews were conducted with the heads, deputies, all heads of year or house and a cross-section of form tutors from each year group. (A total of four heads and 56 teachers was interviewed.)

Although the four schools were introducing similar pastoral changes, the method, form and content differed. Table 7.4 shows the basic content and time allocated.

One of the main differences between the changes made by the 'old' and new heads concerned the origin of the innovation. It should be remembered that almost all the changes found in the 16 case studies originated from the new heads, but in the four schools with more experienced heads not one was the main originator of the change in form tutor work. In School 1, the LEA promoted Active Tutorial Work at a conference for all secondary heads and in School 4 the head of middle school suggested the idea after attending a LEA course. A newly appointed deputy in School 2 was given full responsibility to reorganize the pastoral system and a senior teacher in School 3 suggested that one period should be allocated to tutor work when the school moved to a new 25 period week.

The main reason given by the heads for introducing the change was their concern to improve the existing situation and to offer the form tutors a structure for more constructive work with students . The head of School 1 said,

> I looked at a set of ATW books and thought it was an excellent idea. I felt that the spadework had been done so that we could give it to teachers and they wouldn't have to do the developmental work. But I had some reservations: had we moved far enough in my four years for the staff to accept it? I knew the children would, but some of the teachers liked the old authoritarian regime. With ATW, some of the teachers might be exposed as people – others might see it as trendy. I felt we should add pieces to ATW and adapt it to fit our school.

Although the heads were involved in the initial decision to adopt the change, in each of the four schools the main responsibility was delegated to a senior member of staff, either a deputy or senior teacher. For example, when discussing his role, one head said, 'I delegated it to the deputy head. My input has been to provide materials and I have rubber stamped everything.' Another head said, 'My role was to give it my seal of approval. I think if the head gives this, it matters. I delegated it to the senior teacher who had the expertise in this area.'

INSET was used to prepare staff in a variety of ways in each of the four cases. In all the schools, several key people went on courses to obtain knowledge about tutor work. In three cases these were LEA courses, while in the fourth, as no LEA courses existed, the teachers attended a variety of different courses. Two schools then used their annual INSET closure day to mount school-based activities for all members of staff. At School 1 the key teachers organized after-school training in the form of nine weekly sessions for all heads and assistant heads of house. This was followed by ten weekly after-school sessions for form tutors. Unfortunately, this was rather badly handled by the deputy head, who felt that some pressure was required to encourage teachers to attend. A notice was put up in the staff room, listing the teachers' names and asking them to initial that they would attend. The problem arose from the wording, which said that if they did not attend, their promotional prospects might be affected. Most teachers did attend but, as might be expected, considerable resentment was expressed and a few of the teachers tried to find fault with most of the activities and maintained a negative attitude throughout the course.

In School 3 a working party, consisting of all the heads and assistant heads of year and any interested teachers, met regularly throughout the year to produce their own materials for all year groups. They asked the head for some early closure afternoons to introduce the materials and techniques to the rest of the staff, but the head was unable to grant the time. This meant that no pre-implementation training was possible, apart from one staff meeting where sex education was discussed.

The heads of the four schools all believed the staff had been adequately prepared and expected a mixed reaction, with some teachers being enthusiastic, others negative and the rest in between. They realized that the innovations would make new demands on the staff, particularly in terms of teaching style, but as far as they were aware, there had not been any strong opposition to the change. All said that if there had been a greater negative reaction they would have delayed the start, modified the implementation and tried to persuade staff that the change was needed. The heads were pleased with the way the changes had gone and thought that, in general, the pupils had responded well to the new programme. This was based on informal feedback and discussions in the weekly senior management meetings, but none of the heads had any plans to review or evaluate the changes formally in the near future.

When asked if the innovation had taken up much of their time, the heads said, 'No, not directly, because I delegated it'. One head's response seemed to apply to most of the heads, both new and 'old', in the study:

> Actually, it has been fairly low in terms of time because that is how I have to work. I concentrated while it was being introduced but since then I have not given as much time as I should. There is a danger that once something has been introduced there is always a tendency to forget it and concentrate on more pressing problems or the next change. I know I shouldn't do this, but it is really just a question of time.

Teachers' responses to the changes

Almost every teacher interviewed in the four schools felt there was a need to improve the pastoral work of the school and recognized that previously, registration time had not been used very productively. It was described as 'dossing around time' when the pupils might play cards, finish their homework or read quietly, while the form teacher carried out administrative work or saw individual pupils.

In Schools 1, 3, and 4 most teachers were pleased with the changes as they gave them a structure for their pastoral work and the ATW teacher books for each year group provided a valuable source of ideas. The quality of some of the materials produced by the working party in School 3 were considered to be rather poor, but the staff were sympathetic to the hard work of the teachers and felt sure the quality would be improved the following year. Most of the teachers said they adapted the materials to fit their own use and the ATW books were not seen as a 'bible' but were dipped into selectively for ideas. Little change seemed to have occurred in School 2. The form tutors were simply given a sheet listing 30 to 40 topics which could be used on a weekly basis throughout the year. However, they were expected to try the topics during their 20-minute morning registration time and most teachers found it almost impossible to find adequate time. In addition, they felt they had not been given sufficient guidance or training.

Most change and impact seemed to have been achieved in the two schools where the form tutor period had been put on to the timetable, rather than forming part of morning registration. But many teachers said that care was required in deciding when to timetable the tutor period. They argued that it should not be the last period of the day, nor be seen as the continuation of registration time, which was often reduced by assemblies.

Most teachers felt the pupils had responded well to the innovation and this was especially so for years 1 and 2. Difficulties were encountered in introducing it to years 4, 5 and 6 and many teachers suggested that the scheme should have been started in year 1 and then rolled through the other year groups. In general, teachers thought that the programmes were of considerable value for the pupils, especially the group work and discussions.

When the schemes were implemented, only a few teachers had a clear idea of what they were expected to do. These were the teachers who had been on substantial LEA courses or formed the working party at School 3. The other teachers had little idea of what was required: 'We were just given the ATW books.' This lack of clarity existed even after the school-based INSET, which most teachers spoke of favourably, although a few teachers dismissed the role playing activities as 'just silly games' or 'OK for the kids but not adults'. It should be remembered that the INSET was pre-implementation and although this can raise awareness and motivation, it is not until the teachers try to carry out the innovation in their own classrooms that they really know what is involved. For this reason, regular meetings of form tutor teams and their heads of year are vital, as they provide mutual support and allow teachers to exchange ideas. Information from tutors and year heads showed that although regular meetings occurred in some cases, the innovation was rarely discussed, with most time being allocated to problem children or administration, such as school reports.

The heads of year played an important role in the success or failure of the schemes. Most were keen to implement the new ideas but felt they needed to acquire expertise by attending outside courses. If a working party was used to produce ideas and materials, as in School 3, it was seen as essential to involve all the heads of year. In addition to the regular team meetings mentioned above, a further possible means of support was to encourage the heads of year to visit the teachers during form tutor time, although this was only possible if they did not have a tutor group themselves.

Teachers said the new schemes had increased their workload, as they had to prepare materials for topic work or discussion. But most accepted the increase as necessary for the benefit of the pupils. A few teachers felt they had not been trained to undertake the kind of teaching required in ATW – they saw themselves as subject teachers, not pastoral tutors. In School 1, the staff were unhappy about the lack of consultation before the introduction of the scheme: 'The head suddenly announced it would be school policy, it came completely out of the blue.' Most of the staff also felt that the deputy head had handled the introduction badly and they resented 'being coerced or blackmailed' to attend the after-school course.

In all schools, many teachers felt that form tutor work was not given adequate recognition compared to other subject areas and this was shown by the role of the four heads. All the heads of year/house and form tutors interviewed said the heads had played very little active part in the innovations. When asked if they thought the head fully supported the changes, most teachers said they didn't know. They speculated that the heads must have been in favour or else the changes would not have been introduced: 'But I don't know what his feelings are because he has only said one sentence about it.' Some teachers thought (erroneously) that the change may have been forced on to the heads by the LEA. In all cases, the heads had been seen to delegate the innovation to a deputy or senior teacher and the fact that none of the heads had taken part in the school-based INSET was interpreted as lack of interest or support for pastoral work.

The senior management teams were aware of the role the heads played and knew that they favoured the innovation and wanted the new schemes to be part of school policy. The deputies' knowledge came from discussions about the innovations which occurred during senior management team meetings. But below the level of the senior management team, staff were unaware of the head's views. Most heads of year/house wanted more support from the head and the deputies. They wanted the heads to raise the status of tutor work and demonstrate their commitment and interest by occasionally dropping in on teachers during form tutor time. Many teachers also said they would welcome occasional visits by the head and deputies. The clear message from the teachers was that senior staff had to show through their actions and not just their words that they believed in the innovation. (For other comments on teachers' reactions to ATW, see Bolam and Medlock, 1985; Stagles, 1985; and Tall, 1985.)

Summary and discussion

A major difference between the current project's findings and the previous research outlined at the beginning of the chapter concerns the amount of involvement by heads in innovation. Whereas most of the new heads played a major part in innovation and were the originators of almost all the changes, the North American work suggests that most heads have little involvement in change. Two main reasons would appear to explain the difference: the fact that the NFER study focused on newly appointed heads rather than heads in general and secondly, the cultural differences in the organization of schooling between the UK and North America.

The case studies showed very clearly both that teachers expected a new head to make changes and that the heads themselves were particularly concerned to improve the school in a variety of ways. The research suggests that new heads, especially those appointed from outside the school, initiate a series of organizational and curricular changes during their first year. Most of the major changes are probably implemented by about the third or fourth year and then require fine tuning. The case studies showed differences between the way the new and more experienced heads handled innovation. The new heads initiated almost all the changes and played a major role in seeing them through to implementation. Once it was decided to proceed with an innovation, the 'old' heads were happy to delegate the main responsibility to one of the senior management team or another member of staff and maintain a watching brief.

A clear difference seems to exist between North America and the UK with regard to the power and autonomy of heads and principals. The American research shows that the majority of changes were initiated from outside the schools, largely by central office administrators. While it may be argued that the autonomy of UK heads is being reduced, the NFER study found that relatively few changes came from the LEA office or from national initiatives.

The design of the present project did not permit a study of the changes much beyond the implementation stage. Many of the factors affecting implementation outlined at the beginning of the chapter were found in the NFER research. For example, the majority of teachers interviewed believed the changes were needed but many were unclear about exactly what they were expected to do differently. 'Mutual adaptation' appeared to occur with most changes being modified to fit the particular circumstances of each teacher. Although INSET was often used to help teachers, it was noticeable that almost all of it took place *prior to implementation* and teachers were given little support thereafter.

The pace and timing of change proved to be a major factor, requiring heads to move neither too quickly nor too slowly. Various meetings and working parties were used to allow teachers to express their views and opinions about the innovations. Having set up a working party with a clear brief, heads were expected to take full account of the recommendations and to do all they could to implement them whenever possible. The majority of teachers wanted heads to show through their actions that they were fully behind an innovation, even though day to day responsibility was delegated to a deputy or another senior member of staff. In advocating change, new heads had to be particularly careful not to imply that everything that had happened previously was of little value.

Innovation was a major concern for the new heads and it is hoped that by spending considerable time discussing the ways in which they approached this important topic, a number of points have been raised which will be of use for both present and future heads.

CHAPTER 8
Professional Isolation and Support for Heads

The feeling of isolation and loneliness is a problem generic to all those holding senior management positions, where responsibility for an organization or institution lies predominantly in the hands of specific individuals. The problem therefore applies both to heads of schools and their counterparts in industry and commerce. It is the intention of this chapter to consider the extent to which secondary heads considered themselves to be professionally isolated and to discuss the main factors related to such feelings. It will focus specifically on the main forms of support mentioned as helping to reduce isolation and fulfilling heads' needs for understanding, companionship and the sharing of professional concerns. Finally, consideration will be given to the benefits gained from attendance at a variety of headteacher meetings.

The isolation of headship

The two groups of heads surveyed and the new heads interviewed were asked to comment on the extent to which professional isolation was a problem and to give examples where this had proved to be the case. The question of professional isolation was also raised with the 16 case study heads on each of the researcher's three visits, thus enabling some understanding to be gained of how this may or may not change over time.

An analysis of the replies from the questionnaire surveys showed that the majority of heads experienced some degree of professional isolation. Only 33 per cent of the more experienced heads and 41 per cent of the new heads did not perceive it as a problem. No relationship was found between perceptions of professional isolation and the size of school, the catchment area or, for the 'old' heads, the number of years in post. In other words, the data do not suggest that a greater sense of isolation was felt in large schools or rural areas or that headship became any more or less isolating the longer it was experienced. In addition, no difference was found between male and female heads and the amount of perceived isolation. However, a statistically significant relationship was found between professional isolation and adequacy of preparation; those heads who felt well prepared for the demands of headship were less likely to report feelings of professional isolation. This relationship seems possible as an adequate preparation for headship should include not only a clear recognition that headship brings with it an element of professional isolation, but also an opportunity, possibly as an acting head, to experience the position of ultimate responsibility.

From the surveys it was clear that the majority of heads reported occasionally feeling a sense of professional isolation. For many, this was accepted as part of the head's accountability and feelings of isolation became most evident when they had to make particularly difficult decisions. The transition from deputy head to head was for many rather an abrupt one and even though some had been forewarned of the dangers of professional isolation, it was only on taking up appointment that the reality of the situation became clear.

Many heads made reference to the fact that the relationship between themselves and their teacher colleagues was of a different nature than when they were deputies or senior teachers. As has been shown in Chapter 5, teachers have certain expectations of heads and unlike deputies, who are permitted to plead ignorance and learn gradually, heads were often expected 'to know all the answers immediately'. For a variety of reasons, staff may be wary of what they say to heads and treat them with a certain amount of caution. As such, headship can be lonely and it was suggested by some that every head should be prepared to give up the day-to-day camaraderie of the staffroom. (This may be particularly difficult for those heads promoted internally within the same school.) One head expressed the view of many others when he said, 'it is necessary to be impartial and just, friendly but not familiar, approachable but not easy. Directness, honesty, fairness are all qualities which earn respect though not friendship.' It was felt essential, in order to maintain objectivity and avoid claims of favouritism, that heads did not become too involved with their staff. 'Distancing', in terms of impartiality, was thought by some to be a necessary condition to be attained and that a certain amount of isolation was therefore the strength of the head's position.

In contrast, other heads were conscious of becoming physically distant from their colleagues and were particularly concerned to develop the notion of a 'team'. They felt professional isolation was less likely to be experienced if heads were prepared to leave the sanctity of the office and go 'walkabout', thus developing contacts with the teaching staff. Professional isolation was also less likely to occur, it was said, if heads had a regular teaching commitment and attended subject department meetings. Attempts were made by some to reduce the divide between teachers and management, to show that 'we are all colleagues in education' and to encourage teachers to relate to their heads as fellow professionals.

It was very common for heads to refer to the isolation and loneliness that accompanied being ultimately responsible for making decisions. As a deputy it was possible to avoid decision-making and refer matters upwards; this was clearly not the case for heads. A new head said, 'It is the loneliness of being the final arbiter upon whose word all sinks or swims. It is this power that isolates and daunts.' In practice, the head is the end of the line: 'Governors are lay, officers are only administratively responsible, inspectors do not carry any ultimate responsibility...in the end you are the field officer with no obvious line of responsibility upward.' Another put it more colourfully when he said, 'As the ultimate can-carrier for decisions and the reconciler of disputes, the head is the ultimate coconut in the stall to be shied at'. At the end of the day, the head was responsible for the whole school a responsibility which simply could not be avoided. As many remarked, 'The buck stops here'. It was thought to be important for a head to learn not to take personal responsibility for everything, although this was easier said than done.

For many heads, professional isolation and loneliness were part and parcel of the job itself, something for which in the final analysis they were paid. It was suggested that those aspiring to headship must accept that isolation was a feature of the role: it was 'an inevitable fact of life' and 'part of the initiation ceremony of leadership'. For some, professional isolation was a reality but it was compensated by the many pleasures and rewards that headship brought.

Others commented that isolation was a feature of any hierarchical institution, and that the situation would not be improved until the structure of education changed and more democracy was brought into school management. It was noted that some authorities were seeking to employ heads who would act as team leaders, and that many heads created their own isolation because they refused to share power.

A facet of the role that frequently led to feelings of isolation related to the structural position of the head as mediator between diverse and often conflicting interest groups. Heads dealt with a wide range of people including teachers, parents, pupils, governors, LEA officers and the community at large. Many heads commented that on occasions they felt as though they were 'piggy in the middle', acting as a buffer or bridge between, for example, the education authority and the staff. Feelings of isolation were most acute at certain times, for example during union disputes, when heads were caught between the staff who may see them as 'management' and the LEA who expect them to run the school in accordance with their instructions or advice. This particular situation was experienced by a case study head who although stating during the first and second visits that professional isolation had not been experienced, said at the time of the third interview:

> This term's industrial action has been a real drain on me. As a head you become the meat in the sandwich. Whenever a notice was put up, I am sure it was very carefully scrutinized. It can be a lonely position; all of a sudden you find that the staff are agin you rather than for you. I felt I did not know where I stood and I felt very isolated whilst it was on. There was a feeling that the staff appreciated the difficulties I was under but nevertheless said, "Sorry, but that's life". Now it's over, relations are back to normal.

For some heads, the fact that professional isolation was not perceived as a major problem for themselves was attributed to 'personality factors'. A case study head commented that she had never depended entirely on people and felt this was related to her personality. Others thought such feelings depended largely on the individual's make-up or temperament and that heads should be able to work and stand alone yet be able to mix with others and be approachable. A necessary requisite for heads to withstand and ultimately avoid professional isolation was a 'thick skin', although one new head asked, 'I'm learning not to worry about what the staff might be saying about me, but how thick a skin should I have?'

General feelings of isolation could be exacerbated when promotion to headship involved geographical mobility. In order to achieve headship it may have proved necessary to move to a different location and thus there was the possibility of a physical separation from family and friends. The survey data confirmed, not surprisingly, that more professional isolation was experienced by those heads appointed from outside the LEA compared to within-LEA appointments. A new head in a new area takes time to make friends, whether within or outside education and, paradoxically, the nature of the job may make it difficult for such friendships to develop quickly. The heavy demands of the first year of headship may reduce the amount of time heads can spend with their families and friends, when what is really desired is more time to compensate for the loneliness that the job brings. It was also suggested that an out-of-school social life was important to lessen the stresses and strains of headship, yet time does not seem to allow for it and therefore relaxation becomes difficult. The general problem of isolation brought about by 'settling in' was recognized by an experienced head who commented that although he had not experienced difficulties with making new friends and settling in to a new area and LEA (as he had continued to live in the same house and lead a very similar private life as when a deputy) added 'nevertheless, the shock of isolation can still be considerable'.

A large number of heads made reference to their deputies and, as was mentioned in Chapter 4, relations with the senior management team had a major effect on perceptions of professional isolation. A lot depended on whether the deputies were perceived as subordinates or fellow managers, the latter being more likely if the head had been personally responsible for their appointments. It was suggested the key to breaking down isolation was total trust and full consultation; as one new head said of his management team,

> they must shelter the head from trivia but keep no important secrets and this requires discrimination. Equally, the head has to share his (or her) knowledge and thinking with them, relying on their confidentiality. I enjoy this relationship with my two new deputies: in this I am blessed.

A case study head was in a less fortunate position and, at the time of the researcher's third visit, had not, as yet, been able to overcome the isolation and loneliness of headship. In an earlier interview he had suggested the crucial factor here was the support of the senior management team, without which 'you are on a loser to start with'. He gave an example of an incident that had occurred in the middle of his second year which made him feel particularly isolated. It involved the suspension of a pupil and as the pupil refused to leave the school premises, the head thought he had little choice but to send for the police. After a very traumatic incident, the head returned to the office where neither of the two deputies passed comment and it was left to a head of department, who arriving later, asked if the head was all right. The head said, 'Whether or not they thought I mishandled the situation is immaterial: they should have given me some support and then subsequently they could have been critical of my actions'. For this head, the two deputies were reluctant to commit themselves and nearly always 'sat on the fence', so he did not get the kind of personal support he felt he needed and which he had given the head at his previous school.

Other heads, although agreeing that relationships with senior staff were paramount, made the point that nevertheless, occasionally, there were matters that were so confidential they could not be shared even with senior colleagues. Related to this was the fact that regardless of how well the senior management team worked as a unit, the members were not 'first amongst equals' as the head, by virtue of the position, held final responsibility. As a new head said, 'One carries the banner and the can and only other heads really share the same situation'.

Another factor related to perceptions of professional isolation was the lack of feedback associated with the job. It was felt by a number of heads to be particularly difficult to assess progress and development; furthermore, problems were invariably presented but successes not always noted. Most feedback was therefore negative and related to problems and complaints and this could lead to an unbalanced view. It was noted that self-assessment or developing criteria for judging one's performance was virtually impossible. Professional isolation could partly be explained by having no real way of evaluating success; as a new head asked – is it absence of complaint from parents, being left alone by the LEA or should it be something more?

A number of heads referred to the value of objective comment or criticism from an outsider – a person who could be open and honest about the school. There was a need for a neutral consultant, an individual who could offer disinterested advice and counsel and thus help heads to overcome the problem of lack of feedback. An experienced head thought he was rather fortunate here because at one stage he had had an educational researcher in the school whom he had used as guide, philosopher and friend. Another suggested there was little scope for totally confidential consultation with anyone and that there was a role for neutral consultants at specific times and on specific issues – 'a kind of "phone in" advisory service'. (This issue is pursued further in the following chapter.)

Finally, it is interesting to consider the extent to which feelings of professional isolation may or may not change over time. From the preceding discussion it would appear that such feelings are largely the result of a combination of individual and contextual factors. Of the 16 case study heads, half stated they did not experience feelings of professional isolation, five claimed they did and three changed their minds over the course of the research. Of these three, one initially felt isolated but by the time of the third visit, had developed excellent contacts with other heads in the authority and had found the local convenor of his professional association very helpful. An internally-promoted head felt isolated because he had found it necessary over time to distance himself from the staff, while the third stated she had not initially realized what it meant to be professionally isolated.

The importance of other heads as a form of support and a means of reducing feelings of professional isolation was a constantly recurring theme. A large number pointed to the value of contacts with other secondary heads and both informal and formal gatherings were seen as providing opportunities to discuss issues of common concern. It is to fellow heads and other forms of support that attention is now given.

Fellow heads and other forms of support

Both groups of heads surveyed were asked to indicate, using a five-point scale, the amount of support they had received from various groups and individuals since taking up appointment. The results, which are presented in full in Appendix 2, show that 'Other heads in the LEA' were perceived to be very supportive by the heads. As few as one in ten felt they received little or no support from their fellow heads and approximately 60 per cent saw them as either 'extremely' or 'very supportive' on the rating scale. Further analysis showed that there were no differences between the amount of support received from other heads and the number of secondary heads in the authority. Similarly, no differences were found between the amount of support received by male and female heads. However, as might be expected, a relationship was found between feelings of professional isolation and the level of support received from other heads in the authority. Those who did not experience professional isolation were more likely to report that they had received support from their fellow heads.

The uniqueness of each head's situation was mentioned as a factor affecting the degree to which fellow heads could help allay feelings of professional isolation. For example, an experienced head said: 'One difficulty is that your problems are unique to your own institution, so discussion with others who don't know the personalities, the circumstances, the constraints and so on is not particularly helpful.' Another found other heads supportive but commented, 'We all have to go back to our own schools and to our own circumstances. Headship is walking a tightrope between being a teacher and being a site manager. Other heads are busy walking their own ropes.'

However, it was far more common for those heads who received little support from their colleagues to state that this was the case for two main reasons. Heads explained that they could not or would not confide in other heads in the authority because of personal incompatibility and/or increased competition over pupil numbers.

A case study head explained that he did not share the same line of thinking as others in the authority, adding at the time of the third visit: 'The only support from other heads I find I can get is from another newly appointed head. He is my only ally, he is my soul mate... I don't really trust the other heads in the borough, too many things seem to get back. The image they have of me, I think, is still the young whippersnapper.' Another new head referred to the heads in the area as an 'odd bunch'. Many had predated comprehensive reorganization and others, in the head's view, were reluctant to run comprehensives at all. All the area heads had offered support but the new head saw them as having very different philosophies to his own and therefore he did not think that they would be particularly useful or supportive.

Another case study head felt she had little in common with the majority of her colleagues and found that there were few she got on well with. A new, very young, female head had recently been appointed to a neighbouring school, who phoned her for advice, which, as the case study head commented, 'Is very complimentary and good for my ego, but we are, because of falling rolls, fighting for the same kids, so that might make things difficult'.

Interestingly, a senior education officer in another LEA, also with declining rolls, raised the issue of competition for pupils and related it to the increased use of unprofessional behaviour. The officer referred to the dilemma for heads between professionalism (e.g. don't sell the neighbouring school down the river) and the requirements of the 1980 Education Act to do just that! This was an area that few people were prepared to discuss and one for which new heads were poorly prepared. The officer was sure that the heads in his authority felt threatened by falling rolls and parental choice and stated that they went to extraordinary lengths to attract pupils (e.g. by staging elaborate parents' evenings). In the view of the officer, this was a significant additional external pressure on heads for which they were totally untutored. The heads in his authority were increasingly 'looking over each other's shoulders' and he added that the case study head was not as self-reliant as the others, possibly because he was new. However, he concluded, 'I think a few mistakes on his part will cause him to appreciate this. He cannot afford to let the bloke up the road score a trick off him – he will soon learn!'

The situation in those authorities or areas with falling rolls and possible school closures was not always competitive. One case study head, whose school was about to be merged with another, said in response to a direct question on this theme:

> All the area heads decided that we would not put on special one-off showpiece parents' evenings; there would be no big hard sell. If we all started that, then it would be awful. The hard edge of competitiveness is knocked out of it because we know each other very well as friends. We agreed, for instance, that we would not unload unsatisfactory staff members on one another. We thought to do so would not be a very professional approach.

This case study head also did not experience feelings of professional isolation, mainly because there were a number of heads in the authority whom he knew well and trusted.

A means by which problems relating to incompatibility and competition could be avoided was for heads to form their own informal support groups or establish links with individual like-minded heads. New heads felt that the most useful advice came from other heads, and greatest benefit – in terms of both reducing professional isolation and in providing general support – seemed to be obtained from regular meetings of small groups of heads who discussed various educational topics. However, it was found that regular informal meetings of this kind were not common.

A case study head who had recently completed a 20-day management course (as part of DES Circular 3/83) stated that he strongly hoped four to six course members would continue to meet regularly. Another felt that she would benefit from a weekend meeting, about every six months, with those whom she met on a management course (COSMOS). This particular head was still in contact with a number of individuals from the course and they were going to arrange visits to each other's schools. Similarly, two new heads from neighbouring authorities, who had both attended a one-week residential management course, commented that the five heads from two LEAs were having regular meetings. These arose largely as a result of the last session of the course which raised the question 'where do we go from here?' Such inter-LEA meetings remove the possible rivalry between heads in the same authority, but the main problem as recognized by one of the heads, was that 'as the diary gets fuller then those meetings are likely to be put off'. By the time of the researcher's third visit, the head said of the informal link developed, 'We did not have our meeting last term and we probably will not have one this term. I hope it will not die.'

Finally, another case study head spoke of the need for a small group to be set up, not so much to provide support (although no doubt this would be forthcoming) but rather to provide a means by which new heads could obtain feedback on their own performance and discuss issues of common concern. As mentioned earlier, lack of feedback was seen as an important factor contributing to perceptions of professional isolation. It would be most helpful, it was therefore suggested, if a small seminar group could be formed, whose membership was fairly constant and included people of differing views, but in similar situations. The group could meet every half term or so and would need some professional input to provide its theoretical underpinnings. The case study head also suggested that because of the general mistrust amongst colleagues it would be best if the small group was made up of advisers and heads of non-neighbouring schools.

Before considering other meetings for heads and their value, it is worth noting that another source of support often referred to, but not shown in Appendix 2, was the head's spouse. One new head, who saw professional isolation as a problem, was at least fortunate in that 'my wife listens to all my problems sympathetically and then tells me to mow the lawn, fix the shelf, mend the fuse, etc.!' It is interesting to note that a case study head, who at the time of the first interview made references to his wife as helping to offset fellings of isolation, said at the second visit that he had made a deliberate policy of not talking to his wife about school. The head, who had experienced a particularly difficult first year, initially told his wife about all the problems at school, but found that she took on a 'mother tiger' role; she was upset about what was happening to him and there was nobody to take it out on except him. The head therefore found it was far better to separate school from home completely, and now, much more than before, he talked to other heads and had found the local convenor of his professional association particularly supportive.

Heads' meetings

Whether or not heads set up their own support groups, they were most likely to come into contact with other heads in the authority as a result of attending a variety of both formal and informal meetings. The isolation that heads felt on occasions could be considerably reduced by support obtained from such attendance and, in any one authority, heads' meetings could take a number of forms. The meetings could be arranged by the LEA or the heads themselves, and involve all the heads in the authority or just those within a local area or district. In addition, professional associations organized meetings and it was not uncommon for other informal meetings to take place, for example between consortium heads or between secondary heads and the heads of feeder primary schools. By drawing on data derived, not only from the heads themselves but also from the LEA survey, it is intended to consider the more common meetings and examine their general usefulness. It is proposed to begin by looking at meetings arranged by heads themselves and conclude with a more detailed analysis of LEA arranged meetings for secondary heads throughout the authority.

The LEA survey showed that in very nearly nine out of ten authorities the secondary heads organized their own regular authority-wide meetings. (This figure excludes professional association meetings – for example, the Secondary Heads Association and the National Association of Head Teachers.) LEA officer involvement in these meetings varied, but it was quite common for senior officers to be invited to attend to discuss particular issues, or for a sub-group representing the heads to arrange specific meetings with them.

In general, and like the other meetings heads attended, the authority-wide meetings were helpful in that they allowed the participants to share problems and establish contacts. In those authorities with districts or area education offices (41 per cent) it was not uncommon for there to be additional meetings of heads. These area heads' meetings were invariably arranged by the relevant education officer or the secondary heads themselves, and usually took place on a regular basis. In a few districts, the heads' meetings were more ad hoc and only occurred in response to specific issues.

The area meetings were often seen by heads as more useful than those involving all heads in the authority, as they were more likely to enable small group discussion to take place. There was, however, some criticism voiced that they frequently turned into 'moaning' sessions, or that there was too much discussion of trivia.

One of the case study heads commented that local meetings were not being used as well as they might, so the heads decided, with the LEA's support, to start a programme of termly 'professional days'. The first was on the role of the form tutor and involved outside speakers. The day had proved very successful and the case study head was pleased that the area meetings had been made more worthwhile. He commented that the impression he had formed on attending the earlier meetings was one of disappointment, as they were, at that time, predominantly grousing sessions.

Another case study head referred to the termly meeting of the local secondary heads as the 'best' meeting attended, as the heads shared ex eriences and talked frankly. The head remarked: 'Officers are not usually present at these meetings so you can be very frank without any kind of worries and I found it helpful to listen to others – you may or may not choose to follow their advice, however.'

Most of the new heads had joined a professional association and both the National Association of Head Teachers (NAHT) and the Secondary Heads Association (SHA) held regional meetings. Seventy-three per cent of the cohort had joined SHA and 30 per cent NAHT, while 13 per cent had decided to subscribe to both professional associations. As can be seen in Appendix 2, the professional associations were seen by both groups of heads surveyed as an important source of support. A statistically significant relationship was found between feelings of professional isolation and the amount of perceived support from professional associations. As might be expected, there was a greater tendency for those heads who said they did not find isolation a problem, to state that they received more support from their professional associations.

Many new heads joined the association that the majority of the heads in the LEA belonged to, and saw attendance at meetings as yet another means of getting to know others. A number of new heads interviewed said they found the NAHT and SHA publications particularly useful: for example, the document on legal matters and the short checklist on the head's first day. Other new heads, like the case study head referred to earlier, praised the local convenor as a valuable source of information and support.

The vast majority of LEAs arranged meetings for *all* their secondary heads on a regular basis. From the LEA survey it was found that 42 per cent organized regular annual meetings for all secondary heads, while 86 per cent held more frequent meetings, usually termly. Only five authorities did not themselves arrange meetings for heads. In these instances, meetings were more likely to be organized by the secondary heads and LEA officers would usually be invited to attend. One of the five authorities had occasional weekend conferences for *selected* secondary heads only, which as the LEA respondent remarked, often led to feelings of resentment on the part of those not involved and was thought to indicate which heads were 'well in' with the officers.

Generally, the LEA-arranged meetings functioned both to provide information and to allow discussion of various issues. Many officers stated that the meetings provided a valuable 'sounding board' to obtain heads' views on a range of LEA ideas. One officer commented that it was also very useful for heads 'to get things straight from the horse's mouth' and another saw the meetings as providing an opportunity to bring the Chief Education Officer (CEO) closer to the heads. Regular contact between heads and senior officers was generally welcomed by both parties. Nearly three-quarters of LEAs said their secondary heads met with the CEO or Director of Education on at least one occasion per term. In only one authority was it acknowledged that the CEO never met all the secondary heads in the LEA on a regular basis.

A few officers were critical of the LEA-arranged meetings for all secondary heads, seeing them as of limited value and often involving too many heads to provide an adequate forum for discussion. In an authority in the case studies, the termly meeting was made up of a morning input from the CEO and senior officers and then, after lunch, small group discussion took place with a final plenary session. However, in this particular authority, many heads wanted more structure for the morning session and by the time of the researcher's third visit the format had changed. The heads themselves had drawn up the agenda, chosen the speakers and there were more opportunities for quesions. An officer in another authority saw such meetings as giving heads a chance to let off steam and felt it was a good thing for LEA officers to be in the firing line. The meetings were not simply for information-giving and were useful, he thought, as the LEA was able to try things out and obtain heads' reactions.

In general, the regular meetings arranged by the LEA tended to focus on 'bread and butter' issues pertaining to the authority and were primarily information-giving sessions. The termly meetings tended to be about LEA policy and administrative matters, while annual meetings of secondary heads were more philosophical and discursive in nature. The annual meetings were very often less formal, residential in format and provided opportunities for in-depth examination of issues of current interest. Both types of meeting were seen by most LEAs as useful and an important form of support for heads, especially new heads, allowing them to meet other secondary heads, to share experiences and appreciate that their problems were not necessarily unique.

It is worth noting that in order to maximize the benefits derived from such participation and to ensure that the annual meetings met the needs of secondary heads, one authority regularly seconded a head for one term to be the annual conference director. The main theme of the conference was agreed with the senior officers and usually focused on a current problem or initiative.

Summary and discussion

The research showed that most heads experienced some degree of professional isolation and occasional feelings of loneliness. The survey data showed that only a third of 'old' heads and about 40 per cent of the new heads said professional isolation was not a problem. Further analysis indicated that feelings of isolation were not related to the size of school, its catchment area or whether the head was male or female; this was contrary perhaps, to popular expectations that heads in large urban schools might find isolation more of a problem. Although longitudinal data were not available, a cross-sectional study of the 'old' heads found no relationship between feelings of professional isolation and number of years as head. This suggested that the problem was not more or less severe for heads three years or eight years in post. But whether the situation improves or deteriorates after a longer period of headship remains unknown.

The main cause for feelings of isolation seemed to be the ultimate decision-making role of the head. Loneliness appeared to be most acute at times when heads were faced with particularly difficult decisions. Some heads simply accepted a degree of isolation as a necessary part of the job. The feeling of being a 'piggy in the middle' between the LEA and the staff was experienced most strongly by some of the case study heads during the prolonged period of industrial action. Many heads said that the problem of isolation could be considerably reduced by fully adopting a team approach to management with their senior staff and this has already been discussed in detail in Chapter 4. To reduce the problem further, most heads wanted to be seen as fellow professionals by the staff and stressed the importance of having a regular teaching commitment and playing their full part as a member of a subject department. Heads mentioned the valuable support they received from their spouse and how important it was to have an out of school life which enabled them to 'switch off' from the problems.

Other heads in the authority provided a major source of support. The surveys showed that only 10 per cent of heads felt they received little or no support from their colleagues. A cross-tabulation showed that the more support heads felt they received, the less likely they were to experience professional isolation. Any lack of support was usually due to problems of confiding with other heads with whom they were in direct competition because of falling rolls. The other main reason for feeling a lack of support was due to differences in personalities or philosophies between the heads.

Heads met their colleagues at a variety of meetings organized by themselves, the LEA or their professional associations. Most meetings were seen as useful by both heads and LEA officers in providing information, allowing heads to share common experiences and 'let off steam'. The LEA meetings also acted as a good forum where new heads could develop contacts with other heads, LEA officers and advisers. Although generally praised, some meetings were criticized as simply 'grousing sessions'. Heads thought the meetings needed more structure and could be improved by using the morning to exchange information and devoting the afternoon session to one major topic with a high quality speaker and small discussion groups.

A serious problem for most heads was the lack of feedback on their progress and suggestions were made for the need of an outsider's constructive criticism.

One method already mentioned in Chapter 3 was a mutual support group of heads and LEA officers meeting about once a month to discuss individuals' problems. The LEA survey showed that this type of group was very rare, although some heads had set up informal meetings with colleagues they had met on a course. A strong recommendation from the research is that LEAs should consider how to set up and facilitate small support groups, as the limited experience in this country and the work of Laplant (1981) in the US, show they are particularly valuable for school improvement and in reducing heads' feelings of isolation.

A second suggestion mentioned by several heads was the need for a neutral consultant, similar to those used in industry and commerce. Some examples have been tried in education through various forms of Organization Development work and Gray (1983) provides a useful review. Interviews with the heads in the NFER study showed that many would welcome such an approach and LEAs need to think about the possibilities of this type of work.

CHAPTER 9
LEA Support for Heads

The previous chapter discussed in detail the issue of professional isolation and showed how it was often seen as an integral part of being a head. It also examined the main forms of support for heads which helped reduce feelings of professional isolation and particular attention was given to informal support groups and heads' meetings, including those organized by local education authorities. This chapter examines other forms of support offered to heads by LEAs. It begins by considering the ways in which new heads are introduced to their authorities and then widens the focus to look at the other main types of LEA support offered to all secondary heads, whether old or new.

New heads and induction into the authority

It was most common for LEAs to invite new heads to the central education office or County Hall for an introductory visit or induction day. Eighty-six per cent of LEA respondents stated it was their policy to invite heads for an introductory visit, while several others said the situation was currently under review.

During the introductory visit, the new heads were usually introduced to the various officers responsible for different sections and with whom they would have to deal in the future. The visit enabled them 'to put faces to names' and was an opportunity to find out about LEA procedures. For example, in one LEA the visit was made up of half a day with a senior adviser to discuss matters relating to the school and the LEA, which was followed by an introductory tour to meet key professional and administrative officers whose role *vis-à-vis* the school was explained. In some authorities the introductory visit was arranged by the school's 'pastoral' adviser, who acted as a kind of 'go-between' or bridge between the new head and the LEA, introducing the heads to key administrative officers and familiarizing them with LEA procedures.

Seventy per cent of LEAs with areas or districts said that new secondary heads normally had an introductory visit to the local office. If the structure of the authority was such that the area or district education officer had major responsibility for the oversight of local schools, then clearly a visit to the office to meet the various officers was a considerable advantage to the new head. It is worth noting that in one large county a working party of new heads and senior officers, set up to consider induction in the LEA, recommended that responsibility and provision should be at the area office rather than the county office. They felt that the area officer should be mainly responsible for ensuring that new heads received advice about important issues and knowledge of any school-specific information, while the central education office would provide support in the form of documentation and advisory help.

Induction programmes or courses for newly appointed secondary heads lasting for *more than one day* were provided by just over one-quarter of LEAs. Organized induction programmes or courses were only found in large or medium-sized authorities (i.e. those containing 21 or more secondary schools). Two main reasons were given to account for this. Firstly, a commonly expressed view was that an induction programme was not viable or appropriate, given the number of new secondary heads appointed in any one year. Secondly, several LEAs stressed the importance of the informal approach and claimed that in small authorities informal contact was so regular that formal arrangements appeared unnecessary. However, there were some small authorities who, although claiming to operate informally, also pointed to the need for a more structured induction programme which, given the numbers involved, would have to be provided on a more individual basis. The dilemma between the recognized need for a more structured induction and insufficient new appointments to make such programmes viable was not, however, confined to small authorities. One large authority with over 60 schools, for example, reported that in the last three years it had appointed only *one* new secondary school head!

In the 21 LEAs providing them, induction programmes for newly appointed heads varied in length from two days, to a maximum of 13 days spread throughout the heads' first year. Only four LEA programmes were for more than ten days' duration, while nearly three-quarters of them lasted five days or less. The importance of a residential component was clearly recognized, with over three-quarters of induction courses including at least one residential session. Other LEAs recognized its importance but pointed to recent financial constraints which had necessitated a series of non-residential day sessions.

The content of the induction programmes varied but usually consisted of an introduction to the authority *and* a management course. The range of issues and areas covered was, as might be expected, related to the length of the programme. Several authorities with shorter induction programmes tended to concentrate on the broader issues of headship, preferring to focus on more local matters and procedures during the arranged introductory day visit to the education office(s). An analysis of the main areas covered during induction is shown on p. 136.

The induction programmes themselves, like most management courses, were made up of lectures, talks, workshops and exercises. They were usually the responsibility of LEA senior officers in conjunction with experienced heads, with 'experts' and guest speakers being brought in for specific sessions.

Main areas covered during the induction programmes:

Introduction to the LEA; LEA policy, procedures, support services, officers and advisers.

Finance; buildings, health and safety; law; governors; communication; leadership; decision-making; PR and the media; pupil supervision and welfare.

Forward planning and falling rolls; curriculum development and evaluation; special educational needs; management of change.

INSET; disciplinary procedures re staff; staff development and appraisal; staff appointments.

As part of induction, several authorities arranged visits to local teachers' centres and, where applicable, to centres specializing in, for example, educational technology, urban studies, multicultural education, music, drama and resource-based learning. Familiarizing new heads with the forms of LEA support available to them and their schools was especially important for those heads – the majority – who were appointed from outside the authority. On some induction programmes heads were also able to request visits to particular schools and institutions in order to discuss matters with experienced practitioners and examine certain things in greater depth. These visits could be on an individual or small group basis.

Finally, many of the longer programmes concluded with a course evaluation or review. At least one LEA tried to ensure that the team responsible for organizing the programme included one new head from each phase who had completed the programme in the previous year. As an officer interviewed commented, this in itself can be a salutary experience. Other authorities ensured that experienced heads were part of the team responsible for designing, organizing and running induction programmes.

In one large authority there were plans to facilitate and develop induction by setting up a seminar group comprised of new secondary heads, senior advisers and experienced heads. The group, made up of six individuals, would meet regularly and discuss the organization and management of large institutions. The discussions would be followed by visits to two schools, one similar to the new head's and one not. It was the intention of the visits to facilitate discussion, with established, experienced heads commenting on management and curricular issues. A senior adviser involved in developing the seminar group stated that it was due to commence as a result of the experiences gained from the induction course offered within the LEA. There was a need, he said, to tailor and individualize the support for new heads. It was therefore necessary for new heads to identify their particular problems or weaknesses and for the LEA to respond accordingly. The main constraint, and one that was fully recognized, was, of course, finding sufficient time and resources for the seminar arrangement to take place.

Where induction programmes were found, they were usually available for *all* newly appointed secondary heads; that is, for people promoted from within the LEA as well as those who were entering their first or subsequent headship from outside the authority. The courses themselves tended to take place either in the first term of the academic year (usually beginning in late September or early October) or they were spread throughout the heads' first year. In two authorities, a rolling programme had been devised consisting of a number of modules, thus enabling a new head to enter the programme at any point in the school year. In one of these authorities, for example, a meeting was held in which information about the LEA was given to secondary, middle and primary heads designate and then, on taking up post, the new heads were able to participate in one of the six modules which made up the induction programme. Data derived from the cohort of new secondary heads appointed in 1982–83 show that approximately 50 per cent took up post in September and 25 per cent in January and April respectively. Therefore, the use of a rolling programme into which a head could enter at any stage, is one way in which the problem of different start dates could be minimized.

Finally, what is known about the composition of the participants on induction programmes or courses? Just over 50 per cent of the 21 programmes combined primary and secondary heads, while six were offered for secondary heads only. Interestingly, three LEAs, possibly in order to make a viable group size for the purpose of induction, combined new secondary heads with other new senior staff (usually first deputies).

All the new heads involved in the research were asked to comment on the usefulness of these introductory visits and induction programmes. Most heads made positive comments on the value of the programmes and visits, although many qualified their responses and made suggestions as to how LEA induction could be improved.

What heads particularly liked about the programmes, in addition to obtaining basic information about the LEA's policies and procedures, was the opportunity to meet other new heads and the various officers and advisers of the authority. It was felt extremely useful to meet other heads in similar situations and the new heads valued the opportunities, spread over a period of time, to develop contacts and discuss their initial difficulties and misgivings with their peers. Such opportunities were enthanced when the courses had a residential component. It is worth noting that some LEAs referred to the value of these courses and visits, not only to the new heads but also to the advisers and officers. Attendance at such courses and, for that matter, others put on by the LEA, helped to develop and maintain a genuine partnership between the LEA's heads and its officers, allowing issues to be openly and honestly discussed and helping to counter feelings of professional isolation.

There was, however, criticism levelled at the content of some of the programmes. A few heads were disappointed and thought there was a lack of appreciation of the problems facing newly appointed heads. There was a need for more information about LEA personnel and lines of communication. Some were of the opinion that much of the information imparted could have been written down (for example, in a handbook) and it would have been of greater value to have pursued issues they had already met or were likely to meet in the future. One head added that perhaps such issues and problems could have been discussed together with practising heads and LEA officers. In general, heads appreciated being asked what they wanted pre-course and several spoke of the importance for the authority of a post-course evaluation.

The timing of the induction course was an issue about which the new heads held strongly and occasionally opposing views. Several commented that their introductory visit to the education office, which took place several months after taking up appointment, needed to be much earlier, with one head stating that his own initiatives in visiting County Hall and introducing himself had proved to be more useful. A group of newly appointed heads, asked by their authority to comment on induction, remarked that information and advice were most urgently needed during the head designate period. However, several other heads commented that their introductory visits to County Hall had taken place almost immediately after their appointment and at this stage they were not sure what questions to ask. Another added that on appointment many officers were introduced to the new head, but by the time he took up post, he had forgotten what some of them were responsible for! Similarly, they had been given too much information in too short a time.

There was general agreement amongst the new heads that they wanted time to settle in before attending an induction course. Several expressed a desire at this stage to put their energies into the new school rather than a course. There was a wish to be away from the school for as little time as possible and some heads saw documentation and personal support as preferable to attendance at courses. At least one head deliberately chose not to go to the first session of the LEA's induction programme, as it was held as early as the second week of the head's first term. One authority, although starting its induction programme early, thoughtfully held all meetings for heads, including the induction programme, on the same weekday, thus enabling those heads who so desired to have a regular teaching commitment.

Another issue that evoked a strong response amongst the heads concerned the participants of the induction programme or course. As mentioned earlier, about one-half of the programmes combined new secondary heads with their primary school counterparts. This situation, as might be expected, was a common response in those authorities where the number of new secondary head appointments in any one year was small. However, it was not uncommon for those heads involved in induction programmes for both phases to be highly critical. The need to ensure that induction programme content is appropriate to all phases is obviously important, but not always easy, organizationally, to put into practice. One possible solution is to invite secondary heads to join primary heads' induction programmes only when the matters dealt with are relevant to *both* phases.

It is worth noting that in two small authorities there were no induction programmes specifically for new heads, but there were introductory half days for *all* teaching staff new to the LEA. In one of these authorities a head said he had received a 'routine' letter inviting him as a 'new teacher' to meet the Director of Education and the inspectors. On checking its applicability to new *head* teachers, he went to the central office to meet the director and the officers with all the scale 1 teachers new to the authority. The director sought him out and said a few words, but generally the head thought this arrangement was absolutely hopeless. He later discovered he did not know who did what in the LEA and it was quite difficult to find anyone else who did! Fortunately for the new head, there was a change in one of the senior officers and eventually he was able to use the new person for almost all points of contact. The head was unhappy that nobody had informed him how the authority worked. Since the time of the research, the authority has arranged for new heads to have a half-day visit to the office, where matters relating to the school and the LEA are discussed.

How important is induction to the LEA and, if it is perceived as important, what can be done not only to help it take place, but also to ensure it operates to best effect? Data collected over the course of the project can be used to answer the first question. It will be recalled that all three groups surveyed – new heads, more experienced heads and LEAs – were asked to delineate those areas for which, in their view, heads were *least* prepared (see Chapter 3 for further details). It is interesting to note that responses to this open-ended question gave high priority to familiarization with the LEA (e.g. its routines, procedures, who to contact, services available, etc.). 'Knowledge of the LEA' was perceived to be of considerable importance, being ranked the second most significant area by the experienced heads and third by the two other groups surveyed. The magnitude of the problem is also shown by examining the heads' survey responses to the question on 'Difficulties Facing The New Head' (see Appendix 1). Nearly a quarter of both new and more experienced heads regarded obtaining information about decision-making in the authority as 'a serious' or 'very serious' problem and only one-fifth said it was 'not a problem'. A very similar pattern was found for the related area of obtaining information about areas of responsibility and 'who does what' in the LEA.

How might induction programmes be introduced, bearing in mind the main constraint found in many LEAs – namely, the low number of new appointments in any one year? For those authorities appointing few heads but wishing to introduce induction courses, one possible solution is to act in conjunction with neighbouring authorities. In the LEA survey, five of the 21 authorities offering an induction programme of more than one day's duration, were involved in consortia arrangements and at least two others were examining the possibility of linking with other authorities. The five authorities mentioned above were able to put on the bulk of their induction course at a regional headship unit with the new heads spending occasional half-days or days in their respective education offices. It thus proved possible for individual authorities to link with others and thereby offer lengthy, partly residential, induction courses on LEA procedures *and* general issues of curriculum and management.

Another possible solution to the problem of numbers is to offer an induction programme, as 12 LEAs did, for both secondary and primary heads, or, as three LEAs did, some other combination of new senior secondary appointments within the authority. There are, however, as stated earlier, mixed views about the value of combining primary and secondary heads on such programmes.

Notwithstanding the above, it may still prove impracticable to offer a structured programme because of low numbers, and it may therefore be necessary to devise an induction programme specifically designed or tailored to the needs of the new secondary head. While this may be more time-consuming, it is likely to be more effective, catering as it presumably would for the individual needs of the head. A significant disadvantage of such individually-tailored courses, however, would be the missed opportunities to mix with similarly placed new secondary heads. An individually-tailored programme may also be of greater help than an informal arrangement, as it would mean the new head did not have constantly to contact the LEA officers for information about procedures and regulations. Many new heads were reluctant to do this, and often did so only after exhausting all other possibilities. They were very conscious of running the risk of being labelled by the office as nuisances or, worse still, incompetents.

Several heads, in their comments about induction, referred to the importance of the 'pastoral' adviser. One head said that the authority provided each school with a 'pastoral inspector' and his had become a valuable guide and mentor and had proved more helpful than the induction course. Another, who was unhappy with the authority's induction, claimed that what was needed to improve the situation was the development of links with existing experienced heads in nearby similar establishments, who could advise as and when required. The importance and potential of 'mentor' and 'pastoral' advisers is pursued in more detail later in this chapter.

If those authorities wishing to put on a more structured programme are able to overcome the aforementioned problems and offer a course of some length, the obvious next step is, where possible, to eliminate or minimize heads' critical comments: namely, those concerning programme content, participants and timing. As for timing, there is no universally agreed-on 'best' time for induction, although the working party of secondary heads referred to earlier, suggested unanimously that the LEA should concentrate its efforts to improve induction procedures in the two or three months preceding the date on which new heads take up appointment.

Regular meetings as part of induction, however, are also important as new heads may not be fully aware of the range of problems encountered until they actually take place. The suggestion was made by a head that LEAs should call new heads together after 12 months or so in order to answer questions and hear of frustrations.

Finally, one other factor commonly referred to that would considerably ease induction, was the need for an LEA *handbook* containing, amongst other things, lists of procedures and key telephone numbers. Regardless of whether the authority ran an induction course, many heads wanted a handbook informing them of 'who does what' and what LEA policy was on various issues. However, only 38 per cent of LEAs produced these so-called 'blue' or 'brown bibles' which the new heads, who had them, said they consulted frequently and generally found useful. Just under half of the large authorities and one-third of the small and medium-sized authorities had handbooks. Handbooks act as a helpful reference and the key problem for the LEA of keeping them up-to-date can largely be overcome through the use of ring binders and word processors.

It has been the purpose of this section to describe and document what is known about introductory visits and induction into the authority. Considerable attention has been given to this and to what the heads themselves thought could be done to make their induction smoother. Its importance should not be underestimated, bearing in mind that nearly 60 per cent of all new heads were appointed from *outside* the LEA.

Other forms of LEA support

The previous section examined a very important form of LEA support for *new* heads – namely, induction into the authority. It is now proposed to consider the other main types of support made available by LEAs to both new *and* established secondary heads.

There are a number of factors affecting the amount of support an authority and its officers, both administrative and advisory, can give to its schools. Perhaps the most obvious concerns the number of advisers or inspectors employed by the LEA, and it was found that the school-inspector/adviser ratio varied considerably from one authority to another. Information obtained from the LEA survey enabled a crude quantitative index of inspector/adviser support to be calculated, by dividing the number of secondary schools in the authority by the total number of inspectors or advisers for both primary and secondary schools. The most favourable ratio was found in three authorities which had fewer than one secondary school per adviser, while at the other extreme, two LEAs had as many as six or more schools per adviser. The average ratio for the 78 responding LEAs was 2.4 with approximately two-thirds of authorities having a ratio of 2.5 or less, secondary schools per adviser. The LEA survey also found that about 70 per cent of authorities had an officer who had specific responsibility for *all* secondary schools.

In order to pursue further the levels of support in general that secondary heads obtained from LEAs, the two groups of heads surveyed were asked to indicate, using a five-point scale, the amount of support they felt they had received from various parties, including LEA advisers and administrative officers. Appendix 2 reports the findings and shows how supportive advisers and officers were in general, with over half the heads claiming that both sets of LEA personnel were 'extremely' or 'very supportive'. Approximately one in 15 of the new and one in ten of the 'old' heads surveyed stated that officers and advisers were 'not very supportive' or of 'no support' at all. No relationship was found between the size of school and the amount of support heads felt they had received from LEA personnel.

It appeared to be the policy of most authorities for an officer to visit the new head soon after the beginning of their first term or, less commonly, their second term. This could be the adviser with responsibility for secondary schools, or in some cases a 'pastoral' adviser who, in addition to a subject specialism, also had a general responsibility for a group of schools. However, there were noticeable differences in the number of visits made by senior advisers between one authority and another.

Various administrative officers such as Deputy Directors or Area Education Officers could also be involved in these early visits to new heads. Many of these senior officers and advisers recognized that the new head needed time to settle in and discover possible problems and thus usually waited a few weeks before making their first visit. They felt it was important to provide the head with information from someone outside the school as well as giving general details about how the authority worked. Others saw their role as helping the new heads implement their plans.

One way of doing this was for LEA personnel to make special provision for newly appointed secondary heads. Altogether, 48 LEAs (60 per cent) said they made special provision for new heads, for example by making available extra finance or resources. (No relationship was found between the existence of special provision for new heads and size of authority.) Some authorities gave an additional capitation allowance, while others considered sympathetically any requests for assistance necessary to promote desirable change, the finance usually coming from the advisers' discretionary curriculum fund. Each circumstance was usually considered individually but most authorities gave new heads priority on additional resources and/or minor works.

Several chief advisers made reference to a brief 'honeymoon period' when additional finance was made available. One added that there was always an attempt to counter the inexperience of the new head by improving conditions, and that it was important for an advance or an achievement to be credited to the new head. Most LEAs therefore viewed new heads in a sympathetic light and, while all cases were examined individually, the majority could hope for additional finances or extra resources. An officer commented that although his authority did, in fact, make a special provision, new heads were asked to list priorities, rather than being told, 'Here is your £5000, get on with it!' This, he claimed, made them think about what they wanted to do and how they would go about doing it. Also, in a few cases, new heads were given extra points or staffing, but generally this was not considered necessary or appropriate.

Many administrative officers recognized the need to spend more time visiting schools but said they were often severely limited by time constraints. A senior officer commented that an ideal situation would be to spend half a day a week in schools, but added, 'at the moment, we just tend to be firefighting'. Similarly, several 'old' heads when asked to comment on relations with administrative officers, spoke of the need for more school visits. They claimed that it was only by actually visiting the schools that the officers were able to avoid becoming remote and thus be in a position to appreciate the everyday problems that schools faced.

Head's relationships with LEA personnel

As might be expected some criticisms of administrative officers were made by heads, but in general terms, developing harmonious working relationships with LEA personnel was *not* perceived as a problem. Very rarely were heads as critical as one 'old' head, who said that the officers in his authority wanted a head to be a 'line manager who runs an efficient school with the lowest level of resources, who doesn't ask for any additional financial help, who never suspends any pupils and doesn't say anything at speech day which will embarrass them. Whenever one asks for anything, the impression given is that there are many schools far worse off and one should therefore stop complaining!' Negative comments were the exception, however, and as can be seen from Appendix 1, developing good working relationships with LEA officers was only a problem for a very small proportion of heads. Only 7 per cent of new heads and 8 per cent of 'old' heads referred to 'developing a good working relationship with LEA officers' as a 'serious' or 'very serious' problem. The data show that 'developing good working relationships with LEA advisers' was not a problem either, with only one in 20 of both new and 'old' heads reporting that this was a 'serious' or 'very serious' problem.

The relationship between heads and LEA officers was further explored in the interviews with both new heads and LEA officers. It appeared to be quite rare for heads to have had any direct contact with the Chief Education Officer or Director of Education and only six of the 47 heads interviewed said the officer had actually visited the school, usually for some form of social function. The new heads appreciated the opportunity to meet the director or the CEO. In one large county it was the CEO's practice to see all new heads for lunch and, in another, new heads received a personally written letter of welcome from the Director of Education. In another authority the Chief Education Officer phoned the head on his first day. These were the only instances mentioned by the 47 new heads interviewed and it was clear that it was rare for the most senior officer to be personally involved. Nevertheless, it must be said that the four heads concerned were very impressed by the welcome.

In large authorities, the most frequent contact was between the head and the local area officer, who in almost all cases was seen as extremely helpful and supportive and from whom only two heads felt they had received little help. In some authorities, contact was made at the Deputy or Assistant Director level and heads, again, felt these officers had provided help when it was required.

In a few authorities, the senior advisers made suggestions to the *subject* advisers that they 'drop in and see the new head' or at least tried to give the school priority over others in the LEA. A senior adviser, for example, commented that he would in principle make a visit to a new head, as would the

Area Education Officer, the general adviser for the school and the various subject advisers.

As might be expected, the heads felt the individual subject advisers varied in their effectiveness. A case study head put it well when he said, 'I think the usefulness of the advisory service depends on the individual. Some advisers are very useful; others I wouldn't go out of my way to get their advice.' There was a tendency for new heads to invite the subject advisers into schools at the earliest opportunity and then, after these visits, to make judgements about their usefulness.

Although, as previously mentioned, in some authorities it was incumbent upon advisers to visit new heads, it was far more common for the heads themselves specifically to request a visit or to encourage their own staff to 'get them in regularly'. A head from a small authority stated that he had to initiate *all* contact with the advisers by writing to them individually – none had come in of their own accord. In general terms, however, it appeared that most advisers had been seen during the course of the heads' first year, even if the visit had just been a courtesy call or an occasion to introduce themselves. In a minority of schools this was not the case. For instance, in a case study school, the new head had seen only three advisers in the first year and, although they had proved very helpful, others had been very difficult to contact. One particular subject adviser had failed to reply to two separate letters inviting him to meet the new head. However, those heads who had had difficulty in contacting advisers and arranging for them to visit the school, although finding this rather frustrating, were generally sympathetic to their plight and recognized that the service was often considerably overworked and under-resourced.

Over half the new heads interviewed had had considerable contact with the advisory team and found them very helpful, especially on staff appointments, resources, INSET and curricular advice for various departments. These points were confirmed by survey data from both the new and 'old' heads. The surveys also showed where LEA advisers were of relatively little help: namely, in the areas of home–school relations, reports/assessments, pastoral care, special needs and school management.

With regard to school management, the point was frequently raised that the majority of LEA officers – both administrative and advisory – had little or no experience of senior management in schools themselves and were therefore not in a good position to offer advice. It was most likely for both subject and senior advisers to have come from a head of department background; few, if any, had held headships (especially comprehensive school headships) or even deputy headships, and they therefore often lacked credibility in the eyes of new heads. One of the case study heads was in a very fortunate situation in that the school's 'pastoral' adviser was also the senior (secondary) adviser and had previously worked as a head in the authority. However, having been a head may not, in itself, be a sufficient condition for dispensing sound advice on school management. For example, another of the case study heads had been visited in his second year by a senior adviser with headship experience, and although he was affable and wanted to be supportive, the new head, for a number of reasons, found him to be no use at all.

Others commented that what was often lacking from the advisers, was something that new heads found most helpful – namely, a broad overview of the school and its curriculum. Although some subject advisers were useful as a sounding board for ideas, others had limited definitions of their roles, often defining matters in terms of their own subject rather than in broader, cross-curricular terms. The limitations of the service were put forcefully by one 'old' head who said,

> With one notable exception, I have found the advisers to be so immersed in their own subjects, that they are not able to take an overall view of the school curriculum. None have had management experience in secondary schools and this seems to make them insensitive to the pressure from different areas to which a head is always subject. Most in their own way, would agree with one adviser who told me, "Home economics is the hub of the curriculum!"

Finally, there were interesting variations in the way new heads made use of the advisory service in order to facilitate the change process. For example, one new head discussed with subject advisers new directions for the various departments and, having done this, it was suggested the change process would now be made that much easier. The assumption made was that heads of department were more likely to be persuaded to make changes if suggestions for change came from the advisers rather than from the new head. On the other hand, and much less common, were those heads who wanted to move very fast on the curricular front and were therefore not prepared to involve the advisory service more than was absolutely necessary. One new head, appointed from outside the LEA, commented that he did not know the advisers very well and felt some of them would block his ideas, and therefore they were to be used sparingly.

The role of the 'pastoral' adviser

Reference has already been made on a number of occasions to 'pastoral' advisers and the role they can play in supporting new heads. In general, those heads interviewed who had such advisers attached to their schools made positive comments about their value, although similar caveats were frequently raised concerning such matters as individual usefulness and shortage of school management experience. They were perceived as helpful and supportive and several heads pointed to their value as guides through 'the minefield of department procedures'.

It did appear, however, that there was often a difference between policy and practice, and the potential of the role was rarely fully achieved. As can be seen from the comments of the case study heads below, a system that appeared very good on paper did not always, for the best of reasons, work out as intended.

Of the 16 case study heads, eight did not have an adviser specifically attached to the school and in most of these LEAs there was an area education officer who had responsibility for all the schools within the district. Two of the case study heads had as many as three 'pastoral' advisers in their first four terms of headship. Such a turnover of personnel meant the advisers had proved less useful than they could have been. One of the heads spoke of the potential benefits gained from regular visits by the pastoral adviser and made reference to his previous school where the pastoral adviser used to drop in and see the head once a fortnight. In the head's view, this was very useful as it provided an occasion where ideas and issues could be regularly discussed. Unfortunately, although the new head's three pastoral advisers had all been very good, the head remarked that he saw them infrequently.

The fact that there were many pressures on advisers, including pastoral advisers, was remarked upon by a number or case study heads. It is worth noting that one of them was particularly unhappy with the amount of support he had received from the LEA. In this case the two main forms of support identified by the LEA officer interviewed – namely the pastoral adviser and the LEA induction programme – had clearly proved inadequate. The head had been unable to attend the first session of the induction course and had failed, despite making inquiries, to receive invitations to attend further sessions. As for the other main form of LEA support, the head remarked that the school's pastoral adviser was also solely responsible for computing throughout .the LEA and thus was very busy. In this particular example there was an obvious mismatch between the LEA's intentions and the reality as experienced by the new head. Clearly, as in other areas of the advisory service, a major factor militating against the effective performance of the 'pastoral' role was lack of time.

In another authority, the system of attaching an adviser to the school had gone by default as the advisers were, according to the new head, seriously overworked, badly understaffed and under enormous strain from the politicians. The head thought that the best form of LEA support would be a 'proper' advisory service *and* an adviser attached to each school, making the important proviso that the latter 'have to be good'.

Only two of the eight case study heads with pastoral advisers were very happy with the support they had been given. The head in a large authority said of his pastoral adviser, who incidentally was also responsible for computers, that he could not be faulted. This particular pastoral adviser also attended governor meetings and the head was slightly disappointed when, by the time of the third visit, he had been replaced. The number of schools the pastoral adviser was responsible for had been reduced in recognition of the fact that he was the only computer adviser in the authority.

Pastoral advisers could also be of great assistance to heads in their role as clerical officer to the governors or by simply attending such meetings. It was found, where pastoral advisers did not exist, that many area education officers performed this same function. Pastoral advisers can also play a key role as 'confidants' to both new and more experienced heads, giving information on such matters as the school's history, LEA policy and procedure, staffing and curriculum design.

Confidants, mentors and consultants

The importance of having an individual or group that heads can confide in was an issue raised on a number of occasions. Whether that person or group should be fellow heads (either past or present), senior officers or 'pastoral' advisers was not always clear. What many heads wanted was someone they could immediately contact in times of crisis or when difficult decisions had to be made rapidly. It was often difficult for a head entering a new authority to know with whom matters could be discussed in confidence and it was not unusual, in the early days at least, for new heads to maintain contact with their previous heads and/or develop ties with like-minded individuals.

The issue of a confidant was raised by a case study head without a pastoral adviser, who spoke to an adviser, in what he assumed to be total confidence, only to be later approached by the chief adviser, who wanted to know all about his problems. It should be noted, however, that most case study heads felt their relationships with the officers of the authority were good and that the above situation would have been unlikely to occur.

Many new heads thought that some form of 'mentor' system, where a formal link was arranged between a new and experienced head, would be very helpful. However, the LEA survey showed that, at present, this was used by only 14 per cent of authorities, although several others were considering such a system. There was a recognition by some authorities, that experienced heads, in association with LEA personnel, could be used more effectively to offer support and guidance to new heads. The suggestion was also made that in times of falling rolls there were a number of heads within an authority, who could possibly be used to create a pool of 'confidants' or consultants.

In one of the authorities in which the researchers worked, attempts were being made to instigate a 'mentor' system. An ex-secondary head had been given responsibility for senior management training and part of the three-year contract was to set up an induction course for new heads and to act as confidant and consultant. At the time of the researcher's second visit, the 'liaison officer' had visited all recent secondary head appointments and had also tried to 'plug them into an experienced head in their area'. It was felt there were a number of local problems the schools faced and it would be helpful for a head to have someone they could instantly contact for advice or information.

However, the main problems with such a system, as discussed in the previous chapter, were the issues of compatibility and competition over pupil numbers. Some heads were reluctant to confide in others if either of these factors was present.

It is interesting to note that Dwyer (1984) specifically asked secondary heads if they would welcome the appointment of a 'consultant head', i.e. a member of the advisory team who had extensive and successful past experience as a secondary head and whose role was the advising of heads. Expressed in such a way, it was perhaps unsurprising that 42 of the 50 heads interviewed said yes, although there was concern that the position should not be filled by heads affected by, for example, school closures or reorganization, and for whom such a post would help the LEA solve a problem. Dwyer's own view was that a consultant head would be a significant strengthening of any advisory service and, given current management training initiatives, the consultant head could be responsible for senior staff development within the LEA, along with the 'servicing' of headteacher selection panels, the induction of new heads and the provision of pastoral support.

The NFER research did not ask specific questions about consultancy or consultant heads, but the matter was raised on a number of occasions. For example, one LEA respondent stated that an offshoot of recent, centrally-funded INSET initiatives, was the intention of utilizing course participants to set up a system of consultancy for all heads in the authority. Another LEA referred to its existing organization development consultancy team, which provided a route whereby particular issues could be explored on an individual head and school basis. Finally, one small borough mentioned that it had introduced a new form of support for its heads by employing an independent consultant. The consultant had conducted in-depth interviews with heads in order to identify individual needs and review progress over a period of time. Initial reactions from the heads themselves were positive and it was hoped that a structured programme of meetings would emerge and that those involved would form a mutually supportive group.

Altogether, just over 50 per cent of the LEAs surveyed claimed to have developed some form of small support group for their secondary heads which met several times during the year. However, on closer analysis it appeared that these support groups were broadly defined by the LEAs and included such things as ad hoc working parties, steering committees, local catchment area groups and consortia meetings. A number of other authorities stated that they intended to set up or develop small support groups in the light of recent INSET developments (e.g. DES Circular 3/83). Southworth (1985) has argued that LEAs should seriously consider how they might encourage groups of heads, both within or across-LEAs to come together, not only to help reduce stress and ease feelings of professional isolation, but also to demonstrate their belief in the validity of support.

The case study head with the LEA liaison officer mentioned in the previous section, commented at the time of the third visit, that he had become involved in a group of four heads who met every three or four weeks. This group had been set up by the LEA's liaison officer and the new head admitted it had provided very good contact for him. He qualified his enthusiasm, however, and said he had no really close link with any head. Most heads had previously been deputies in the LEA and there was a strong inner-circle effect, of which the new head, who was appointed from outside the authority, did not feel part.

INSET provision

A very important form of support that authorities offered their heads, both new and more experienced, was the opportunity to participate in courses, either provided by LEAs themselves or by outside agencies. The opportunities such course attendance provided, both in terms of skill and knowledge acquisition, *and* in providing occasions to meet other senior staff have already been discussed in Chapter 3. However, it is worth noting that several LEA officers and heads suggested that support for heads could be improved by providing greater opportunities for INSET for all senior staff with a management responsibility. Heads could be considerably assisted by authorities encouraging their deputy heads to attend management courses, or by facilitating residential courses for senior management teams from a number of schools. Also, regarding training opportunities, a limited number of authorities had introduced courses for governors and, very occasionally, new heads had been given the resources for weekend residential courses for the entire teaching staff. An officer interviewed referred to several occasions in his authority when a new head was able to take advantage of an entire school staff conference. In one school, the staff held very entrenched attitudes and the conference tried to generate an atmosphere where change could take place. In another, staff morale was extremely low: the teachers felt that nobody cared and that they had been left alone for too long. The officer suggested that, given adequate resources, whole-school staff conferences could be used profitably for all schools and not just for those with new heads. The reality of the situation in the current financial climate is, of course, that such conferences are likely to become even less common.

Two further features of LEA in-service support concern school closure days and full-time secondments for headteachers. When asked if any of the secondary schools in the authority had had an INSET closure day in the last 12 months, just over two-thirds of LEA respondents answered in the affirmative. The LEAs were also asked to give details concerning the number of secondary heads seconded for *full-time* in-service activities (excluding 3/83 courses) for the academic year 1982–83, and the results can be seen in Table 9.1. It is worth noting that just under half of the authorities seconded secondary heads for various periods and that the total number of secondments (158) was equivalent to approximately 5 per cent of all secondary heads in the 80 LEAs who completed the questionnaire.

Additional forms of LEA support

In this final section it is intended to examine briefly various other forms of LEA support for secondary heads. One form of support occasionally mentioned by respondents was that of financial support to assist new heads towards the cost of removals and setting up home. Although it is not known how many LEAs give such financial support, two of the case study heads

Table 9.1   Number of LEAs and secondary heads involved in full-time secondments (1982–83)

	Number of LEAs	Number of secondary heads released*
One year or longer	13	22
Two terms	3	3
One term	21	42
Less than one term	20	91
Total	39**	158

* the figures do not include those involved in 3/83 courses
**LEAs can appear under more than one category
NB 39 of the 80 LEA respondents (49 per cent) seconded secondary heads

claimed the move to headship had personally cost them about £5000. Both said they had received no help from their employers and one of the heads had specifically expressed his concern to the LEA, especially as the authority continued to give financial assistance to new advisory appointments but not new heads!

A very important form of LEA support for heads concerned ancillary staff; most notably, secretarial and administrative assistance within the school itself. Certainly, some of the new heads spoke positively of the help they had received from their administrative staff, but others thought there was a need for a closer analysis by LEAs of support systems in general. A case study head, for example, when asked what would be the most effective means of LEA support, suggested that there was a need to ensure that schools were getting the best out of their technical, secretarial and ancillary staff. One area, which as a new head he did not feel well prepared for, was the monitoring of the support staff and he asked, for example, how you ensured that you were making the most effective use of the secretary's time. The head suggested that the authority should think hard about this area, perhaps allowing schools to make use of consultants in office management to permit a thorough analysis of existing systems.

Related to this is the need for an administrative officer, or bursar, for all schools, regardless of size. It could be argued that such an appointment could go a long way towards unburdening heads of many of the routine administrative tasks they currently undertake. It would permit the higher paid and more senior staff in schools to focus on their more educational role as leading professionals. The roles of secondary school secretaries and bursars are considered in more detail by Hart (1985), Handy (1984) and Spooner (1984).

Teachers' centres and their leaders are potentially another important source of support for secondary heads. The research found, however, that teachers' centre leaders or wardens were seen as not very helpful by both new and 'old' heads (see Appendix 2). Although neither group obtained much help from centre leaders, there were significant differences between the two in that new heads appeared to receive less assistance and support than the more experienced heads. This could be because a period of time is necessary to establish a working relationship between the head and the local centre leader. A national study of teachers' centres (Weindling *et al.*, 1983) found that there was a need for centre leaders to increase the amount of work undertaken with secondary schools, as their main orientation tended to be primary focused. It is possible that the level of support given by teachers' centre leaders could increase because of the emphasis being placed on both school-based and school-focused INSET.

Two of the case study heads made specific reference to the structure of their respective authorities and commented on how this seemed to hinder rather than facilitate LEA support. Both heads worked in authorities with an area or divisional structure and one spoke of the need to send copies of everything to both central and area offices and noted how easily channels of communication became blocked.

The other head was more critical of the fact that the authority operated in a very informal and *laissez-faire* manner and, in his view, lacked any formal structure and saw heads as largely autonomous. The head, along with other new appointments to the authority, gained some insight into levels of LEA support when they were informed by the Director of Education during an induction day that, 'You win your spurs by surviving'. At the time of the second interview, the case study head said:

> One can ask for support, but the difficulty is knowing whether one should be asking or not. There is nothing on paper, you are simply expected to get on with it. A LEA handbook would be very helpful. I don't know what the role of the advisers is, for instance. Do I ask for help? What is the function of the senior adviser in the authority? and so on... This LEA seems to rely on muddling along and tremendous emphasis seems to be placed on the great autonomy of the head. I think it is too often an excuse for doing nothing or for not involving themselves. Each division does its own thing, it runs its own show and heads are expected to do the same. That's OK in times of plenty but in times of falling rolls and cutbacks, this can be divisive... More information from the centre is needed.

The LEA officer interviewed reinforced many of the head's points, adding that although an informal system is a 'civilized way of doing things', it can amount to a tremendous strain on a new head, especially if appointed from outside the authority. When asked what could be done to improve the means of support currently offered by the authority to its heads, the officer spoke of the need for: a) an administrative infrastructure to ensure that things flow smoothly and b) a sensible restructuring of the advisory service so as to be able to offer the kind of support that heads want. Perhaps unsurprisingly, the third area that the LEA officer made reference to was the need for a structured induction course over a head's first year.

The situation found in the case study above highlights the lack of general agreement concerning heads' autonomy and the amount of LEA support. It is also a reminder of the difficulties that LEAs have in establishing the right balance between going into schools too often and being seen as intrusive, and not going into them often enough and being seen as unsupportive.

Summary and discussion

Although most LEAs invited new heads for an introductory visit to the central office, only a quarter provided an induction course lasting more than one day. These courses were more likely to occur in the large and medium-sized authorities with over 20 secondary schools. The content usually consisted of an introduction to the LEA and a range of management topics such as finance, law and leadership. Most courses lasted for less than five days and contained a residential component, guest speakers, visits, talks and workshops. New heads found these induction courses valuable and welcomed the residential opportunity to meet other heads and LEA officers but were critical of some of the content. They wanted less theory and more of practical relevance, especially discussion of the problems facing new heads.

LEAs also need to consider which components of the induction course are suitable for both primary and secondary phases, as a number of secondary heads felt that some of the content was not relevant.

Two LEAs had rolling programmes consisting of a number of modules which new heads could enter at any point in the school year. This flexibility was particularly valuable as the survey showed about half the new heads started in September, 25 per cent took up post in January and another 25 per cent began in April. Time is needed to settle in before going on an induction course and some heads said they were reluctant to leave their school during the first few months.

An obvious limitation for LEAs in providing induction courses is the number of heads appointed each year. Small authorities should discuss the possibility of consortia arrangements with neighbouring LEAs, as one group found it was very effective to run a joint course at a regional headship unit. A valuable alternative is to tailor-make an induction programme for each new head. While this may be more time-consuming, it is likely to be more productive, as it concentrates on the needs of each individual.

The research shows that a well constructed induction programme is an important form of preparation for a new head and it is recommended that all authorities should provide more than just an introduction to the LEA office:

An additional recommendation is that all authorities should provide heads with a handbook of LEA procedures and contact names. The survey showed that only 38 per cent of LEAs had a handbook, which new heads said they found most helpful.

The LEA advisers offered support to heads in a variety of ways. The survey data showed that over half the heads rated advisers as 'extremely' or 'very supportive' and only 10 per cent felt they received little or no support. Heads usually invited advisers to the school and found their usefulness varied from individual to individual. The main areas of help were on curriculum matters, staff appointments and INSET. Little help was obtained on pastoral care, special needs, assessment, and home–school relations. Heads rarely sought advice on school management because advisers were seen to lack a broad overview of the school and few had experience of headship themselves. While heads sympathized with the workload of the advisers, they found it difficult to contact some individuals even by letter. Although new heads usually received a visit from an officer or adviser in their first term, there was agreement by heads and officers that more visits to schools were necessary but pressure of work made this difficult.

Only 14 per cent of LEAs said they used a 'mentor' system of linking a new head with an experienced head and in one of the case study areas an ex-head had been given the role of a 'consultant' head. It would seem that a mentor or consultant head system has much to recommend it, as the research showed that heads usually seek advice from other heads and not from advisers and officers.

This chapter has shown that, while most LEAs provide a variety of forms of support for both new and established heads, some authorities did little to help their secondary heads. Heads are, of course, appointed to run their schools and there may be a fine line between offering help and being seen as too intrusive. Giving support of any kind can be a delicate undertaking; this should not, however, deter authorities from considering carefully both the amount and the form of the support they currently offer.

CHAPTER 10
The Management of External Relations

Each of the various attempts at analysing heads' managerial tasks discussed in Chapter 3 included a component concerned with the management of external relations which usually encompassed the parents, the wider community and the media. The other major aspect involved accountability to both LEAs and governing bodies. The previous chapter has discussed the part played by the local authority and it is now intended to focus on other aspects of the management of external relations, specifically those concerning governing bodies. Contacts between heads and the wider community will also be examined, and particular reference made to parents, the media and public relations in general.

In order to gain an overall picture of difficulties facing new heads, the two groups surveyed – those new to headship and those with three to eight years' experience – were asked to indicate the problematical nature of various 'external' issues. The results are reported in full in Appendix 1, but for the purpose of this chapter, the five-point scale has been collapsed into three to simplify the presentation of data. Table 10.1 shows that with the exception of 'creating a better public image of the school', and to a lesser extent 'liaising with feeder schools', the vast majority of heads did not consider the external issues listed to be 'very serious' or 'serious' problems. 'Developing a good relationship with governors' and 'issues arising from local party politics' were, for example, perceived by over half of both new and 'old' heads as 'not a problem'. Although 'dealing with parental problems' was a serious problem for only one in ten heads, over two-thirds saw this area as a 'moderate' or 'minor' problem. While some differences between the 'old' and new heads are shown in the table, none was found to be statistically significant. This suggests the levels of concern on these issues during the early years had remained fairly consistent over the time period covering the two groups of heads.

As part of the research, the heads were asked to give details of the areas for which they felt *least* prepared prior to appointment. These were reported in Chapter 3 and governor-related issues (e.g. relations with governors, meetings, head's report) were mentioned by approximately one in every eight heads. For many of these heads the first governors' meeting attended was as a head. Others remarked that they had been more fortunate and their

Table 10.1 Difficulties facing the new head – external issues

	New Heads (%)			'Old' Heads (%)		
	Very serious or serious problem	Moderate or minor problem	Not a problem	Very serious or serious problem	Moderate or minor problem	Not a problem
Developing a good working relationship with governors	6	42	52	6	34	60
Dealing with parental problems	10	67	23	9	71	20
Dealing with local community groups and services	6	48	46	5	53	42
Issues arising from local party politics	9	31	60	12	36	52
Dealing with the media (e.g. local press)	8	49	43	9	51	40
Creating a better public image of the school	42	43	15	42	44	14
Liaising with feeder schools	18	45	37	16	51	33
	N = 188			N = 228		

Chi-square on 3-point scale and original 5-point scale (Appendix 1) not significant between the two groups.

introduction to this area had been facilitated through having had prior experience of governing bodies and meetings. This may have been gained as teacher representatives, parent governors or when they had been acting heads or deputizing for their previous heads. Also, in some cases, as deputies, they had been invited to attend governors' meetings by their previous heads. Those who had had prior experience of governors' meetings found it a valuable preparation, although it was remarked that attendance per se was limited in that it did not enable one to have direct experience of what it was like to being 'in the hot seat'. Nevertheless, attendance was useful and several said they now involved their deputies in governor meetings to 'better prepare them for headship'.

It is worth noting that when LEA survey respondents were asked to identify, from experience, the main areas for which new heads were least prepared, 29 per cent made reference to governors and governing bodies. Why there was such a difference between the heads' perceptions and those of the senior advisers and officers completing the LEA questionnaire is, however, a matter for speculation.

In many authorities, the clerk to the school governors was an LEA officer whose expertise and contacts could be used to the advantage of the governing body. The clerks were also of considerable value to heads and could act as advisers or consultants. An area education officer interviewed remarked how his new head's governing body was made up of a number of very influential and powerful people, including the chairperson of the education committee. The officer said the new head could not afford to make mistakes or show deficiencies, adding that in his role as clerk to the governors, he tried to give heads as much support as possible by discussing their reports and fully briefing them beforehand. Recent research into school governing bodies, funded by the DES and based at Brunel University (Kogan *et al.*, 1984), has made reference to the problem of the dual loyalty of clerks who were LEA employees. The researchers suggested the officer must serve the governors without ambiguity or divided loyalties and underlined the value of governing bodies being clerked by someone familiar with the LEA and its workings.

The Brunel team also remarked that school governing bodies had little opportunity to develop a corporate identity as they met so infrequently. The NFER case study school governors usually met termly, with some schools having additional meetings when needed to discuss particular issues. In one school the governing body met monthly, although the meetings usually lasted only an hour. Most governors' meetings lasted one-and-a-half to two hours, although one case study head was rather surprised when his first meeting lasted only 20 minutes, while another found hers went on for four hours! In some authorities the meetings were open to the public and the press but, in practice, attendance by individuals not specifically invited to attend was uncommon.

The composition and size of the case study school governing bodies varied considerably: some were made up primarily of LEA and political appointees who often had responsibility for a large number of schools, while others included teacher, parent and pupil representatives. The size of the governing body varied from ten to 20 members, some of whom were more active than others and meetings were held either in the afternoon or evening. It was often remarked during the course of interviews with officers, chairpersons and heads, that the composition and size of the governing body would soon alter as the LEA was attempting to introduce changes in line with the 1980 Education Act. The Act has set down rules and guidelines to be introduced gradually for all state school governing bodies and many of the recommendations arising from the Taylor report (DES, 1977) will be implemented. The intention is for all schools to have their own governing bodies and membership will consist mainly of LEA appointees (number unspecified), teacher and parent representatives. The legislation states it is desirable to appoint governors from industry, commerce and the community and governing bodies have additional powers to include other individuals, such as non-teaching staff or pupils. Under the terms of the Act, it will no longer be possible to be a member of more than five governing bodies (thus preventing the situation of one head involved in the research, who referred to a councillor who was governor for 27 schools!) and governors will cease to hold office if they do not attend meetings (without consent) for 12 months. (More recently, the 1986 Education Bill builds on the 1980 Act and proposes further changes concerning the composition, organization and functioning of school governing bodies.)

In the case study school, a typical agenda for the governors' meeting consisted of minutes from the previous meeting, matters arising, reports from sub-committees, LEA circulars and any other business, but the bulk of the meeting was taken up with the head's report. The Brunel team found heads' reports varied considerably in the type of information they provided, while Bacon (1978) reported they were often given and listened to in a rather perfunctory manner. A chairperson of governors involved in the NFER research who was a governor for nine schools, remarked that some heads' reports were more like diaries, merely informing the governors that on particular dates certain events had taken place. Little detail was given and the chairperson had tried to put pressure on heads to give more information in their reports, but had found a number hard to persuade. He did not include the new head in this category and remarked that the latter's report was a very comprehensive one. In fact, in several of the case studies, the chairperson of governors commented how the previous head's report was very brief and said how much they welcomed the new head's attempt to keep them fully informed of developments in the school.

A problem for the new heads was knowing how much information to include in their reports. Some used the reports of their predecessors as a guide, but gauging the 'right' amount of input was difficult. A case study head commented, 'You need to keep the governors fully informed, but you don't want to bore the pants off them!' (For some guidelines on report preparation, see Hinds and Litchfield, 1984.) One new head thought his governors were pleasantly surprised by his long report as 'the previous head had only given them half a page' and added that the detailed report made them feel involved with the school, while another pointed to a further benefit of having to produce a report for each meeting. It was, she suggested, a very valuable exercise as it made her stop and consider what had recently taken place in the school; it was an opportunity to 'take stock'.

In another case study school, the chairperson stated the head's report was the most important document of the meeting. It was discussed in detail, paragraph by paragraph, and the governors could raise any points they liked. The vast majority of chairpersons interviewed saw the new heads as cooperative, consultative and willing to discuss matters arising. Only one chairperson thought the new head was 'not telling us everything', and this, the head remarked at the time of the third interview, was largely because, in her view, the governors were unsupportive and uninterested in the school. She said, 'The problem with the governors is they don't really know what is going on in the school and they don't come into the school enough to see. So I've found myself not giving them very much information at the governors' meetings.'

The Brunel team noted that heads had differing views on the role of governors and they suggest that the head's attitude is a major factor influencing the way in which governing bodies operate. They also felt that with the appointment of a new head the role of the governing body became open for renegotiation. The vast majority of the 47 new heads interviewed in the NFER research had a very clear picture of the role of governors and governors' meetings. In general, they thought it important for governors to be kept fully informed to enable them to make decisions and participate in meaningful discussion. They wanted governors' meetings to be a forum for discussion – a critical sounding board – and not a rubber-stamp for decisions already made. Similarly, they wanted governors to be involved in the school and encouraged them to enter the school whenever possible. A case study head echoed a common sentiment when he said,

> The governors hadn't been very much involved before. I think they were seen very much as a threat to the head's authority; I don't see it like that. I want the governors to be more involved, I want them to visit the school regularly. They are helpful and willing and I want to encourage them to find out about the school.

A variety of means were employed to help governors find out more about the school and generally become better informed on educational matters. Examples included: inviting community representatives to address the governors; distributing information to governors before meetings; instituting regular governor visits to the school with feedback to meetings; encouraging governors to 'adopt' individual departments and asking departmental heads to report to governors' meetings; termly displays of departmental work put on for governors and parents and encouraging governors to attend INSET days, staff conferences and other school activities.

One case study head had instituted a system whereby two governors visited each term and spent a day at the school and then gave a verbal report to the next governors' meeting on what they had seen. The head worked out a timetable for the day and ensured, via the staff newsletter, that teachers knew of the governors' whereabouts. In another school a similar system had been set up, but in this instance the two governors were 'let loose' to do whatever they wanted and as a result were receiving a tremendous amount of information.

In several case study schools, the chairperson of governors remarked that the head's report usually had a head of department's report attached, The relevant departmental head usually attended and the governors were, over time, discussing different areas of the curriculum. It was suggested that this helped governors understand the work of departments and made them feel less isolated from the school.

The involvement of governors in the school was seen as beneficial to all parties and some heads, as mentioned in Chapter 6, saw this as an important means of improving staff morale. However, it must be said others were disappointed with the response of some individual governors. It was perhaps unrealistic to expect a high level of support and involvement on the part of *all* the school's governors for, as several heads and chairpersons remarked, governors are volunteers and many cannot spare the time to become more involved or to meet more frequently.

A few heads said they did not want greater involvement as the governors were political appointees and were often perceived as having little or no interest in the school. Others remarked that the general response of political appointees was to use meetings as political battlegrounds and a few spoke of how excellent relations with the governing body had been detrimentally affected by a change in political representation. A case study head, with a politically constituted governing body, was very disappointed with his governors and thought he had not succeeded in persuading them of the need for a partnership. Although he was happy with some individual governors, collectively they were not interested in participating in a discussion. The head remarked that the atmosphere was not very pleasant and that they had no real contact with the school. He gave the example of a recent school function, put on by pupils and staff over three nights, when five of the governors did not even reply to the invitation. Also in this school, two of the governors had lost their positions because they had not attended three successive meetings. (By the time of the researcher's third visit, however, the head reported that relations with governors had improved significantly.)

Data from the case studies and surveys showed that these were minority responses and many heads commented that although they had political appointees, the governors were highly supportive and put the school's interests above party politics. Another case study head, for example, whose governors were responsible for a set of nine schools in the same catchment area, felt the governors' meetings were very good and that the governors had a genuine interest in the school.

Although the majority of new heads wanted greater governor involvement it was not always easy to bring about given the nature of the system, and the suggestion was made that if frequent school visits were expected, then it was necessary for governors to be retired or unemployed or able to absent themselves easily from their place of work. It will be interesting to see if the increasing LEA provision of training for governors and the implementation of the 1980 Act, and the 1986 Education Bill have a positive effect on overall governor involvement and interest.

In general terms, however, and as can be seen from Appendix 2, the majority of heads involved in the surveys perceived their governors to be 'extremely' or 'very supportive'. The key relationship in determining the amount of support received was, in most cases, that between the head and the chairperson of governors. Most chairpersons interviewed were involved in the appointment of the new heads and for that reason it was reasonable to expect them to be very supportive of *their* candidate. This was largely true, but there were occasions when it was not. For example, a few chairpersons remarked that the successful candidate was not their first choice ('although I am very pleased to have been proved wrong') and one thought that, without strong support from the LEA, he would not have been appointed. In other schools the incumbent had changed, occasionally as a result of incompatibility between the new head and the chairperson. In one school, for example, the chairperson described his predecessor as 'Conservative with a capital C' and added that she resigned soon after the new head was appointed, as they did not get on at all well.

In a few of the schools, the heads expressed disappointment that their chairperson had not been as supportive as they had hoped. Some were said to be unenthusiastic about the school or difficult to contact. One case study head remarked that the chairperson had never, apart from governors' meetings, visited the school. (A deputy claimed that in his eight years at the school he had yet to see the chairperson.) The LEA officer, similarly, saw the chairperson as unsupportive and the chairperson described his relations with the head as 'businesslike'. At the time of the researcher's third visit the head described the support from individual governors as 'good', but would have welcomed greater support from the chairperson. To give an example, the case study head referred to his last governors' meeting where he had prepared a full report on sixth-form provision. After he had submitted it, the chairperson had no questions whatsoever, whereas the vice-chairman, who had obviously read the report, asked a number of very pertinent questions. In the head's view, 'The chairman does not really support, but neither does he really hinder. His main aim is to get the meetings over as quickly as possible and at the moment his main preoccupation is getting re-elected.' On one occasion when the meeting was chaired by the vice-chairperson it lasted twice as long, which the chairperson implied was largely a result of 'unnecessary chit-chat'. The chairperson's view was that governors should play a minimal role in school government and that providing things were going well, 'Heads should be left to get on with it'.

Similar views about the general role of governing bodies were expressed by other chairpersons – the business of education should largely be left to the professionals with governors playing a supporting and back-up role (see also

Bacon, 1978). But most chairpersons were aware of the importance of regular contact with the head, tried to be available when needed and described the relations between them as good. (Where relations were not perceived in such favourable terms, chairpersons had contemplated resignation.) Most recognized that heads needed support from governors and some were aware of the problem of professional isolation and loneliness that headship can bring, seeing their role as one of lending support and, when needed, 'providing a shoulder to cry on'.

Chairpersons were described most favourably by heads when they were supportive in personal terms and sympathetically critical in institutional terms, and heads welcomed the opportunity to discuss problems openly and frankly with someone involved, but at the same time detached. Heads were also grateful for their advice and insights into the local community. This can be a problem for any head settling into a new area and the chairperson can keep heads informed of local nuances and customs as well as introducing them to individuals within the community.

Kogan *et al.* (1984) remarked that governing bodies benefited from having a chairperson who was also a member of the education committee. The heads in the NFER study were particularly pleased when the chairperson, or other governors, were local councillors or members of the education committee. Those without such representation were trying hard to change this. ('It's important that the school has a voice in County Hall.' 'We could do with a bit of "clout" on the education committee.') However, having a governor on the local council was not necessarily beneficial. One case study head said that the councillor on the governing body was, unfortunately, the only governor who had never come to a meeting.

Another case study head used his governors' report to provide a detailed description of the idea of bringing the community into the school. The chairperson explained that the governors were very happy with the new head's idea, and about ten individuals, representing the governors, the police, the social services and Justices of the Peace had, on a weekly basis throughout the term, come into the school and taken a small group of less able pupils. The chairperson thought this was a 'tremendous idea' and it had made all those involved much more aware of the difficulties of teaching. He added that even after one period he went home quite exhausted!

Other heads also thought it necessary to make the school much more of a community resource and focal point by, for example, involving adults and using the school and its facilities after normal school hours. There was a general recognition by many of the significance of relations with the local environment. Although Table 10.1 shows that for the majority of both groups of heads, dealing with the local community was not seen as a major problem, further analysis showed that this was more problematic for the heads of larger schools.

The heads who stressed the importance of school–community links had willingly taken up invitations to join local groups, attended community meetings and served on local committees. The school was seen as belonging to the community and the need for it to become a focal point was all the greater, it was suggested, in areas characterized by parochialism and insularity or where catchment areas constituted a set of disparate villages. However, although community aspects of schooling were seen by some as key issues for the 1980s, the comment was made by a case study head that it was an area heads were poorly prepared for and there was a need for more training.

Although the interviews with the 47 heads took place soon after their appointment, it was interesting to note that a quarter made reference to initiatives being made on the community front. Most of these heads, however, saw these community developments as taking place over a period of time, as something they were gradually working towards. One case study head explained, at the time of the researcher's third visit, that the school had already embarked upon a number of initiatives. The Parent-Teacher Association (PTA) had sponsored an educational forum and an exponent of community education (the new head's previous head) had addressed the staff. The deputies had held meetings with the local community social worker's network group (linking a number of agencies) and it was decided to set up a youth and community centre at the school. Also, on the community front, there were Gujerati classes at the school and many other meetings were being held. The school had held two very successful computer evenings and, in general, the new head was very excited by the fact that these community initiatives 'were really taking off'.

Another case study head strongly believed in the community ethos and wanted the school to move in that direction. A working party had been set up following a residential INSET weekend and several papers and other information had been submitted to the authority. However, over a year later, a decision had still to be made by the LEA as to whether or not the school would be designated a community school and thus eligible for additional resources.

The majority of new heads were conscious of the need for good public relations and were particularly concerned to promote the school's image. As can be seen from Table 10.1, 'creating a better public image of the school' was a 'very serious' or 'serious' problem for over 40 per cent of both groups of heads surveyed. For only one in seven heads was this 'not a problem'. New heads were particularly aware of the necessity to promote their school, partly in order to attract more pupils, but also to present the school in the most favourable way possible.

A variety of means were used to promote the school's image and included, for example: developing relations with parents and parent groups; improving the quantity and quality of school literature (e.g. brochures); heads making 'public' appearances; introducing school uniform; better liaison with feeder primary schools and establishing links with the news media. For some heads, positive moves had been made in the public relations sphere, not only to improve the school's image, but also as a means of raising staff morale (see Chapter 6). Analysis of the survey data found there was a statistically significant relationship between a school's catchment area and whether creating a better school image was a problem. Heads of schools located in predominantly urban areas were more likely to perceive 'creating a better public image of the school' to be a serious problem.

Table 10.1 shows that 'dealing with the media' was rarely a 'very serious' or 'serious' problem, although further analysis showed that this was more of a problem for the heads of larger schools. Several heads interviewed remarked on how the school had had a number of bad experiences with the local press or how their predecessors had eschewed all forms of publicity. It was intended to change this and some were already sending news items to the local press. Two case study heads were in the fortunate position of having an editor's child in the sixth form, while another had planned to invite the local editor for lunch. Several new heads commented that they had asked teachers to act as press secretaries or liaison officers to develop and improve relations with the local media. It was felt important to promote the good things about the school and where possible obtain favourable publicity.

Obtaining favourable publicity was not always easy and several heads remarked upon the size of the task ahead ('my biggest problem has been to convice local parents that the school is not a glue-sniffing haven for delinquent rowdies'; 'Estate agents grimace when the school's name is mentioned!' It was commented that sensational stories concentrating on the school's problems made for better copy and there was a noticeable lack of interest in the good things about schools. ('It is much more difficult to get good academic and sporting success published than a good scandal!') It was also noted that one front page article showing the school in a bad light could do a great deal of damage to a school's reputation and take a considerable time to rectify.

A case study head remarked that he was trying to establish a relationship with the local press; relations between the press and his predecessor had broken down because a local newspaper had behaved irresponsibly over a certain matter. It came close to libel, so the previous head simply cut off relations. The new head thought it very important 'to get the local papers on the side of the school' and at the time of the second visit he explained that relations were much better, although they had experienced some difficulty over an unsubstantiated accusation about playground violence. The head had written a reply but said, 'with the local press you have to take the good with the bad and they will get it wrong now and again but, on the whole, it tends to balance out'.

Parents were not interviewed as part of the research project, but it was clear the majority of heads were concerned to improve relations with parents and to keep them fully informed of events taking place in the school. In some instances, PTAs were formed or revived and the heads were keen to attend all meetings of parents and keep them fully involved. It was thought to be important for heads to take the initiative for, as a case study head remarked, 'You cannot expect parents to come to you'. Communications with parents were improved with the introduction of, for example, weekly news bulletins, half-termly newsletters, parent evenings, school brochures and booklets on option choice. (It was noticeable that many heads also spoke of improving the quality of published materials.)

Several heads remarked that their predecessors did not want parents involved in the school, whereas virtually all the heads involved in the NFER study did and found parents and PTAs a very important source of support (see Appendix 2).

Summary and discussion

Clearly, the head occupies a crucial position as mediator between the school and the wider community. For the majority of heads, however, the management of external relations was not perceived to be problematic. The one area where it was most likely to be seen as a problem was the need to promote a better public image of the school. Heads seemed to be aware of the importance of public relations, in part brought about by falling rolls and parental choice, but also due to the desire for the school to be seen in a positive light. For many new heads, a high priority was therefore given to public relations and the importance of 'selling the school' was stressed.

Developing good working relations with governors was not a problem for the majority of heads, although some were slightly disappointed that they did not receive the level of governor involvement that they had hoped for initially. Governors, especially chairpersons of governors, were however seen as a very significant source of support and an important means of reducing feelings of professional isolation. It was also noted that the head's attitude was an important factor in the way governing bodies operated in practice. Finally, other research has commented on the ambiguity of the present role of governing bodies and it will be interesting to see how this develops under the provisions of the 1980 Education Act together with those proposed in the 1986 Education Bill.

CHAPTER 11
Headship Styles

Although various aspects of the head's role have been discussed in earlier chapters, particular attention is now given to the head's leadership style. After a short review which indicates how difficult and elusive this topic has proved, NFER data are used to examine leadership style and the issues of communication, consultation and decision-making by comparing the views of heads and teachers. Later sections deal with internal promotion to headship and possible differences between male and female heads.

The concept of leadership style has been given a great deal of attention in social psychology and has attracted interest for its relevance to business management. Recently, its application to education as a way of examining the behaviour of heads and principals has also been attempted. Yukl (1982) provides a detailed review of most of the major theories of leadership and usefully points out their strengths and weaknesses. Mazzarella (1981) looks at a smaller number of theories but carefully considers their practical relevance for heads and principals, and the following section draws heavily on her review.

The theorists differ in their definitions of what constitutes leadership style, but Sergiovanni and Elliot (1975) provide a useful general statement of style as, 'the ways in which the principal expresses leadership, uses power and authority, arrives at decisions and in general interacts with teachers and others'. This definition contains most of the elements of leadership style used in this chapter to describe the heads in the NFER research.

Views on leadership have changed during the last 50 years or so. The early research assumed that 'leaders are born, not made' and attempted to find the personality traits of good leaders. But as the list of factors grew too large to make sense of, attention was switched to leadership behaviour and the concept of style was developed. The search for the most effective behaviour often compared 'autocratic', 'democratic' and *laissez faire* leaders. While much of the research seemed to indicate that democratic styles of leadership were the most effective, a new perspective emerged, suggesting that the particular situation was the main determinant and that different styles were needed for different situations. The new studies argued that effective leadership resulted from an interaction of style and inherent personality traits and thus leadership ability was partly learned and partly inborn.

Mazzarella points out that although most authors agree that style is an important component of leadership and something each individual needs to be aware of to improve their performance, there is agreement on very little else. There is no consensus about the major elements of leadership style: whether it ought to vary according to the situation, whether it is flexible at all and whether personality traits have any effect on style.

A number of studies have found that leaders could be seen as either giving more importance and attention to the task or to the relationships of people in the group. Fiedler (1967), a major worker in the field of leadership, termed these 'task-orientation' and 'relationship orientation' and saw them as each end of a continuum. His 'contingency theory' suggests that people tend to be one or the other, but both orientations can be effective, depending on the situation. Gates, Blanchard and Hersey (1976) believe the style a leader chooses should depend on the 'maturity of the followers' which involves:

the followers' capacity to set high but attainable goals;
their willingness and ability to take responsibility;
their education and experience.

As follower maturity can change over time, the authors believe the appropriate leader behaviour should also change. When followers are low in maturity they need leaders who are heavily task-orientated. As maturity increases, leaders can move their emphasis from 'tasks' to 'relationships'. While this theory is useful and has training implications for heads and principals, care is needed in assuming that any one factor, such as 'maturity of followers' can adequately explain leadership style.

Some authors, such as Fiedler, maintain that style is very difficult to change, but Hersey and Blanchard (1969) insist 'successful leaders can adapt their leader behaviour to meet the needs of the group'. They saw four possible combinations of task and relationship-orientated behaviours each of which could be effective: 1) Task only; 2) Relations only; 3) Task and Relations; 4) Neither. Some leaders, they believed, were able to modify their behaviour to fit any of the four styles, while others could only utilize two or three styles; for example some were more flexible than others and were likely to be more effective in jobs that required considerable adaptability. As followers became more mature and able to operate on their own, successful leaders would be able to change their style while unsuccessful ones could not. Reddin (1970) had a similar theory and thought that the best leaders have three important abilities: 'situational sensitivity', which enables them to diagnose situations; 'style flexibility', which allows them to match their styles to the situation; and 'situational management skill', which helps them to change the situation to fit their styles.

Mazzarella concludes her review by saying it is not yet possible to produce an overall theory of leadership and the data are not clear on whether leaders can change styles or what the most important components of style should be.

She produces a comparison chart showing each of the theories' similarities and differences and provides a synthesis as a guide 'to becoming a better leader'.

Where researchers have examined heads' or principals' leadership styles, most studies have found considerable variety and flexibility. For example, although Rutter *et al.* (1979) did not look in detail at the heads of their 12 case study schools in London, their informal observations indicated that 'no one style was associated with better outcomes. Indeed, it was noticeable that the heads of the more successful school took widely differing approaches.' Manasse (1985), in a review of principal effectiveness, concluded, 'There are no conclusive data on leadership style. All of the studies have found a wide range in personal style among effective principals.' This is exemplified by Dwyer *et al.* (1983) who in their study of '5 Principals in Action' developed the idea of the 'mode' (style of approach) principals take as they lead their schools. They found the mode was closely associated with characteristics of the principals and was 'highly personalistic and varied', spanning the continuum of strategies from direct, authoritarian styles to indirect and catalytic. The principals were 'able and willing to change modes, to step outside their usual frameworks of behaviour, when specific situations indicated the need for change'. The most unobtrusive, indirect, democratic principal in the study proved very capable of decisive, autocratic behaviour in certain circumstances, indicating that personal and situational factors affected the principal's behaviour. While some of the literature suggests that changing the predominant style or mode may have a deleterious effect on the setting, Dwyer *et al.* found no instances where this had occurred and they speculate that 'successful principals may have a greater range of modes – a larger bag of tricks'.

In the NFER study, one of the case study heads made a similar point about the flexibility of style:

> As a head, you have to learn to be very adaptable. You must be capable of adapting your style to suit the situation and the needs of the school. You have to manage the situation that you find yourself in. For example, within the school there are people who want to lead and those who want to be led. So, when you know your staff, you know what you can do.

Another example is provided by Trethowan (1984) who looked back over a ten-year period to when he became head of a secondary modern school which was about to become comprehensive. At the beginning he had used a strong 'dictatorial style' to introduce change, but argued that:

> There is no single right or wrong style of leadership. The problem for the leader is to make an accurate diagnosis and then select an appropriate style. If the new management training movement does nothing but help heads choose the appropriate style for each situation, it will have a long-lasting, powerful and beneficial effect upon our schools.

Communication and consultation

In the NFER study, both groups of new and 'old' heads were asked to assess the kinds of difficulties they faced during their early years. The complete chart is shown in Appendix 1 and while parts have already been referred to in various chapters, Table 11.1 shows a number of factors which relate to the way the heads carried out their role.

To simplify the presentation, the original five-point scale of difficulties has been collapsed to a three-point scale indicating 'very serious' or 'serious', 'moderate' or 'minor' difficulties and 'not a problem'. The similarities between the 'old' and new heads' perceptions is marked and no statistical differences were found for any of the items shown. The table indicates that the most frequently rated serious difficulties were those associated with consultation, communication and the practice and style of the previous head. 39 to 50 per cent of each group of heads saw these as being 'very serious' or 'serious' problems. For the cohort of new heads, problems of communication were perceived as more serious in larger schools.

As shown in Chapter 7, one of the first changes many new heads made was to introduce a calendar of regular meetings at various levels. Information obtained from the interviews with the 47 new heads showed that in almost every school the senior management team met for several hours once a week, in addition to their daily informal meetings. The pattern for other types of meetings was not so clear, and the arrangements varied across the 47 schools. It was most common to have monthly meetings for the heads of department or curriculum committee, and the heads of year/house or pastoral committee. But there was considerable variety with some meeting every two weeks, three weeks or half-termly. A meeting of the whole staff most commonly occurred every half term, but other patterns were monthly or termly meetings and five of the 47 schools only held staff meetings 'as required'.

The new heads usually produced the agenda and chaired the senior management team meetings and the full staff meetings. In some schools, the new heads chaired the heads of department and heads of year/house meetings, but it was more common for the curriculum and pastoral deputies to take on this role. Several heads said the full staff meetings were not a decision-making forum and that discussion was difficult with a large number of staff. The meetings enabled information to be given out and acted as a sounding board to gauge staff feelings.

To improve communication, many heads had introduced daily or weekly briefing sessions when they spoke to the staff for about ten minutes and provided information on current and forthcoming events. In most schools, consultation occurred through the regular meetings of heads of department and heads of year/house. While some decision-making occurred at these meetings, most of the major decisions were finally made by the senior management team.

Working parties were used in almost all the case study schools to encourage staff participation. In the main, the new heads did not chair these groups, as

Table 11.1 Difficulties facing the new head in the first two years of headship

	New Heads			'Old' Heads		
	Very serious or serious	Moderate or minor	Not a problem	Very serious or serious	Moderate or minor	Not a problem
	%	%	%	%	%	%
Establishing/improving consultation procedures within the school	45	46	9	50	44	6
Establishing/improving channels of information within the school	39	52	9	46	50	4
Difficulties caused by the practices and style of the previous head	45	40	15	44	41	15
Coping with a wide range of tasks	29	51	20	24	52	24
Establishing your priorities	21	54	25	27	51	22
Dealing with a large number of decisions	20	61	19	21	58	21
Obtaining information about curricular areas other than your own	13	68	19	11	70	19
Finding out about the daily routine of the school	8	55	37	5	50	45
	N = 188			N = 228		

Chi-square on 3-point scale and original 5-point scale (Appendix 1) not significant between the two groups.

they felt their presence inhibited some of the more junior members of staff. The heads monitored the progress of the groups through the written minutes, by informal talks with the chairperson, or by occasionally sitting in on working party meetings. A few of the new heads had introduced a staff forum once or twice a term to encourage the discussion of a major educational topic. However, the industrial action meant these had had little chance to establish themselves during the period of the research.

The previous head

As shown in Table 11.1, considerable numbers of both the new and 'old' heads felt that the practice and style of their predecessor had caused serious difficulties during their early years of headship. Clearly, 'stepping into someone else's shoes' can often be a problem and Gordon and Rosen's (1981) review of the leader succession literature from a variety of fields concludes that, 'the personality and style of a predecessor can create lasting effects making change by a successor difficult to achieve'. They believe it is necessary to consider whether, 'the former leader is a hero to be lived up to, or a bad act which is easy to follow? ... The popular predecessor who was all things to all people can make any successor's job extremely difficult.' The NFER study suggests that this is not always the case. In one of the schools, the new head took over from a very popular predecessor but was well received by the staff, who spoke highly of him in their interviews.

Gordon and Rosen provide evidence that the frequency of succession is an important factor: 'Too many managerial replacements in too brief a period can be disruptive.' This seems to be borne out by an analysis of the 16 case studies, which showed that two of the schools had four previous heads in the last 10–15 years, three had two previous heads and 11 had only one change. Staff in the first two schools were unhappy with the large number of changes and were clearly unsettled.

The lasting effect of the previous head was described by one of the case study heads, who said: 'One of the biggest problems for a new head is not what you do or do not do, but rather something which is out of your hands, namely what sort of relationship existed between your predecessor and the staff. It's annoying because there is nothing that you can do about it.' Another of the heads had attempted to discover as much as possible about the way the previous head worked and then to introduce changes carefully to enable a gradual transition between his style and that of his predecessor.

To obtain perceptions of style, the cohort of new heads were asked in their questionnaire, 'From what you know and have heard of the previous head, how would you say your style compares with that of your predecessor?' The replies showed considerable consistency with the new heads believing themselves to be more consultative and involving more staff in decision-making. They thought they delegated more to their senior management team; were more accessible and open to other people's ideas; used a more personal approach to both staff and pupils and established closer links with the LEA and the community.

The next section uses interview data from heads to explore further their views on style, while the following section provides details from the teachers' perception as a comparison.

Style of headship

During the interviews with the 47 new heads, they were asked to describe how they operated as a head. The most common response was to say they operated an 'open door' policy for staff, pupils and parents. They literally tried to keep their office door open most of the time. One head contrasted his open approach to that of his predecessor by saying that when he arrived he was horrified to find there was no bulb in the 'enter' sign outside his office! This produced a fantasy of an endless queue of people waiting hopelessly outside the head's door. The majority of heads talked about getting around the school as much as possible and not being 'office-bound'. They felt it was important to be seen in the corridors at break-time, to observe lessons and take assemblies. Some did most of their office work after school in order to be free in the day to go round the school and be available for staff, pupils and parents.

Another theme mentioned by most heads was the need to spend a lot of time listening to the staff and getting to know their interests and problems. It was important to talk to groups and individuals and listen to their points of view. The stress throughout was on face to face relationships and some heads refused to accept memos from staff, saying that they preferred teachers to come and see them.

Almost all the heads wanted a participatory style of management and said they tried to involve as many staff as possible in consultation. But they recognized that a truly democratic approach was not feasible and many had made it clear that while they would discuss and listen to the staff's views, they retained the right to make the final decisions as 'the buck stops here'. One of the heads explained how he had genuinely tried to involve staff in making a democratic decision about the allocation of an extra scale point which could be given to one teacher in school.

I told the staff that I had a spare point and I suggested that they submit suggestions to me as to which area of responsibility it should go to. This would go through the participatory machinery and then be decided at a staff meeting. Fourteen suggestions were tabled and at the heads of department/ principal subject teacher committee (half the 43 staff were present) somebody said, 'I move that this matter be left to the head'. The matter was seconded and carried. My deputy head, however, amended this so that it was left to the senior staff to decide what to do with it. We spent two long hours on the matter and in the end it went to computer studies.

This seemed to be a clear case of the staff saying 'You get paid to make this kind of decision, why ask us to do it?'

A small number of the 47 heads described themselves with phrases such as: 'a cunning, jovial dictator', 'a benevolent despot' and 'a bit Machiavellian'. Others stressed honesty and integrity and most felt it was very important to 'lead from the front' and to be 'prepared to take your coat off and get on with it'. Heads needed to have a 'bird's eye' view of the school and also be seen to be involved, sympathetic and supportive.

The amount of informality and degree of distance varied among the 47 heads. Some wanted to be called by their first name and liked to spend their coffee breaks in the staffroom, talking informally. Others wanted to preserve a social distance from the staff and rarely went into the staffroom. Which of these alternatives they stressed seemed to be largely determined by the personality of the individual, but the 'right' amount of distance from the staff was of concern to most of the new heads.

A good working relationship with the senior management team was mentioned by a number of heads, but the amount of delegation varied. As discussed in Chapter 3, while some heads found it relatively easy to delegate tasks, others wanted to be involved in almost everything.

The case study heads were asked during the second visit if they felt their style had changed over the first year. Two of the 16 spoke of a definite change in their approach. The head who had used a very autocratic approach to introduce rapid change (see Chapter 7 for details) now felt he could 'relax the hard leadership line and move step by step'. Another head said he had become more Machiavellian and scheming because he felt his ideas were being blocked by the senior management team and some of the middle managers. Three of the heads said they had become harder and tougher over the year. They found they had to tell some teachers off and learn to say 'no' to staff. On occasions they had to be more authoritarian and directive than they had been originally and sometimes say, 'I am sorry, but this will happen'. The rest said their style had not really changed over the year and they now felt more relaxed and confident. In reply to a separate question, most of the case study heads did not believe there was a significant difference between how they would like to operate and how they, in fact, worked. A difference arose for four of the heads who found they were not able to be as open and democratic as they had wanted to be because of the staff they had inherited.

An issue explored with each of the 47 new heads was the amount of teaching they did and the reasons they felt this was important or not. Only 11 heads did not have a regular teaching commitment during their first year. The reason commonly given for not teaching was that they wanted to settle in and be as available as possible. Most of the 11 said they would take on a regular commitment in their second or third year. The amount of regular teaching undertaken by the rest of the 47 heads averaged 20 per cent or eight periods in a 40-period week, but varied from a minimum of two to a maximum of 12 periods. All the heads, including the 11 without a regular teaching commitment, were on the 'cover' list and taught when staff were absent. Most heads said it was essential to teach and provided a number of reasons to support their argument. For some, part of the heads' credibility was related to their performance in the classroom. This meant leading from the front and working with difficult and disruptive classes to show staff they were prepared to take their share of the teaching load. A regular teaching commitment allowed the head to stay in touch with 'the pulse of the classroom' and to be aware of teachers' problems as well as maintaining contact with reports, homework and marking. Many of the heads said it was important for the pupils to know them as teachers and not just as the headteacher, and it also helped them in getting to know the children. An additional reason was simply that most of the heads really enjoyed teaching.

Despite these reasons, many heads saw a problem in taking on a regular commitment and pointed out that it could be detrimental to the pupils, as they often had to attend meetings instead of being in the classroom. 'There is a dilemma for heads – it's good to teach to keep your feet on the ground and for staff to see you teach, but LEA officers expect you to be available and it's bad for the pupils if you are out for too many meetings.' Another head said, 'I used to feel it was important for a head to have a regular teaching commitment, but now I am not sure. I enjoy it, but perhaps this is self indulgent and the time could be better spent. By doing cover you have contact with many more children and can get to grips with the more difficult ones.'

It was evident that all the new heads were working extremely hard and putting in long hours both at the school and at home. All the case study heads arrived well before school started and stayed long after it finished. However, it seemed that some heads dealt with rather general administrative matters, which with adequate secretarial help, or better still a bursar, could have been delegated. An example of such a matter occurred during the researcher's visit to one of the case study schools when the head received a telephone call about using the school's playing fields for a charity football match on Sunday. This took up a considerable amount of time, as the head had to negotiate the matter with the caretaker. On the same day the head spent further time in completing LEA forms about the amount of electricity consumed by the school. Most of the case study heads found themselves involved in similar routine administrative matters. (The need for school bursars has been mentioned in Chapter 9.)

During the second and third visits, each of the case study heads was asked if they felt the job was getting easier or more difficult. Almost all said it was getting easier, although factors such as falling rolls, low teacher morale and financial restraints counteracted this to some extent. After a year in post, the heads were becoming more confident as they had been through the whole cycle once. It took time to get to know the teachers and for the staff to get to know the new head. Generally, this meant relationships became easier, but it also meant heads became aware of teachers' limitations and vice versa. For a few of the heads, matters had become easier with the appointment of a new deputy, releasing the heads from some tasks they had previously undertaken. The heads became more relaxed with time and the pace was less hectic. One head after a year in post said, 'Last week was the first time that I was able to say "what shall I do first?" Before this, there was no question of choice!' For most heads the volume of work remained high, but they became more confident and were beginning to delegate and pace themselves better towards the end of their second year.

Teachers' views

During each of the case study interviews, teachers were asked for their views on communication, consultation and decision-making in the schools. In most cases it proved difficult to find a clear consensus, but in two schools the majority of teachers who were interviewed expressed strongly negative reactions. Details from one of these schools has already been provided in Chapter 7, which showed how the head forced his ideas through with apparently little regard for the views of the staff. Teachers at the school felt there was a lack of communication and very little consultation. Having set up working parties, the head ignored their recommendations and so the staff believed they had no role in decision-making. In the second school, the situation differed in that little change had actually been implemented. Most of the teachers, nevertheless, were equally unhappy with the lack of consultation about changes planned for the following year. For example, they had been told that option blocking was being trialled during the present year and there would be an opportunity to discuss the matter. About half a dozen heads of department had seen the deputy head (curriculum) individually to complain and each had been told they were 'the only one opposed to the idea'. One teacher had canvassed the opinion of about half the staff and found a 50:50 split for and against subject blocking. The staff felt their views were being ignored and they were incensed when they found out that next year's timetable had already been constructed with subject blocking before it could be discussed at a heads of department meeting. In this case, some of the resentment was directed towards the deputy head, although the head was blamed for being weak and indecisive. All the staff interviewed at this school said how poor the head was at communication – 'He just talks us to death with his excessive verbiage'.

In the other 14 case study schools, the questions on consultation, communication and decision-making produced mixed responses from the staff. Many teachers believed decisions had already been made, even though the heads said they wanted to consult the staff. In several schools the heads of department felt they played a minor role. The heads of department meetings were seen as talk shops, which simply 'rubber stamped' the senior management team's decisions. In only one school was there general agreement that there was a free exchange of ideas at the head of department meetings and that major policy decisions were genuinely discussed.

The views of scale 1 and 2 teachers varied across the schools and seemed to depend on whether they thought their head of department or year adequately expressed their opinions at middle management meetings. But many other factors were involved: for example, whether regular departmental or year meetings were held and whether individual teachers wanted to express their views at all.

In those schools where the new heads had introduced a weekly or daily staff briefing, the majority of teachers welcomed this as a good means of giving information. Most of the teachers interviewed thought full staff meetings were necessary to allow people to express their views but a number of common criticisms appeared across the 16 schools. The large number of staff present was recognized as an inhibiting factor which meant that most people were reluctant to speak. Teachers felt that much of the time was often taken up with 'trivia' and a lot of the information could have been provided in written form. Staff objected when heads 'lectured' them and in one school 'mouths dropped open' when the head launched into a tirade because some departments were late with their curricular reviews. They felt the head should have seen the individuals concerned and not blamed everyone in such a wholesale manner. Meetings were often too long or over-ran and in one school, during the industrial action, a union official decided to make his point most strongly. During a staff meeting he had set an alarm clock to ring in his bag and at the prearranged time all the union members walked out. Some of the staff meetings were described as 'noisy affairs' and many teachers found them boring and non-productive, as they believed decisions had already been made. However, despite this, most teachers thought they were useful in helping to clear the air. Scale 1 and 2 teachers, in particular, were concerned when the number of staff meetings was reduced although, paradoxically, many teachers complained that since the new head's arrival there were too many meetings of one form or another. The interview material confirmed how difficult it was for heads to 'please most of the people, most of the time'. While two heads were criticized for their lack of consultation, others seemed to err by too much discussion. One head of year illustrated this by saying, 'School reports came up at the pastoral meeting, then at the heads of department meeting, then it was discussed by the management team and then at the full staff meeting. I thought, oh my goodness, not again! So I switched off and thought about my shopping list.'

In addition to questions about consultation and communication, teachers were asked how open they thought the head was to other people's opinions and to compare the style of the new head with that of the previous head. Table 11.2 summarizes their views in the form of the desirable and undesirable characteristics of headship style.

Most of the teachers did not think the heads were very open to other people's ideas and opinions. Only one of the 16 heads was perceived as genuinely open and two were believed to either ignore or not listen to the staff at all. The other heads were seen as open and willing to listen but unlikely to change their minds on key issues. Teachers generally felt the heads knew what they wanted, were quite determined or even stubborn, and were only prepared to modify their views slightly. Most teachers wanted heads to be consultative

Table 11.2   Teachers' views on style of headship

Desirable	Undesirable
Leads from the front or by example	Low profile, unobtrusive
Firm and fair	Favours certain individuals, groups and/or departments; evasive
'Makes haste slowly'	Impatient
Good organizational and admin. qualities	Bureaucratic (e.g. over-reliance on paper, memos, etc.)
Systematic	'Spins too many plates' i.e. should focus on one thing at a time
	Operates according to rule-book
Operates informally	Too formal a style
A 'relaxed' style, easy-going	Too informal a style (especially to pupils)
Prepared to get involved	Gets bogged down in trivia
Accessible, approachable	Too approachable
Good manager of people	Poor interpersonal skills
Gives credit, full of praise	Little contact with rank and file teachers
Gets out of office	
Good at PR	Poor speaker; shuns PR
Timetabling skills	
Teaches	Does not teach or visit classrooms
Prepared to teach any group	
Supports staff	Supports parents and pupils before staff
Not reluctant to discipline staff or pupils	Too soft, reluctant to discipline staff or pupils
Stands up to LEA	
Listens and accepts advice	Ignores advice
	Only 'get on' if concur with head's views
Encourages participatory approach	
Gives teachers a role in decision-making	Working party recommendations ignored
Open and consultative, encourages discussion	Too much consultation
	Not open, fixed views
Meetings finish on time	Meetings over-run
Keeps staff informed	Poor communicator, forgets to pass on information
Decisive and makes own decisions	Indecisive, slow decision-making
	Easily swayed
Delegates	Finds delegation difficult
	Delegates too much

and listen to the views of staff, but then make a clear decision. They disliked indecisiveness and slow decision-making, which often placed new heads in the difficult position of having to make decisions without having all the necessary information. One head was specifically criticized for too many 'get backs', as he frequently said, 'I'll get back to you on that'. If time was required for heads to make a decision, it was very important not to forget to 'get back' to the teachers concerned.

Teachers welcomed the 'open door' approach adopted by most of the heads but, in one case, staff found it very difficult to see the head because of the constant queue of pupils waiting outside his door. From the first week the head made it clear that pupils could go directly to him and they did so. Several teachers thought this had 'backfired' because many pupils saw him as an 'easy touch' and he had lost their respect.

Most staff liked the heads to be seen around the school in the corridors and the playgrounds. They also wanted heads to visit more classrooms, something which many had done at the beginning but found little time to do later. Teachers appreciated heads who taught, especially if they were prepared to take some of the more difficult classes, but disliked those heads who frequently missed lessons because of meetings.

The degree of informality and the correct distance of the head from the staff and the pupils was something that teachers did not agree on. Most seemed to welcome an informal, relaxed style with the staff but felt that a certain distance was required with the pupils to maintain their respect. The majority of teachers who were interviewed, liked the head to come into the staffroom and to join in various social events. However, the correct balance was difficult and a few heads were criticized for being 'too chatty and matey and trying to be one of us', while in another school a teacher complained that the head was not prepared to join the cricket team or accompany the staff for a drink. They had tried to be polite and sociable but, much to their annoyance, they had been spurned.

All the new heads were seen as very hard working, but this in itself was not enough; teachers wanted clear leadership and while many of the heads were able to provide this, in some schools the staff were not impressed. 'He is pleasant and never makes waves, he works hard, but I don't feel there is anything that 5000 other people couldn't do – there is no dynamism.' In another school a teacher said, 'The head should be on the bridge as captain of the ship. But where is our head? Down in the stores, trying to sort things out!'

Information about the previous heads of the 16 case study schools was obtained from the interviews with each teacher. As shown in Chapter 1, only three of the previous heads had moved on to another school and 13 had retired (five of these due to ill health). An analysis of the teachers' views and opinions of the previous heads suggested that overall, four were seen positively, four negatively and views were mixed in the remaining eight schools. In nine of the 13 schools where the heads had come to the end of their careers, teachers felt the previous head was 'winding down and coasting to retirement'. These heads, according to the teachers who were interviewed, had become rather *laissez faire* and were letting things slide.

Most of the new heads' predecessors had delegated a considerable amount to the senior staff and only four of the previous heads were seen as autocratic in their decision-making and failing to consult staff on major issues. With regard to decision-making, five of the previous heads were specifically referred to as 'indecisive' and only two of the 16 were seen to make firm decisions. Just under half the heads were seen as 'not wanting to rock the boat' and tending to compromise or 'sit on the fence'.

The pen-portraits from the teachers suggested that many of the heads conformed to the rather stereotyped image of the traditional headmaster. The seven ex-grammar school heads were all seen in this way, often wearing gowns and adopting a very formal approach. Half the heads, some ex-grammar school and some ex-secondary modern, were described as 'the perfect gentleman'. A negative point made against seven of the previous heads was their general patronizing and paternalistic attitude to the staff, particularly the women and more junior teachers.

Five of the heads were felt to be very poor at public relations, shunning publicity and having little to do with the community.

Only one of the heads was described as 'extrovert, dynamic and charismatic' and this was a man who moved to his second headship after seven years at the school. Teachers at his school spoke highly of him; he was very popular and well liked and when he left 'a dozen or so staff literally cried'. A senior member of staff at the school felt there were three types of head, 'Those who like to be at the middle of the circle, like our previous head; those at the top of a pyramid; and the mushroom types, who keep you in the dark and hurl manure at you'.

Teachers in ten of the 16 schools were particularly concerned with the ability of the previous heads to cope with comprehensivization. These heads had never worked in comprehensive schools and seemed to find the change from a small grammar or secondary modern school to a larger institution, with a wider student ability range, a very difficult transition to make.

The appearance and personal characteristics of the previous heads were mentioned by a number of teachers and clearly influenced their perceptions. 'He didn't look like the head and people thought he was the school doctor or caretaker.' 'He was a very lonely man and almost grateful if he was drawn into a joke. We were unfair to him in many ways. He was odd to look at and had some quirky ideas, for example, he was a nudist and lots of stories went round about him.'

In a few schools, teachers provided totally contradictory views on the previous head and clearly showed differing perceptions. Thus, in one school a teacher said, 'He was a lovely man and very approachable', while another said, 'He was an isolated man, not highly thought of by the staff'. The same head was also described as, 'more humane and concerned about staff than the new head', but another teacher said, 'the new head is more interested in you as a person than the previous head who drove a woman teacher to tears because she resigned on the last day possible'. Some of the contradictions can be explained by differences in teacher status as this particular head seemed to have little contact with the junior members of staff, who tended to express more negative attitudes compared to those of the senior staff.

In one of the case study schools, the situation seemed to be particularly difficult and all the teachers who were interviewed spoke badly of the previous head, who had left after three years for another headship in the authority. The staff believed he had been sent in by the LEA to close the school down and extremely vitriolic comments were made about him: 'He lied and bullied and didn't support the staff.' 'There was a total abuse of power. He left mid-term with no farewell ceremony, which I think says something.' At one period there were eight separate grievance procedures against him all going on at the same time. The staff were never behind him and could not trust him. Thus the new head arriving at this school inherited a very difficult situation and considerable mistrust, which took delicate handling and several years to reduce.

Internal promotion to headship

The number of heads who were internally promoted from being a deputy in the same school was quite small, and for the 1982/83 cohort of new heads the figure was only 10 per cent. It appeared that some LEAs had a policy of not appointing heads internally. Although the number of heads was small, a separate analysis was carried out to identify any possible differences between the internal and external appointments. No differences were found in the heads' perceptions of difficulties apart from the obvious ones that internally appointed heads had less of a problem 'finding out about the daily routine of the school' and 'obtaining information about the strengths and weaknesses of staff'. Of more interest was the fact that 'persuading members of staff to accept new ideas' was perceived as less of a problem to internal heads, but as shown in Chapter 7, they generally implemented fewer changes than the external heads. As a group, internal heads rated themselves as less well prepared for headship than the rest of the cohort. Although no significant difference was found on the degree of professional isolation, some internal heads said they found it more difficult to establish the right distance between themselves and the rest of the staff, especially the senior staff who were previously their peers. The advantages to be gained from appointing an internal candidate seemed to be quite small and were probably outweighed by the disadvantages. Certainly, if large-scale changes were needed at the school, then an external appointment seemed a better way of achieving them, a point confirmed by Hoy and Aho (1973) in the United States. In their review of the leadership succession research, Gordon and Rosen (1981) also point out that promotion from within is not always good for the organization and they cite some evidence which suggests that succession from outside produces better results. It is interesting to note that two of the case study heads felt it would *not* have been in their previous schools' best interest to have appointed them as heads because they felt, 'schools need new blood'. The early research by Bernbaum (1976) on heads in this country also found that being a member of the existing school staff was one of the factors which they would least like their successor to possess.

Male and female heads

There has been considerable interest, especially in the United States, in the different leadership styles and administrative behaviours of male and female heads. Most of the research has focused on primary and elementary schools and has suggested female principals are most likely than their male counterparts 'to involve themselves in instructional supervision, to exhibit democratic leadership style, to be concerned with students and to seek community involvement' (Adkinson, 1981). Cochran (1980) in a paper entitled 'When the Principal is a Woman', notes that

> multiple studies have indicated the following trends when female administrators are present:
> 1) Teacher morale in schools with women principals is either equal to or higher than in schools with male principals.
> 2) Women principals are more effective at resolving conflicts with staff members.
> 3) Teachers believe there is no difference in the leadership abilities of men and women principals.
> 4) Women principals emphasise and bring about a greater amount of productive behaviour on the part of their teachers.
> 5) Women principals speak and act more as representatives of the group.

Similarly, two recent reviews of the research literature have noted, 'The research does not appear to support the myth that women cannot succeed as educational leaders. Quite the contrary, they appear to equal or excel men in these roles on all significant dimensions' (Fauth, 1984) and 'women's performance in the administrative field is equal to or, in some cases better than that of their male counterparts' (Haven *et al.*, 1980).

Little research into gender differences in managerial behaviour has been conducted at the secondary school level. Why this is the case is not clear, although it is worth noting that despite the fact that women constitute nearly half the high school staff in the US, they make up only 1 per cent of high school principals (Cochran, 1980). A small-scale qualitative study of high school principals has been carried out by Berman (1982), who undertook interviews with five principals of each gender and observed them for four days each. An analysis of their performance, using Mintzberg categories, found there were no real differences in the task behaviours of male and female principals.

Although the NFER project was interested in examining styles of headship and leadership qualities, it was not the intention to focus deliberately on gender differences in managerial behaviour. Reference has already been made to the fact that female heads were relatively uncommon (see Chapter 2); only three of the 47 new heads interviewed were women (two of whom became case study heads) and only 66 of the 416 (16 per cent) new and 'old' heads involved in the surveys were female (nearly 60 per cent of whom were heads of girls' schools). An analysis of the survey data did show, however, that there were statistically significant differences between male and female heads on 'finding out about the daily routine of the school' and 'establishing/improving consultation procedures within the school'. The fact that female heads perceived these to be less of a problem could be explained, in part, because a higher proportion of women were promoted to headship from within their existing school.

Analysis of the interviews with the three female heads did not bring out any obvious differences in headship style or difficulties faced. It would seem that staff and school-based factors were more crucial variables than gender. One head said she was rather surprised the research had not focused more on gender-related difficulties, but when asked to describe the ways in which they were important or problematic, the head replied they were not! The only real problem of being a woman, she felt, had been with some traditional working-class parents who simply believed that a woman should not be in charge of a school. In the two case studies there were no obvious differences or difficulties resulting from having a female head and the range of teacher responses was very similar to that in the other schools.

Reference was made in Chapter 2 to the POST team's findings on the position of women candidates. They suggest that, in the selectors' eyes, appointing women involved a greater risk than appointing men and that a key factor in assessing suitability was being able to maintain discipline. One of the female heads involved in the NFER research remarked how she had been angered at the time of her interview when a member of the panel asked if having a woman as a head would have a deleterious effect on the school. (She also thought her anger had not done her chances of appointment any harm!) The NFER evidence, although based on a relatively small number of female heads, shows that there were *no* major differences between male and female heads. As such, it suggests that those responsible for appointing heads should not allow their decisions to be influenced by whether the candidates are women or men.

Summary and discussion

The cohort of new heads saw themselves as being more consultative and open to the views of staff than their predecessors and they felt their style of headship involved an 'open door' approach towards staff, pupils and parents. New heads tended to establish a pattern of regular meetings and a system of staff briefings to improve consultation and communication in the school, factors which seemed to be problematic for most heads. Although they wanted teachers to express their views and opinions, the heads retained the right to make final decisions.

The new heads wanted to 'lead from the front' and by example. Interviews with 47 heads showed that the majority had a regular teaching commitment which they felt was important in providing a 'leading professional' role for the staff. All the case study heads were working long hours before and after school, but there were indications that some of the time was taken up with administrative work, which with adequate secretarial support or a bursar, could have been delegated. Most of the heads in the 16 case studies said the job had become somewhat easier by the second year as they got to know the strengths and weaknesses of their staff and became more confident themselves. With time, they tended to delegate more to the senior staff and did not try to do everything themselves.

The surveys showed that only 10 per cent of new heads were promoted from within the school, and that only 16 per cent of all heads were women. Although the data were limited there were indications that internally promoted heads made fewer changes than externally appointed heads and found greater difficulty in establishing a degree of social distance with the staff. Research from the United States supports the idea that, given an equal choice between internal and external candidates, it is probably better to appoint the person from outside the school. Other American research, mainly from the elementary school, suggests that women 'equal or excel' as principals compared to men. The design of the NFER research and the limited numbers involved do not permit firm conclusions to be drawn, but it is worth pointing out that no major differences were found between male and female heads. This suggests that selectors should not consider that being a women is a hindrance for a head.

Staff at nine of the 13 case study schools where the previous head had retired, saw them as 'winding down' at the end of their career and tending to let things slide. About half of the 16 previous heads were believed to be men who compromised and did not want to 'rock the boat'. Most had delegated a great deal to their senior staff and only four were seen as very autocratic in their decision-making. In ten of the 16 schools, the staff felt the previous heads had experienced considerable difficulty in running a comprehensive school after being a grammar or secondary modern head. The picture produced from the interviews with staff portrayed most of the previous heads as the 'traditional headmaster' – rather paternalistic, 'a father figure' and a 'perfect gentleman'.

The teachers' views of the new heads often produced phrases such as 'chalk and cheese' when comparing them with the previous head and numerous differences were given. Table 11.2 summarizes teachers' views about aspects of headship style which they liked or disliked. Most staff welcomed the opportunity to be able to express their opinions, but felt that the major decisions had already been made by the new head and the senior management team. Only one of the 16 new heads was seen by most staff to be genuinely open, while two others were believed to totally ignore the staff's views. The rest were seen as willing to listen but unlikely to change their minds on important issues. Teachers wanted heads to consider their views and then make a clear and firm decision. Many of the teachers who were interviewed liked the new heads' informal, relaxed style with the staff but wanted them to retain a certain distance from the pupils. However, it was not possible to please all the teachers and a small number of the staff disliked the informal approach adopted by many of the case study heads towards them. This is clearly a complex matter and depends both on the personality of the head and that of each individual teacher. The project did not study heads' leadership style by observation but the interviews suggest, as does much of the previous research presented at the beginning of the chapter, that heads need to be flexible and adapt their styles to particular situations.

CHAPTER 12
Conclusions and Recommendations

This final chapter attempts to draw together the main points of the research and provide a set of recommendations in the form of statements. The necessity of putting these in the form of short sentences means that some may appear to be common sense and rather obvious. For the reader who wishes to see the detailed research base underlying the recommendations, the relevant chapter is indicated by the number at the end of each statement in the box. Some of the main findings and implications of the research are given in the text which follows each set of recommendations. The recommendations focus on four main groups: deputies who wish to become heads; various INSET providers; new and experienced heads; and local education authorities.

EFFORTS TO IMPROVE PREPARATION FOR HEADSHIP SHOULD BE CONCENTRATED ON ASPIRING DEPUTY HEADS

* Heads need to play a more important part in preparing deputies for headship. (3)

* Heads should rotate deputies' job responsibilities. (3)

* Deputies need to spend more time standing in for the head. (3)

* Deputies should attend governors' meetings. (3, 10)

* Deputies should have greater opportunities to attend substantial management courses. (3)

* Visits, exchanges and secondments to industry and other schools are important for deputies. (3)

Most heads in the research felt that preparation for headship required both a variety of school experience and attendance at a number of management courses. Although various skills and knowledge were acquired at each stage of the path to headship, there was general agreement that the most important learning period was as a deputy head. However, the research showed that most heads did not deliberately prepare people for headship. The quality of preparation could be considerably improved if heads consciously undertook a staff development role for their deputies. This could include the rotation of job responsibilities about every two or three years to ensure that deputies encountered all aspects of school management. New heads who felt well prepared often spoke about their breadth of experience as deputies.

The move from deputy to head was felt to be a very large step and the initial experience of being a head was problematic for most people. Obviously, it is difficult to prepare for this, as it has to be experienced first hand, but a period as acting head or deputizing in the head's absence can provide an element of 'sitting in the hot seat'. Only one-third of the new heads had stood in for their previous heads for a continuous period of more than two weeks and it must be hoped that, as more heads attend substantial management courses, a beneficial spin-off will be the experience gained by the deputy in running the school.

One of the areas where new heads wanted more help was in working with the governors. As this was less of a problem to those who had attended governors' meetings before becoming a head, an obvious way of improving preparation is for more deputies to attend the meetings with observer status.

There was some evidence from the more experienced heads to suggest that courses prior to headship were more useful than those after becoming a head. In the first year of the DES initiative on management training over 300 secondary deputies attended 20-day or OTTO courses. This was very reassuring and LEAs must continue to encourage and release deputies for these and COSMOS courses.

In addition to formal training courses, extremely valuable experience can be gained by allowing deputies more time to visit other schools. An exchange scheme, where two deputies work in each other's schools for a term, is very rare. The method seems useful, both to refresh and broaden the experience, and needs to be given greater consideration. Secondments to industry are more common and provide a useful perspective on the school–industry link as well as some insight into industrial management.

PROVIDERS SHOULD TAILOR THEIR SENIOR MANAGEMENT
COURSES MORE CAREFULLY TO THE NEEDS OF LEAs,
HEADS AND DEPUTIES

* More consultation is required prior to the course. (3)

* Courses need to be of more practical relevance. (3)

* Greater use could be made of experiential learning methods. (3)

* A component of the course should focus on coping with a weak member of the senior management team. (4)

* More attention should be given to disciplinary and dismissal procedures. (6)

* Interviewing, counselling skills and more training in personnel management are needed. (6)

* Providers should reconsider how much of the course focuses on problems with external agencies. (10)

Most heads had attended at least one major management course prior to headship and found these a useful preparation. LEAs welcomed the DES initiative but wanted more consultation with the providers about the content and form of the 20-day or OTTO courses. Residential components of a course allowed the participants to share common problems, exchange information and discuss issues of concern. Generally, less theory was wanted and more practical relevance to the course members' schools was required. One way of achieving this was to use experiental learning, where small groups discussed the problems of each individual and drew upon their own experiences to offer advice. At the time of the research relatively few courses were using this approach, but those that had, together with work from industrial management, suggested the technique had considerable benefits.

Information was collected from heads about the skills and knowledge they felt could be acquired or developed by training. Although many of the topics (listed in Chapter 3, Table 3.2) already form part of existing courses, providers could use the data as a checklist. The research also highlighted other problem areas for heads which management courses specifically need to address. Thus, about a fifth of new heads reported that coping with a weak member of the senior staff was a problem. This was a particularly difficult and sensitive area in which heads had been given little help by training courses or their LEA. Similarly, when heads were forced as a last resort to institute dismissal proceedings, some found they had to teach themselves the necessary procedures. In fact, many heads felt they needed greater preparation in various aspects of personnel management and training courses should increase the amount of time devoted to this area.

Perhaps surprisingly, after so much has been written elsewhere about the growing pressures from outside the school, the management of external relations was not a major problem for most heads. For some promoting a better public image of the school was a concern, but most seemed quite capable of devising a variety of strategies to improve the situation. This suggests that providers should reconsider how much time is spent on this aspect during the course.

NEW HEADS SHOULD FULLY RECOGNIZE THE IMPORTANCE OF THEIR RELATIONSHIPS WITH THE SENIOR MANAGEMENT TEAM

* Deputies must be fully involved in the planning and
  implementation of change.   (4, 7)

* New heads have to learn how to delegate.   (4, 11)

* The head must not allow a large gap to develop between
  the senior management and the rest of the staff.   (4)

* A mix of new and experienced deputies make a
  good senior management team.   (4)

* Senior management team meetings need more
  careful planning.   (4)

Almost all the heads in the study advocated a team approach to management and the quality of the relationship between the new head and the senior management team was extremely important in determining how well the head settled in. Without the support of the deputies, new heads found it difficult to introduce change, as the case study in Chapter 4 illustrated.

At first, new heads found it hard to delegate and tried to do most things themselves, even though they knew they ought to delegate. This was clearly something they had to learn and after their first year all the case study heads said they thought they had improved. It seems likely that during the year they were gauging the strengths and weaknesses of the staff and determining what could be delegated with what result.

The deputies provided an invaluable link between the head and the teachers and some new heads were aware of the possible danger of drawing the senior management team towards them and creating a large gap with the staff. This seemed to be more likely when the new head was able to appoint one or more new deputies. The data from the 1982–83 cohort showed that about half the new heads had appointed at least one new deputy during their first two years in post. As the heads were usually able to recruit someone with similar philosophies to their own, care had to be taken to avoid a division in the team between the established members and the newcomers. Several case study heads spoke of the benefits, if this potential problem was overcome, in having a blend of new and experienced deputies, as this provided a balance of new ideas and stability.

Most heads saw the deputies informally each morning and the senior management team usually met once a week. These meetings seemed to work quite well in terms of exchanging information, but less so with regard to discussion and decision-making on major policies. Observation and interviews with the heads and deputies indicated that heads needed to plan the meetings more carefully so that less time was spent on relatively low level topics and more attention was devoted to major issues.

To achieve their objectives in the school, heads have to work through the staff. While this may sound obvious, some of the new heads in the case studies were criticized by staff for not putting enough time and effort into establishing good working relationships with the teachers.

Interviews with teachers showed that, as might be expected, they used their knowledge of other heads to make judgements about the new head. The research indicated that the relationship between the previous head and staff was a particularly important factor and emphasized that new heads do not start with a clean slate. The new heads should obtain and compare information about their predecessors from as many sources as possible, e.g. the previous heads themselves, the staff, chairperson of governors, LEA officers, etc. The new head should recognize that in some cases the information and opinions will agree well, while in others there may be discrepancies. The research generally found a coherent picture of the previous head was produced and that differences were often due to the different status and position of people. But this in itself was often revealing, for example, a previous head who had had

---

NEW HEADS SHOULD CONCENTRATE MUCH OF THEIR
EFFORT IN ESTABLISHING GOOD WORKING RELATIONSHIPS
WITH THE STAFF

* The new head should obtain information about the
  relations between the staff and the previous head. (5)

* The first staff meeting must be handled with
  particular care. (5)

* Methods of improving communication and
  mechanisms to establish consultation procedures
  have to be carefully considered. (5, 11)

* The allocation of scale points and internal appointments
  must be handled carefully. (5, 6)

* New heads must not be seen to favour particular
  individuals or departments. (5)

* New heads need to develop a variety of strategies
  to deal with incompetent staff. (6)

* The number of references made by the new head
  to their previous school should be kept to a minimum. (5)

---

little to do with junior staff was perceived quite differently by the deputies and the scale 1 teachers.

The interviews in the 16 case study schools showed that most staff had very high initial expectations for the new head which frequently proved unrealistic. Heads need to be aware of this and handle their first staff meeting very carefully. While it is far too early to present a blueprint, staff want to have some idea of the direction in which the head wishes to move. The new head must show a strong commitment to the school and demonstrate a belief that, jointly, the staff and new head can improve the school.

Most new heads set up a pattern of meetings soon after their arrival. Staff welcomed improvements in communication such as weekly briefings and staff newsletters, but consultation was far more problematic. Most heads said they believed in consultation, but retained the right to make the final decision. Staff wanted to be consulted about major issues, but not minor ones, and allowed the opportunity to express their views before decisions were taken. However, in many cases teachers believed the head and senior management team had already made up their minds and that their views made little difference.

A source of dissatisfaction for teachers in some of the case study schools was the way the new head handled staff appointments. It was particularly important that posts were advertized on notice boards with job descriptions which allowed more than one teacher in the school to apply. Staff were unhappy when internal candidates were not interviewed or given adequate counselling if unsuccessful, and this required courtesy and tact on behalf of the head. A common dilemma facing heads when allocating scale points was how to reward experience and also encourage rising young talent. New heads wanted to use points to change aspects of the curriculum, but often found few scale points were available and it was difficult to reallocate these from one department to another. Heads had to be seen to be fair and not show favouritism to particular departments or individuals. But in many cases the heads seemed unaware that their behaviour was being interpreted as favouritism by some staff.

Although the number of incompetent staff was very small, when serious difficulties occurred the head had to devote considerable time and effort in attempts to help the teacher concerned. Different kinds of problems arose depending on the position of the teacher (e.g. scale 1 or head of department) and the case studies illustrated the need for the head to develop a range of strategies to provide support.

Many new heads made the error of frequently referring to their previous school in comparison with the new school. While it was natural to use their past experience to gauge the value of an idea, too many references were interpreted by the staff as criticism of their school. There was also a tendency for the new head to believe that 'because it worked at my last school it will work here', without fully considering the different situations.

NEW HEADS NEED TO LEARN MORE ABOUT THE MANAGEMENT OF CHANGE

* New heads should carefully consider the appropriate strategies for each stage in the change process. (7)

* The pace of change is crucial. (7)

* Heads must show through their actions that they fully support the innovations. (7)

* Various types of INSET activity are required throughout the process of change and not simply prior to implementation. (7)

* Heads should consider how to evaluate the success of the innovation more thoroughly. (7)

* New heads should capitalize on their 'honeymoon period' by establishing the groundwork for major changes and achieving a short-term objective. (5)

The introduction of change to improve the school was a major concern for the vast majority of new heads. Recent research has provided a clearer understanding of the process of innovation and heads need access to this information in order to use the appropriate strategies during each phase. Similar methods were used in the case study schools and included curricular reviews and a series of discussion papers, usually produced by the new head. Most schools also used a number of working parties whose brief needs to be clearly stated. Various forms of INSET were used to prepare staff for the changes, but it was noticeable that most took place prior to implementation.

As teachers only fully realize the problems involved once they begin the innovation, it is essential that time is allowed to discuss difficulties and successes *after* implementation has taken place.

The new heads initiated most of the changes and played a major role in the early stages. After implementation responsibility was usually delegated and the heads maintained a watching brief. The deputies were heavily involved throughout the process in most of the case study schools.

It was difficult for heads to judge the correct pace of change and interviews with teachers showed that it must not be too fast *or* too slow. The heads had to show through their actions, not just their words, that they fully supported the innovations.

Almost all the teachers expected the new head to introduce change and thought the innovations were needed. Heads were given a 'honeymoon period' and although the length varied, it was important to show that something positive could be achieved, as well as starting the process for major curricular and organizational changes.

In the case studies the heads felt that almost all the changes which had been implemented were going well, but no formal evaluation was used or planned. The heads seemed to use informal feedback from their deputies and other staff to judge the success of the innovation. A more careful appraisal of the changes is needed using a periodic review to obtain the opinions of staff and depending on the innovation, pupils, parents and others. The main problem seemed to be the lack of time and the heads' desire to move on to the next change on their list. There was a tendency for heads to assume that once a change had been implemented there was little need for further review. However, more careful evaluation is necessary to assess the effects of change.

LEAs SHOULD HAVE A PLANNED PROGRAMME OF INDUCTION FOR NEW HEADS

* More time is required for heads designate to visit their new school. (2)

* LEAs should require all outgoing heads to produce a full written report on the school. (2)

* LEAs need to carefully plan introductory visits to the central and local office for all new heads. (2)

* LEAs should provide an induction course of several days for new heads. (9)

* Each authority should produce a handbook for heads giving details of LEA procedures and personnel. (9)

* Each new head should be linked to an experienced 'mentor' head for their first one or two years. (9)

In 1982/83 about 80 per cent of all secondary headship vacancies in England and Wales were filled by first-time heads, the majority of whom had moved to a different LEA to take up their posts. These two facts taken together show why more attention needs to be given to the induction of the 250 new secondary heads who start each year.

For most people, the head designate period lasted several months from the time of their selection and appointment to the time they actually took up post in their new school. The majority of heads were only able to spend a total of between one and three days visiting the school during this period. With the cooperation of the head of their present school, the outgoing head and the LEAs, far better preparation could be achieved in what is currently a time of limbo for the head designate. During this time the new head usually obtains information about the school from the outgoing head and some of the senior staff. With more time available for visits, the new head would also be able to talk to heads of department, heads of year and a number of other staff. Additional information would be obtained by the new head if LEAs required all outgoing heads to write a detailed report on the school. Few, if any, LEAs seem to operate such a system at present, but it would be relatively easy to introduce and would certainly be of benefit to new heads.

In most authorities new heads were invited to the central and area office to meet a variety of LEA personnel. The research showed that these visits have to be planned carefully if they are to be of any value. In some cases too many people were introduced and the new heads found the faces just became a blur. In other instances, a poorly planned visit meant that few key staff were free to meet the new heads, who found it simply a waste of time. Obviously, a balance has to be obtained with regard to the number of people being introduced and in a large LEA two visits may be needed. Someone to guide the head on these visits is required and this is probably best done by an officer or adviser who is directly linked to the school.

In addition to these introductory visits which are useful in putting 'faces to names', an induction programme totalling several days is required for new heads. The research showed that at present, only a quarter of the LEAs ran induction courses for heads which lasted more than one day. These courses provided an introduction to the authority and allowed people to meet officers, other new heads and some more experienced heads. The content of the course should be highly practical and related directly to the needs of new heads.

If an LEA has only a small number of new heads each year, consortium arrangements with neighbouring authorities should be considered. One group of LEAs had introduced this scheme and it seemed to be working well. Another method used by some authorities to overcome low numbers was to run a combined course for primary and secondary heads. This can work successfully for some general components of the course, such as LEA procedures, but for other topics it is best to divide heads into separate groups, as many new secondary heads felt their needs differed from their primary colleagues. As new heads may start at different times, a modular approach spread throughout the year may be worth considering so that people could join at any point. Some indication of the starting pattern is given by the 1982–83 cohort where about 50 per cent of new heads took up post in September, 25 per cent in January and the other 25 per cent began in April. Ideally, individual induction programmes tailored to each head's needs are likely to prove most productive, but would require more time on behalf of officers, advisers and experienced heads.

At the time of the research, 38 per cent of LEAs provided a handbook for heads. These were a very useful source of reference for new heads about 'who does what' and general LEA procedures. It is strongly recommended that all authorities should produce such a handbook. The use of word processors and loose-leaf binders would allow the information to be updated as required.

A system of linking new heads to an experienced 'mentor' head was used by only 14 per cent of LEAs. The research showed that many new heads were reluctant to seek managerial advice from officers and advisers, and found the most useful source of help was often the other heads in the authority. A mentor system would allow each new head to quickly obtain by telephone, information and advice on a variety of problems. There is however, a need to avoid pairing heads who are competing for children in the same catchment area and to ensure that the heads have reasonably similar educational philosophies. This type of scheme, which is easy to set up, should be provided by all authorities.

LEAs NEED TO CONSIDER WAYS OF IMPROVING THEIR SUPPORT FOR HEADS

* LEAs should establish mutual support groups
  of heads.   (3, 8)

* A system of 'consultant' heads should be established.   (9)

* Authorities need to consider the possibility of using
  external consultants to provide advice to schools.   (8)

* LEAs should consider ways of improving their
  regular meetings for heads.   (8)

* LEAs need to produce a management development
  plan and consider how to best use their course 'graduates'.   (3)

* LEAs should consider the benefits of management
  development by working with whole senior
  management teams as well as individuals.   (4)

Although the research focused upon newly appointed heads, information was also obtained on LEA support for all heads. The surveys and case studies showed that both the amount and type of support varied from one authority to another; some LEAs offered considerable help, while others provided very little. The following points and recommendations should be considered by authorities as a means of improving their support for all heads whether new or more experienced.

An effective means of reducing heads' professional isolation would be to establish small support groups which met regularly, for example, on a monthly basis. The small number of groups which exist at present are often the result of informal contacts made by heads on various courses, but without formal status from the LEAs they do not usually last for very long. Although problems of competition between the heads due to falling rolls might exist, a more structured approach by the authority is likely to be highly beneficial. Whether these groups should consist of heads, advisers and academics or only heads, is open to debate and needs further discussion by the possible participants.

While heads found LEA advisers and officers a useful form of support on the curriculum, staffing and INSET, they were seen as less helpful on other school management issues. Authorities need to consider the possibility of establishing a number of experienced heads as 'consultants' who would be able to offer specific school management advice to other heads. Obviously, care would be needed in the selection of these heads, who would have to have high credibility and respect from their peers. The research also highlighted the need for heads to be able to talk to someone who was outside the authority and played a 'neutral' consultancy role. At present, LEA officers and advisers are expected to offer help and advice, but the case studies showed that heads spoke far more openly to the researchers on many issues which they said could not be discussed with LEA staff. There appears to be a strong case for the use of outside consultants working with schools in a similar way to the Organization Development (OD) approaches used in industry and commerce.

All LEAs organized a variety of regular meetings for their heads which usually worked quite well in terms of information giving. If authorities wish the meetings to serve more than this purpose, they need to consider their form and structure. Many heads seemed to prefer a morning session devoted to administrative matters, followed by discussion of one major topic in the afternoon.

As the National Development Centre at Bristol has already emphasized, LEAs must begin to organize management development policies for their senior staff. Authorities need to consider the best method of using heads and deputies who have attended 20-day and OTTO courses, and how to capitalize on their experience once they return to school. A support network needs to be established by the LEA to facilitate the follow-up from courses both within and outside the schools. Some authorities have begun working on management development with the complete senior management team of a school and this should be taken into consideration in addition to the training of individuals.

It should be pointed out that many of the changes suggested as a result of the research do *not* have major financial implications and if some or most of the recommendations are carried out, the preparation and support of secondary heads would be improved considerably.

While much of the NFER research has focused on the difficulties and problems of the early years, it is important to emphasize that mose of the heads involved in the project thought the positive aspects of headship considerably outweighed the negative ones. Very similar views were expressed by both new and 'old' heads on this matter, as they were for almost all of the themes dealt with by the research.

Many heads referred to the wide variety of tasks associated with headship. As one head said rather colourfully – 'Life is never dull, heads may die of coronaries, but never of boredom!' Heads liked the relative freedom they had to develop the school for the benefit of both pupils and staff. They derived satisfaction from having the opportunity to plan and implement change and seeing innovations progress. Meeting a wide range of people also appealed to many of the heads, who felt rewarded when they received compliments about the school from parents, pupils and members of the community.

Some of the more experienced heads pointed out that the job had become more difficult and that they were facing greater pressure from such groups as the teacher unions and the education authority. Despite this gradual erosion of autonomy, most agreed with the head who said: 'The variety, the challenge and the rewards cannot be equalled – it's the best job you can have.'

Appendices

Appendix 1   Difficulties facing a new head during the first two years of headship

	New Heads (%)					'Old' Heads (%)				
	Very serious	Serious	Moderate	Minor	Not a problem	Very serious	Serious	Moderate	Minor	Not a problem
a) Internal issues										
Establishing your priorities	7	14	32	22	25	5	22	31	19	22
Coping with a wide range of tasks	7	22	32	19	20	6	18	28	24	24
Dealing with a large number of decisions	6	14	34	27	19	6	15	32	26	21
Finding out about the daily routine of the school	2	6	22	33	37	1	5	18	32	44
Obtaining information about curricular areas other than your own	2	11	33	35	19	2	9	31	40	19
Establishing better standards of discipline	9	18	28	23	22	9	18	29	25	19
Establishing/improving consultation procedures within the school	14	31	31	15	9	18	32	29	15	6
Establishing/improving channels of information within the school	11	28	35	17	9	13	33	33	17	4
Dealing with school finance	6	13	26	32	23	4	11	24	32	29
Dealing with a contracting education budget*	11	24	27	24	14	8	14	31	19	28
Difficulties caused by the practice and style of the previous head	16	29	20	20	15	22	22	23	18	15
Dealing with problems relating to school buildings	16	33	27	17	7	–	–	–	–	–
b) External issues										
Developing a good working relationship with:										
LEA advisers	2	3	12	22	61	1	4	12	20	63
LEA officers	3	4	17	25	51	3	5	12	22	58
School governors	2	4	14	28	52	2	4	11	23	61

*Chi-square significant at 5 per cent level between new and 'old' heads.

Appendix 1 (continued)

	New Heads (%)						'Old' Heads (%)				
	Very serious	Serious	Moderate	Minor	Not a problem		Very serious	Serious	Moderate	Minor	Not a problem
Dealing with parental problems	1	9	27	40	23		2	7	31	40	20
Dealing with local community groups and services	1	5	19	29	46		1	4	17	37	41
Issues arising from local party politics	4	5	12	19	60		5	7	14	22	53
Dealing with the media (e.g. local press)	0	8	17	32	43		1	8	16	35	40
Getting information about decision-making in the LEA	8	18	32	23	19		8	15	31	27	20
Getting information about areas of responsibility – 'who does what' – in the LEA	7	17	26	25	25		4	13	28	31	25
Obtaining information about what has been tried in other schools	6	9	27	30	28		3	8	33	31	26
Creating a better public image of the school	17	25	28	15	15		16	26	25	19	13
Liaising with feeder schools	3	15	18	27	37		4	12	25	26	33

Appendix 1 (continued)

c) Staff and staffing	New Heads (%)					'Old' Heads (%)				
	Very serious	Serious	Moderate	Minor	Not a problem	Very serious	Serious	Moderate	Minor	Not a problem
Obtaining information about the strengths and weaknesses of staff	5	11	34	27	23	7	13	35	27	17
Promoting staff professional development/INSET	6	24	31	29	10	8	23	32	25	12
Dealing with poor staff morale	12	24	27	24	13	11	20	30	22	17
Persuading members of staff to accept new ideas	8	39	30	17	6	11	20	30	22	17
Coping with a weak member of the senior management team	19	19	17	19	26	24	22	15	11	28
Dismissal/redeployment of incompetent staff	16	21	18	14	31	19	32	14	16	28
Issues arising from previous head's allocation of points	22	32	19	14	13	24	32	19	11	14
Attracting suitably qualified applicants for teaching posts	6	18	25	21	30	6	19	24	26	24
LEA restrictions on staff recruitment*	15	27	26	16	16	10	11	26	25	28
Staff reductions as a result of falling rolls	19	17	22	12	30	–	–	–	–	–
Issues arising from non-teaching duties of staff	5	17	28	26	24	3	20	28	26	23
Dealing with staff unions and professional associations	4	16	21	28	31	3	9	19	37	32
Issues concerning non-teaching staff	6	13	22	35	24	5	9	19	39	28
	N = 188					N = 228				

*Chi-square significant at 5 per cent level between new and 'old' heads.

Appendix 2 Support received (where applicable) from the following groups or individuals

	New Heads (%)						'Old' Heads (%)				
	No support	Not very supportive	Moderately supportive	Very supportive	Extremely supportive		No support	Not very supportive	Moderately supportive	Very supportive	Extremely supportive
LEA advisers/inspectors	0	6	39	32	23		0	9	33	39	19
Other LEA officers	2	5	41	35	17		1	11	34	35	19
School governors	1	5	23	34	37		1	7	18	39	35
Parents/Parent Teacher Association	2	5	25	40	28		1	5	26	35	33
Other heads in the LEA	1	9	28	42	20		1	9	32	38	20
Teachers' centre leader/warden*	42	18	23	14	3		28	15	36	16	5
Local FE/HE institutions	21	23	35	20	1		17	27	39	12	5
Secondary Heads Association	6	9	36	32	17		2	12	34	32	20
National Association of Head Teachers	12	11	35	28	14		9	11	28	27	25
	N = 188						N = 228				

*Chi-square significant at 5 per cent level between new and 'old' heads.

References

ACLAND, H. (1973). Social determinants of educational achievement. PhD thesis, University of Oxford.

ADKINSON, J. (1981). 'Women in school administration. A review of the literature', *Review of Educational Research,* **51,** 3.

ASSOCIATION FOR TEACHER EDUCATION IN EUROPE AND NATIONAL ASSOCIATION OF HEADTEACHERS (1982). Training for Heads (School Leaders) in Europe. Report of Conference, Gatwick, UK. Brussels: ATEE; Haywards Heath: NAHT.

AUSTIN, G.R. (1978). Process Evaluation: A Comprehensive Study of Outliers. Maryland State Department of Education.

BACON, A. (1978) 'Democratic values and the managerial prerogative: a case study of head teachers and democratised school boards', *Educational Studies,* **4,** 1, 29–44. Also in BUSH, T. *et al.* (Eds) (1980), see below.

BAILEY, A.J. (1982). Patterns and process of change in secondary schools. DPhil thesis, University of Sussex.

BALDWIN, J. and WELLS, H. (1979). *Active Tutorial Work Books 1–5.* Oxford: Basil Blackwell.

BALLINGER, E. (1985). 'Headship in the 80s': Evaluation Report. National Development Centre, University of Bristol.

BALTZELL, D.C. and DENTLER, R. (1985). *Selecting American School Principals: A source book for educators.* Washington, DC: National Institute of Education.

BARKER, B. (1982). 'Root-based leader or cloud-based manager?' *Times Educational Supplement,* 8 October.

BARNETT, B. G. (1985). 'Peer-assisted leadership: using research to improve practice', *The Urban Review,* **17,** 1, 47–64.

BARON, G. (1956). 'Some aspects of the "Headmaster Tradition"', *Researchers and Studies,* 14. Also in HOUGHTON, V. *et al.* (Eds) (1975), see below.

BARON, G. (1979). 'Research in education administration in Britain', *Educational Administration,* **8,** 1, 1–33. Also in BUSH, T. *et al.* (Eds), see below.

BELL, L. A. (1979). 'The planning of an educational change in a comprehensive school', *Durham and Newcastle Research Review,* Spring, 1–8.

BERMAN, J. (1982). 'The managerial behaviour of female high school principals: implications for training'. ERIC microfiche ED217–516.

BERMAN, P. and MCLAUGHLIN, M. (1975). 'Federal programmes supporting educational change', *The Findings in Review, vol. IV.* Rand Corporation, Santa Monica, Calif.

BERNBAUM, G. (1973). 'Headmasters and schools: some preliminary findings', *Sociological Review,* **21,** 3, 463–84.

BERNBAUM, G. (1976). 'The role of the head'. In: PETERS, R. S. (Ed) (1976), see below.

BLANCHARD, B. E. (1981). 'The qualities of the high school principalship rated by secondary teachers', *Scientia Paedogogica Experimentalis,* **18,** 1, 5–20.

BLATCHFORD, R. (Ed) (1985). *Managing the Secondary School*. London: Bell and Hyman.

BLUMBERG, A. and GREENFIELD, W.D. (1980). *The Effective Principal: Perspectives on School Leadership*. Boston: Allyn and Bacon.

BOLAM, R. (1986) 'The first two years of the NDC: a progress report', *School Organization*, **6**, 1, 1–16.

BOLAM, R. and MEDLOCK, P. (1985). *Active Tutorial Work Training and Dissemination: An Evaluation*. Oxford: Blackwell for the Health Education Council.

BOLAM, R., JERVIS, P. and HOYLE, E. (1985). 'Training heads in Bristol fashion', *Education*, 165, 9, 192–3.

BRIMER, A. *et al.* (1978). *Sources of Difference in School Achievement*. Slough: NFER.

BROOKOVER, W. B. *et al.* (1979). *School Social Systems and Student Achievement: Schools Can Make a Difference*. New York: Praeger.

BUCKLEY, J. (1985). *The Training of Secondary School Heads in Western Europe*. Windsor: Council of Europe–NFER-NELSON.

BURGESS, R. (1983). *Experiencing Comprehensive Education: A Study of Bishop McGregor School*. London: Methuen.

BURNHAM, P. W. (1964). 'The role of the deputy head in secondary schools'. In: BUSH, T. *et. al.* (Eds) (1980), see below.

BUSH, T. *et al.* (Eds) (1980). *Approaches to School Management*. London: Harper and Row.

CARLSON, R. O. (1962). *Executive Succession and Organizational Change*. Chicago: Midwest Administration Center, University of Chicago.

COCHRAN, J. (1980). 'When the principal is a woman'. ERIC microfiche ED184–247.

COLEMAN, J. S. *et al.* (1966). *Equality of Educational Opportunity*. Washington, DC: Government Printing Office.

COLLIER, V. (1982). 'The role of school management in the process of change', *Durham and Newcastle Research Review*, **9**, 48, 335–9.

CRANDALL, D. and LOUCKS, S. (1983). *A Road Map for School Improvement: Executive Summary of the Study of Dissemination Efforts Supporting School Improvement (DESSI)*, vol. 10. Andover, Mass.: The Network Inc.

DEAN, J. (1984). *Managing the Secondary School*. Beckenham: Croom Helm.

DEPARTMENT OF EDUCATION AND SCIENCE (1977). *Education in Schools: a consultative document*. Welsh Office (Cmnd 6869). London: HMSO.

DEPARTMENT OF EDUCATION AND SCIENCE (1977). *A New Partnership for our Schools*. Taylor (chairman). London: HMSO.

DEPARTMENT OF EDUCATION AND SCIENCE (1977). 'Ten Good Schools: a secondary school enquiry.' Discussion paper by some members of HM Inspectorate of Schools. London: HMSO.

DEPARTMENT OF EDUCATION AND SCIENCE (1982). *The Secondary School Staffing Survey: Data on teachers' characteristics and deployment and on average class sizes in England and Wales*. Statistical Bulletin 5/82.

DEPARTMENT OF EDUCATION AND SCIENCE (1982). *The New Teacher in School*. A survey by HM Inspector of Schools. London: HMSO.

DEPARTMENT OF EDUCATION AND SCIENCE (1983). *Statistics of Education: Teachers in Service in Maintained, Assisted and Grant-aided Schools and Establishments of Further Education in England and Wales*. London: HMSO.

DEPARTMENT OF EDUCATION AND SCIENCE (1983). *The In-service Teacher Training Grants Scheme*. Circular 3/83. London: HMSO.

DICKINSON, N. B. (1975). 'The headteacher as innovator: a study of an English school district'. In: REID, W. A. (Ed) *Case Studies in Curriculum Change*. London: Routledge and Kegan Paul.

DOYLE, W. and PONDER, G. (1977). 'The practicality ethic in teacher decision making', *Interchange*, **8**, 3, 1–12.

DUKE, D. *et al.* (1984). 'Transition to leadership. An investigation of the first year of the principalship'. Educational Administration Program, Lewes and Clark College, Portland, Oregon. (Shortened version to appear in *School Organization.*)

DWYER, D., LEE, G., ROWAN, B. and BOSSERT, S. (1983). 'Five principals in action: perspectives on instructional management.' Far West Laboratory, California. ERIC ED231–085.

DWYER, J. (l984). Preparation for Secondary Headship. A report on a two-term secondment, September 1983 to April 1984. Whitley Bay High School, North Tyneside.

EDMONDS, R. (1979). 'Effective schools for the urban poor', *Educational Leadership*, **37**, 15–24.

EDUCATION ACT (1980). London: HMSO.

EDUCATION BILL (HL) (1986). An Act to amend the law relating to education. London: HMSO. 19 February.

EKHOLM, M. (1983). 'Research on the School Leader Education Programme in Sweden'. In: HEGARTY, S. (Ed) (1983), see below.

EVERARD, K. B. (1982). *Management in Comprehensive Schools – What Can Be Learned from Industry?* Centre for the Study of Comprehensive Schools, University of York.

EVERARD, K. B. and MORRIS, G. (1985). *Effective School Management.* London: Harper and Row.

EVERARD, K. B. (1986). *Developing Management in Schools.* London: Blackwell.

FAUTH, G. C. (1984) 'Women in educational administration: A research profile', *The Educational Forum*, **49**, 1, 65–79.

FIEDLER, F. E. (1967). *A Theory of Leadership Effectiveness.* New York: McGraw Hill.

FIELDING, M. (1984). 'Asking different questions and pursuing different means; a critique of the new management training movement.' In: MAW, J. *et al.*, see below.

FRITH, D. (Ed) (1985). *School Management in Practice.* York: Longman.

FULLAN, M. (1982). *The Meaning of Educational Change.* New York and London: Teachers College Press.

FULLAN, M. (1985). 'Change processes and strategies at the local level', *Elementary School Journal*, **85**, 3, 391–421.

GALLOWAY, D. (1976). 'Size of school, socio-economic hardship, supension rates and persistent unjustified absence from school', *British Journal of Educational Psychology*, **46**, 40–7.

GATES, P. E., BLANCHARD, K. H. and HERSEY, P. (1976). 'Diagnosing educational leadership problems: a situational approach', *Educational Leadership*, **33**, 5, 348–54.

GILBERT, V. (1981). 'Innovativeness in a comprehensive school: the head as Janus,' *Educational Administration*, **9**, 3, 41–61.

GLASMAN, N. S. and BINIAMINOV, I. (1981). 'Input–output analyses of schools', *Review of Educational Research*, **51**, 4, 509–39.

GORDON, G. E. and ROSEN, N. (1981). 'Critical factors in leadership succession', *Organizational Behaviour and Human Performance*, **27**, 227–54.

GRAY, H. L. (Ed) (1982). *The Management of Educational Institutions: Theory, Research and Consultancy.* Lewes: Falmer Press.

GRAY, H. L. (1983). 'Organization Development (OD) in education', *School Organization and Management Abstracts*, **2**, 1, 7–19.

GRAY, L. and WAITT, I. (1983). 'If you want to get a head. . .', *Times Educational Supplement*, 24 June.

GREENFIELD, W. D. (1982). Research on public school principals: a review and recommendations. Paper presented for NIE national conference on the principalship, October.

HALL, G. *et al.* (1984). 'Effects of three principal styles on school improvement,' *Educational Leadership,* February, 22–27.

HALL, G. and LOUCKS, S. (1978). 'Teacher concerns as a basis for facilitating and personalising staff development', *Teachers College Record,* **80**, 1, 36–53.

HALL, V., MACKAY, H. and MORGAN, C. (1986). *Secondary School Headteachers.* Milton Keynes: Open University Press.

HANDY, C. (1981). *Understanding Organizations.* Harmondsworth: Penguin Books.

HANDY, C. (1984). *Taken for Granted? Understanding Schools as Organizations.* Schools Council Programme One. York: Longman.

HART, J. (1985). 'The secondary school secretary – some hidden and developmental aspects of the secretary's role', *Educational Management and Administration,* **13**, 2, Summer, 131–9.

HAVEN, E.W., *et al.* (1980). *Women in Educational Administration: The Principalship – a literature review.* Washington, D.C.: National Institute of Education.

HEGARTY, S. (Ed) (1983). *Training for Management in Schools.* Windsor: Council of Europe–NFER-NELSON.

HELLER, H. (1982). 'Management development for headteachers'. In: GRAY, H. L. (Ed) (1982), see above.

HERSEY, P. and BLANCHARD, K.H. (1969). *Management of Organizational Behavior: Utilizing Human Resources.* Englewood Cliffs: Prentice-Hall.

HILSUM, S. and START, K. (1974). *Promotion and Careers in Teaching.* Windsor: NFER–NELSON.

HINDS, T. and LITCHFIELD, B. (1984). 'The head's written report', *Education,* **164**, 17, 336.

HOPES, C. (Ed) (1981). European Forum on Educational Administration. Deutsches Institut für Internationale Pädagogische Forschung, Frankfurt.

HOUGHTON, V. *et al.* (Eds) (1975). *Management in Education 1: the Management of Organizations and Individuals.* London: Ward Lock.

HOY, W. K. and AHO, F. (1973). 'Patterns of succession of high school principals and organizational change', *Planning and Changing,* **4**, 2, 82–8.

HOYLE, E. and MCMAHON, A. (Eds) (1986). *The Management of Schools.* World Yearbook of Education. London: Kogan Page.

HUBERMAN, M. and MILES, M. (1984). *Innovation Up Close.* New York and London: Plenum Press.

HUGHES, M. (1973). 'The professional-as-administrator: the case of the secondary school head', *Educational Administration Bulletin,* **2**, 1. Also in: PETERS, R. S. (Ed) (1976), see below.

HUGHES, M. (1975). 'The innovating school head: autocratic initiator or catalyst of cooperation', *Educational Administration,* **4**, 1, 43–54.

HUGHES, M. (1983). 'The role and tasks of heads of schools in England and Wales: research studies and professional development provision.' In: HEGARTY, S. (Ed), see above.

HUGHES, M., CARTER, J. and FIDLER, B. (1981). Professional development provision for senior staff in schools. Faculty of Education, University of Birmingham.

HULING-AUSTIN, L. *et al.* (1985). High school principals: their role in guiding change. Paper presented at American Educational Research Association (AERA), Chicago.

IMISON, T. (1985) 'How to get a head', *Education,* **165**, 3, 57.

JACKSON, A. (1976). *Heading for What? A Study of the Role of the Head.* Leeds: University of Leeds Counselling and Career Development Unit.

JENCKS, C. *et al.* (1972). *Inequality: A Reassessment of the Effect of Family and Schooling in America.* New York: Basic.

JONES, A. (forthcoming). *The Impotent Head.* London: Heinemann Educational Books.

KATZ, R. (1974). 'Skills of an effective administration', *Harvard Business Review*, September–October.

KMETZ, V. and WILLOWER, D. J. (1982). 'Elementary principals' work behaviour', *Educational Administrative Quarterly*, **18**, 4, 62–78.

KOGAN, M. *et al.*, (1984). *School Governing Bodies*. London: Heinemann Education Books.

LAMBERT, K. (1984). 'The changing nature of headship skills and public confidence: a personal view.' *Educational Management and Administration*, **12**, 2, 123–6.

LAPLANT, J. (1981). 'Improving school practice through principals' inservice.' ERIC ED208–518.

LEITHWOOD, K.A. and MONTGOMERY, D.J. (1985). 'The role of the principal in school improvement'. In: AUSTIN, G. *et al.* (Eds). *Research on Effective Schools*. New York: Academic Press.

LINDELOW, J. (1981). 'Leading meetings', Chapter 9 in SMITH, S. C. *et al.*, see below.

LODGE, B. (1986). 'Fewer want to become heads', *Times Educational Supplement*, 17 January.

LYONS, G. (1976). *Heads' Tasks: A Handbook for Secondary School Administration*. Windsor: NFER.

LYONS, G. (1981). *Teacher Careers and Career Perceptions in the Secondary Comprehensive School*. Windsor: NFER-NELSON.

LYONS, G. and STENNING, R. (1986). *Managing Staff in Schools: A Handbook*. London: Hutchinson.

MCGEOWN, V. (1979). 'Organizational climate for change in schools', *Educational Studies*, **5**, 3, 251–64.

MCKELVEY, J. and KYRIACOU, C. (1985). 'Research on pupils as teacher evaluators', *Educational Studies*, **11**, 1, 25–32.

MCPHERSON, A., GRAY, J. and RAFFE, D. (1983). *Reconstructions of Secondary Education*. London: Routledge and Kegan Paul.

MCQUEENEY, J. (1985). 'The development of secondary school organization and staff management: the headteacher as principal protagonist', *Educational Management and Administration*, **13**, 2, 106–12.

MADAUS, J. *et al.* (1979). 'The sensitivity of measures of school effectiveness,' *Harvard Educational Review*, **49**, 2, 207–30.

MANASSE, A. L. (1985). 'Improving conditions for principal effectiveness: policy implications of research', *Elementary School Journal*, **85**, 3, 439–63.

MARTIN, W. J. and WILLOWER, D. J. (1981). 'The managerial behaviour of high school principals', *Educational Administrative Quarterly*, **17**, 1, 69–90.

MATTHEW, R. and TONG, S. (1982). *The Role of the Deputy Head in the Comprehensive School*. London: Ward Lock Educational.

MAW, J. *et al.* (1984). 'Education Plc? Head Teachers and the New Training Initiative'. Bedford Way Papers, 20, University of London, Institute of Education.

MAZZARELLA, J. A. (1981). 'Leadership styles'. Chapter 3 in SMITH, S. C. *et al.*, see below.

MINTZBURG, H. (1973). *The Nature of Managerial Work*. New York: Harper and Row.

MISKEL, C. and COSGROVE, D. (1985). 'Leader succession in school settings', *Review of Educational Research*, **55**, 1, 87–105.

MORGAN, C., HALL, V. and MACKAY (1983). *The Selection of Secondary Headteachers*. Milton Keynes: Open University Press.

MORRIS, V. C. *et al.* (1981). *The Urban Principal*. NIE Report, University of Illinois, Chicago.

NATIONAL ASSOCIATION OF SCHOOLMASTERS/UNION OF WOMEN TEACHERS (1985). 'Headteacher Selection and Training.' Birmingham.

NICHOLLS, A. (1983). *Managing Educational Innovation*. London: Allen and Unwin.

NOCKELS, A. (1981). The Problems, Issues and Strategies of the First Years of Secondary Headship. Mimeographed report to Oxfordshire LEA.

O'SHEA, A.T. (1983). *Management in Secondary Education.* Belfast: Northern Ireland Council for Education Research.

PAISEY, A. (1984). *School Management: A Case Approach.* London: Harper and Row.
PENNINGTON, R. C. and BELL, G. H. (1983). Headteacher education and training in England', *Collected Original Resources in Education* (CORE), **7**, 2.
PERSELL, C. (1982). Effective principals: what do we know from various educational literatures? Paper presented for NIE national conference on the principalship. October. ERIC ED224-177.
PERT, D. and WEEKS, J. (1985). 'Headship in the 80s under scrutiny', *Education,* **165,** 1, 9.
PETERS, R. S. (Ed) (1976). *The Role of the Head.* London: Routledge and Kegan Paul.
PLOWDEN REPORT, DEPARTMENT OF EDUCATION AND SCIENCE. CENTRAL ADVISORY COUNCIL FOR EDUCATION (1967). *Children and their Primary Schools.* London: HMSO.
PURKEY, S. C. and SMITH, M. G. (1983). 'Effective schools: a review', *Elementary School Journal,* **83,** 4, 427–52.

REDDIN, W. J. (1970). *Managerial Effectiveness.* New York: McGraw-Hill.
REINHARD, D. *et al.* (1980). Great expectations: the principal's role and in-service needs in supporting change projects. Paper presented at AERA.
REVANS, R. (1980). *Action Learning.* London: Blond and Briggs.
REYNOLDS, D. (Ed) (1985). *Studying School Effectiveness.* Lewes: Falmer Press.
REYNOLDS, D., JONES, D. and ST.LEGER, S. (1976). 'Schools do make a difference', *New Society,* 29 July, 223–5.
ROSENBLUM, S. and JASTRZAB, J. (1980) *The Role of the Principal in Change: The Teachers Corps Example.* Cambridge, Mass.: ABT Associates.
ROSENHOLTZ, S. J. (1985). 'Effective Schools: Interpreting the evidence', *American Journal of Education,* **93,** 3, 352–88.
RUTHERFORD, W. L. and MURPHY, S. C. (1985). Change in high schools: roles and reactions of teachers. Paper presented at American Educational Research Association (AERA).
RUTTER, M. (1983). 'School effects on pupil progress: research findings and policy implications', *Child Development,* **54,** 1, 1–29.
RUTTER, M. *et al.* (1979). *Fifteen Thousand Hours: Secondary Schools and their Effects on Children.* London: Open Books.

SAYER, J. (1980). 'How women are stopped from getting ahead – and a headship', *Education,* **155,** 10, 258.
SECONDARY HEADS ASSOCIATION (1983). 'The selection of secondary heads: suggestions for good practice', *Occasional Paper No. 2,* London.
SERGIOVANNI, T. J. and ELLIOT, D. L. (1975). *Educational and Organisational Leadership in Elementary Schools.* Englewood Cliffs, N.J.: Prentice-Hall.
SIKES, P., MEASOR, L. and WOODS, P. (1985). *Teacher Careers.* Lewes: Falmer Press.
SMITH, S. C., MAZZARELLA, J. A. and PIELE, P. K. (1981). *School Leadership: Handbook for Survival.* University of Oregon: ERIC Clearinghouse on Educational Management.
SOUTHWORTH, G. (1985). 'Primary heads' reflection on training', *Education,* **165,** 25, 560.
SPOONER, R. (1984). 'The value of appointing a bursar', *Education,* **163,** 24, 492.
STAGLES, B. (1985). 'What teachers like about "Active Tutorial Work"', *Pastoral Care in Education,* **3,** 1, 13–23.
STRAKER, N. (1984). 'The role of the senior teacher in secondary schools', *School Organization,* **4,** 1, 55–64.

TALL, G. (1985). 'An evaluation of the introduction of Active Tutorial Work in a Birmingham Comprehensive School', *Pastoral Care in Education,* **3,** 1, 24–31.

206 *Secondary Headship: The First Years*

TAYLOR, K. (1983). 'Heads and the freedom to manage', *School Organization,* **3,** 3, 273–86.

THOMAS, M. (1978). *A Study of Alternatives in American Education. Vol 2. The Role of the Principal.* Santa Monica, Calif.: Rand Corporation.

TODD, R. and DENNISON, W. (1978). 'The changing role of the deputy headteacher in English Secondary Schools,' *Educational Review,* **30,** 3, 209–20. Also in: BUSH, T. *et al.* (Eds) (1980), see above.

TRETHOWAN, D. (1983). 'Managing to learn', *Times Educational Supplement,* 25 November.

TRETHOWAN, D. (1984). 'I'm going to make this school the best...', *Times Educational Supplement,* 13 January.

TROWN, E. A. and NEEDHAM, G. (1981). 'Headships for women: long term effects of the re-entry problem', *Educational Studies,* **7,** 1, 41–5.

TURNER, L. T. (1981). Preparation for headship. Unpublished BPhil(Ed) dissertation, University of Birmingham.

WADDILOVE, J. (1981). 'Planning a curriculum change', *School Organization,* **1,** 2, 139–48.

WALSH, K., DUNNE, R., STOTEN, B., and STEWART, J. (1984). *Falling School Rolls and the Management of the Teaching Profession.* Windsor: NFER–NELSON.

WEINDLING, R. *et al.* (1983). *Teachers' Centres: a focus for in-service education?* Schools Council Working Paper 74. London: Methuen Educational.

WILLIAMS, G. (1984). *Improving School Morale.* Pavic Publications: Sheffield City Polytechnic.

WILLIS, Q. (1980). 'The work activities of school principals: an observational study', *Journal of Educational Administration,* **18,** 1.

WOLCOTT, H. F. (1973). *The Man in the Principal's Office.* New York: Holt, Rinehart and Winston.

WOOD, A. (1983). 'The management game', *Times Educational Supplement,* 6th May.

YUKL, G. (1982). Managerial leadership and the effective principal. Paper presented for NIE national conference on the principalship: October.